W9-BWP-794

Sociology

Reference Sources in the Social Sciences

American Military History: A Guide to Reference and Information Sources. By Daniel K. Blewett.

Psychology: A Guide to Reference and Information Sources. By Pam M. Baxter.

Sociology: A Guide to Reference and Information Sources. Second Edition. By Stephen H. Aby.

SOCIOLOGY

A Guide to Reference and Information Sources

Second Edition

STEPHEN H. ABY
The University of Akron

1997
Libraries Unlimited, Inc.
Englewood, Colorado

Libraries Unlimited, Inc.
P.O. Box 6633
Englewood, CO 80155-6633
1-800-237-6124
www.lu.com

Production Editor: Kevin W. Perizzolo
Copy Editor: Louise Tonneson
Proofreader: Marcus Elmore
Indexer: Kay Meredith Dusheck
Typesetter: Kay Minnis

Library of Congress Cataloging-in-Publication Data

Aby, Stephen H., 1949-
Sociology : a guide to reference and information sources / Stephen H. Aby. -- 2nd ed.
xv, 227 p. 17x25 cm.
Includes bibliographical references and index.
ISBN 1-56308-422-8
1. Reference books--Sociology--Bibliography. 2. Sociology--Bibliography. 3. Reference books--Social sciences--Bibliography. 4. Social sciences--Bibliography. I. Title.
Z7164.S68A24 1997
[HM51]
016.301--dc21 97-26613
CIP

CONTENTS

Part IV
SOCIOLOGICAL FIELDS

ACKNOWLEDGMENTS

Many individuals contributed to the completion of this bibliography. Specifically, I would like to thank Mark Tausig, Dick Gigliotti, Neal Garland, McKee McClendon, Rebecca Erickson, Jim Kuhn, David Brink, J. B. Hill, Gay Kitson, Rudy Fenwick, Frank Faulk, and Peggy Tonkin for some helpful suggestions. I would also like to express my appreciation to the University of Akron, which granted me a Professional Improvement Leave for Spring 1996 and thereby helped expedite the completion of this work. Additionally the staff at Libraries Unlimited were professional and supportive throughout this project. Finally, I want to thank Martha McNamara for her tireless support and encouragement. Thanks to all of these individuals, this bibliography is better than it otherwise would have been. However, the remaining mistakes, whether of omission or commission, are my responsibility alone.

INTRODUCTION

Scope and Purpose

This second edition of *Sociology: A Guide to Reference and Information Sources* is intended to provide undergraduate and graduate students, faculty, librarians, and researchers with descriptions of 576 of the major reference sources in sociology, its subdisciplines, and related social sciences. Indexes, bibliographies, handbooks, databases, World Wide Web sites, dictionaries, and other print and electronic reference and information sources published from 1985 through 1996 are cited. Works that precede this period are also selectively included if they are considered classics, if more recent works in a subject area do not exist, or if their coverage is historical. The sources are in English, and works from the United States, Great Britain, Australia, and Canada predominate, though some other important international sources are included. The addition of approximately 250 new titles and electronic sources, as well as the inclusion of many newer editions of previously cited works, makes this a substantial revision of and complement to the first edition.

Entries follow the *Chicago Manual of Style* (14th ed.) bibliographic format and are descriptively annotated, with occasional evaluative comments. Annotations range in length from approximately 60 to 250 words, except in the sections on journals, organizations, research centers, and World Wide Web/Internet sites, where the annotations are briefer. Virtually all sources have been examined and annotated by the compiler.

Organization

The guide is divided into four major parts for the classification of entries. The first part, subdivided according to the type of reference source, includes those titles of use to all social sciences, but particularly to sociology: social science guides, bibliographies, indexes and abstracts, handbooks and yearbooks, dictionaries and encyclopedias, statistics sources, directories, and biographical sources. Within these categories, entries are arranged alphabetically by author or editor, or lacking this, by title; this arrangement is used throughout the book.

In a few instances, for well-known titles or works with supervisory editors, title entries are used.

The second part, subdivided according to social science disciplines other than sociology, cites some major sources that may be particularly useful to sociologists: anthropology, economics, education, history, political science, psychology, and social work. (Political science is new to this second edition.) Entries within each discipline are arranged first by the type of reference source, then alphabetically by author or editor.

Parts 3 and 4 comprise the most important and largest sections and include reference sources dealing specifically with sociology and its subdisciplines. The third part includes general sociological guides; bibliographies; indexes, abstracts, and databases; handbooks and yearbooks; dictionaries and encyclopedias; research centers; general World Wide Web and Internet sites; journals; organizations; and directories. The section for research centers is very selective, listing only some of the centers that are mentioned in the book's citations and abstracts. For a much more thorough listing of potentially useful centers, one should consult the *Research Centers Directory* (see entry #54). The World Wide Web and Internet sites are new to this second edition. Their citations include not only a description of the Web site, but also an address (URL) and date last accessed. A selective list of Web sites for the specific subdisciplines in sociology are located in those particular chapters. Additional Web sites can be found through the general sociology sites mentioned in this section. Finally, suggestions by sociology faculty and graduate students contributed to the selection of entries for the chapter on journals. A selective list of major indexing sources accompanies each journal entry.

The fourth part covers reference sources in specific sociological areas, though it excludes some specializations because of the paucity of appropriate reference sources. Within each subject area, entries are arranged first by type of reference source, then alphabetically by author/editor or, lacking this, by title. Most of the standard subdisciplines within sociology are represented in this section. These include: clinical or applied sociology; criminology, law, and deviance; sociology of education; marriage and the family; gerontology and aging; social indicators; medical sociology; research methods and statistics; social change, movements, and collective behavior; social networks; sociology of organizations and groups; population and demography; social problems; race and ethnic relations; sociology of religion; rural sociology; socialization, social psychology, and gender roles; sociology of sport; social stratification; sociological theory; urban sociology; women's studies; and sociology of work. Subdisciplines are combined into one section when their subject matter is closely related or where the number of entries is modest. Examples include the combining of criminology and the sociology of law, and the combining of social psychology, socialization, and gender roles. No slight is intended, nor are the valid distinctions between the areas minimized.

The section on social problems is a collection of works on specific problems, such as drug abuse, alcoholism, violence, suicide, rape, and homelessness. While this is not an exhaustive list of social problems, it does represent some major problems currently treated in reference works. Many other problems, such as poverty or child abuse, are covered within other subject sections and are further accessible through the subject index.

The section devoted to race and ethnic relations includes general sources as well as sources on particular racial and ethnic groups. For space considerations, only sources on African Americans, Native Americans, Asian Americans, and Hispanic Americans are included. For sources on other racial or ethnic groups, the indexes, abstracts, databases, and other reference works in the general sources section should be consulted.

Women's studies, an interdisciplinary subject, is included because some of its reference works address concerns that are central to a number of sociological areas. These include the roles of women and men in society, social inequality, the feminization of poverty, marriage and the family, and more. In fact, one could easily argue that few areas in sociology are not illuminated by the growing literature in feminism and women's studies.

The book's citations include information on the author(s), title, publisher, location of publisher, date of publication, paging, indexes, series, price (if in print), and LC/ISBN and ISSN numbers. Prices for books in print and for serials are included, though not for online databases and government documents. *Books in Print* primarily supplied book prices. Index, abstract, and journal prices were drawn from the sources themselves or, in some cases, from *Ulrich's International Periodicals Directory*, *Faxon Guide to Serials*, *CD-ROMs in Print*, and the *Readmore Periodicals Catalog*. Journal prices are for institutional subscriptions and, as with books and index prices, are subject to change.

Arrangement of the book by subject and type of reference source should make locating titles fairly straightforward. However, additional access to entries is provided by the author/title and subject indexes.

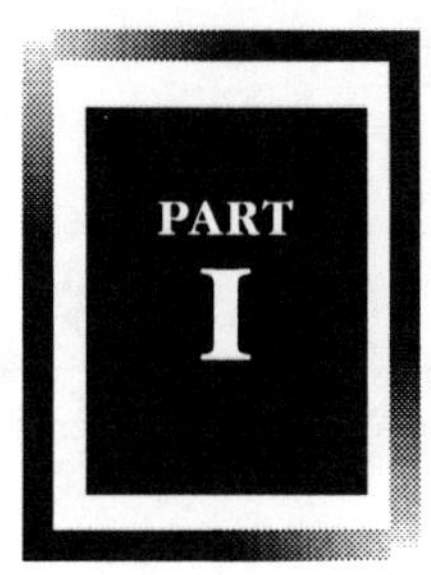

General Social Science Reference Sources

GUIDES

1. Balay, Robert, ed. **Guide to Reference Books.** 11th ed. Chicago: American Library Association, 1996. 2,020p. index. $275.00. LC 95-26322. ISBN 0-8389-0669-9.

Like its earlier editions, this is an excellent guide to reference sources in the various disciplines. It is arranged by a subject classification scheme. This includes a broad category for "General Reference Works," subdivided by type of reference source, and subsequent chapters for the specific disciplines. The chapter for sociology has subtopics for social conditions and social welfare, social work, aging, alcoholism and drug abuse, childhood and adolescence, death and dying, disabilities and the disabled, homelessness, marriage and the family, population planning, poverty and the poor, sex and sexual behavior, urbanization, ethnic groups, and women. Reference works are fully cited and briefly annotated within each of these categories. Other interesting sociological reference works can be found under different headings. For example, the "Psychology" chapter includes social psychology. Statistics and demography sources have a chapter. A combined author/title/subject index is provided.

2. Day, Alan, and Joan M. Harvey, eds. **Walford's Guide to Reference Material: Volume 2, Social and Historical Sciences, Philosophy and Religion.** 6th ed. London: Library Association Publishing, 1993. 1,156p. index. $210.00. ISBN 1-85604-044-5.

Part of a three-volume set, this volume identifies almost 8,200 reference sources across a range of social science and related disciplines, including sociology. The annotated entries are arranged according to a classification scheme, which includes major headings for philosophy and psychology; religion; social sciences; and geography, biography, and history. "Social Sciences" includes a section for sociology reference sources, which are further arranged by sociological specialty, type of reference source, and place. Other sociology-related reference sources can be found under additional subject headings, including religion, statistics, labor and employment, psychology, social services and welfare, and education. While the classification scheme of the guide is somewhat idiosyncratic, this does not appreciably detract from its usability. Author/title and subject indexes provide additional access to the entries.

3. **ESRC Data Archive Bulletin.** Colchester, United Kingdom: ESRC Data Archive, 1982- . 3 issues/yr. ISSN 0307-1391.

This is a guide to resources and services available at the ESRC (Economic and Social Research Council) Data Archive. Other print and electronic resources are also identified. The bulletin typically includes sections for archive news, data news, notices of forthcoming events, book reviews, and lists of newly acquired datasets by the ESRC and the ICPSR. Also included is an insert section titled "ESRC Software Bulletin," where relevant new software programs and workshops are described, accompanied by addresses, phone numbers, and E-mail and Web addresses.

4. **Guide to Resources and Services.** Ann Arbor, Mich.: Inter-university Consortium for Political and Social Research, ICPSR, 1977– . annual. index. free (members). ISSN 0362-8736.

The Inter-university Consortium for Political and Social Research (ICPSR) is a major source of machine-readable social science data from over 130 countries. Its archive includes over 3,000 studies, with approximately 200 studies added every year. This guide provides descriptions of those datasets, which are readily obtainable, if not already owned, by the consortium's 325 college, university, and international members.

The main body of the guide is devoted to the classified list of the archival holdings and is organized by social science area of investigation. Broad topics of interest to sociologists include population characteristics, community and urban studies, elites, organizational behavior, and social institutions and behavior. Within each subject and subsection, studies are arranged alphabetically by investigator. Study descriptions typically include not only a summary and ICPSR study number (used in indexing), but also the number of variables, number of cases, file structure, and record length. For studies released before May 1994, the guide indicates the degree to which the data have been processed by ICPSR.

Title, investigator, and subject indexes, as well as information on how to obtain datasets (via tape, diskette, CD-ROM, or ftp) and codebooks are provided in the guide. The *ICPSR Bulletin* (issued four times a year) provides updated information on newly acquired or updated datasets. Most of the information in these print sources is now available at the ICPSR World Wide Web site (see entry #267).

5. Herron, Nancy L., general editor. **The Social Sciences: A Cross-Disciplinary Guide to Selected Sources.** 2d ed. Englewood, Colo.: Libraries Unlimited Inc., 1996. 323p. $43.00. LC 95-26359. ISBN 1-056308-309-4.

In this second edition, Herron and the contributing authors provide well written, thorough, and comparative annotations for 1,030 reference sources in the general social sciences and its subdisciplines. Entries are organized into four parts comprising 12 chapters, each written by a subject librarian specializing in that discipline. Part one covers sources in "General Social Sciences" that should be of use to all of the social science disciplines. These are further subdivided by the standard reference categories, such as guides, handbooks, indexes, dictionaries, directories, etc. Part two has specific chapters for reference works in political science, economics and business, history, law and legal issues, anthropology, and sociology. Here again, reference works are cited under traditional reference book categories. The "Sociology" chapter includes 84 reference tools for accessing the literature, with good coverage of basic indexes, abstracts, and reviewing sources. Part three provides similar coverage to "emerging" social science disciplines, specifically education and psychology. Part four covers the "related" disciplines of geography and communication. Author, title, and subject indexes are provided.

6. Li, Tze-Chung. **Social Science Reference Sources: A Practical Guide.** 2d ed., rev. and enl. Westport, Conn.: Greenwood Press, 1990. 590p. (Contributions in Librarianship and Information Science, Number 68). $85.00. LC 90-2733. ISBN 0-313-25539-3.

Originally designed as a textbook for a course on reference sources in the social sciences, this second edition now includes approximately 2,200 titles. (The original edition contains 800 titles.) It is written in bibliographic essay style and is divided into two sections. The first section generally covers the social sciences. This includes chapters defining the social sciences and chapters dealing with specific types and titles of reference sources of use to social scientists. Newly added is a discussion of online database vendors and CD-ROM producers; few specific databases are covered. The second section includes reference works that specifically address the subdisciplines of the social sciences, including cultural anthropology, business (new), economics, education, geography (new), history, law, political science, psychology, and sociology. The chapter on sociology has almost triple the number of reference sources covered in the first edition, from 46 to 136. Besides the general reference sources for sociology, some specific works are cited for many of the field's subdisciplines. As with the first edition, the titles covered are thoroughly discussed. This is a generally solid overall treatment of the social sciences. The book is well written and the bibliographic essay style lends itself to comparative evaluations, though this may be less useful to sociologists than to librarians.

7. O'Brien, Jacqueline Wasserman, and Steven R. Wasserman, eds. **Statistics Sources: A Subject Guide to Data on Industrial, Business, Social, Educational, Financial, and Other Topics for the United States and Internationally.** 19th ed. Detroit: Gale, 1995. 2v. $385.00/set. ISBN 0-8013-9091-4.

This regularly updated source now includes approximately 100,000 citations to existing sources of data focusing on the United States and foreign countries. The arrangement is alphabetized by subject, with a significant number of subject headings devoted to countries. These in turn are broken down by subtopics. While most references are to published sources, some are to statistical offices that may have unpublished data. The guide is much stronger in its coverage of Western or industrialized countries. Data sources for Eastern European countries are still somewhat uneven. Sociologists and other researchers interested in development issues and social indicators may find this most useful.

8. Webb, William H. **Sources of Information in the Social Sciences.** 3d ed. Chicago: American Library Association, 1986. 777p. index. LC 84-20494. ISBN 0-8389-0405-X.

This is a revised and updated edition of Carl White's *Sources of Information in the Social Sciences* (1973). The subject coverage and organization of this edition are identical to the second edition. It consists of nine chapters, including an introductory chapter on the social sciences in general and subsequent chapters on its constituent disciplines. These include history, geography, economics, business administration, sociology, anthropology, psychology, education, and political science. Each chapter, in turn, is subdivided into two parts, one dealing with major works in the discipline and the other with major reference works. These parts are organized by subdiscipline and reference type, respectively. Specific works are discussed in a bibliographic essay style, which provides a concise introduction to the topic, not unlike an encyclopedia entry. Following this discussion, the key books are listed in standard bibliographic format. Reference works are arranged and annotated in alphabetical order under each reference type. A combined author/title/subject index in included. A notable deficiency is that many of the works cited as important to the sociological subdisciplines are now 20 or more years old, though this is not a problem with "classic" works.

9. Young, Copeland H., Kristen L. Savola, and Erin Phelps. **Inventory of Longitudinal Studies in the Social Sciences.** Newbury Park, Calif.: Sage, 1991. 567p. index. $65.00. LC 91-11195. ISBN 0-8039-4315-6.

Because of the time and expense involved in longitudinal study, researchers may want to identify and investigate existing studies on areas of interest. This guide, which describes over 200 longitudinal datasets held in the Henry A. Murray Research Center of Radcliffe College, helps expedite such pre-research investigation. The Center archives both machine-readable data and original subject records. The studies are listed alphabetically in the directory by principal investigator and cover a range of topics, including child and adolescent development, family functioning, educational intervention, deviance, mental health, personality development, aging, and other sociologically relevant topics. For each study, the directory identifies the principal investigators, contact person (with address and phone), topics covered in the study, sample characteristics, sample attrition, constructs measured and instruments used, representative references, and the status of the study. Criteria for inclusion in the directory are discussed in the introduction. Supplementary lists of the datasets by author/investigator and title, as well as author and subject indexes are also included. This complements other guides to existing datasets, such as ICPSR's *Guide to Resources and Services* (see entry #4).

BIBLIOGRAPHIES

10. **London Bibliography of the Social Sciences.** Vol. 1 - Vol. 47. London: Mansell, 1929-1989. annual. ISSN 0076-051X.

These volumes comprise a subject index to the major social science collections in London. Most titles are from the catalog of the London School of Economics and many date back to the early 1800s. While the subject coverage is broad, some aspects would be particularly useful to sociologists. The retrospective coverage allows a historical study of earlier approaches to and explanations of social problems and issues (e.g., crime, inequality). Another advantage is its international coverage; works from the United States, Great Britain, and Europe are cited, thus facilitating comparative study. Author indexes in volumes 4, 5, and 6, provide coverage through May 1936. However, author access is lacking in subsequent volumes. More recent supplements list additions to the holdings of the British Library of Political and Economic Science and the Edward Fry Library of International Law.

11. Wepsiec, Jan. **Social Sciences: An International Bibliography of Serial Literature, 1830-1985.** London: Mansell, 1992. 486p. index. $130.00. LC 90-20252. ISBN 0-7201-2109-4.

For researchers trying to identify periodical titles from the recent or distant past, Wepsiec has compiled a historical list of social science periodicals and arranged them alphabetically by title. For most serials, information includes the: 1) beginning date and volume; 2) ending date and volume (if it is no longer published); 3) name of the publisher and issuing body; 4) journal titles it has superseded or been continued by; 5) title that indexes the journal's articles; and 6) frequency of publication. *See* references direct the user from unused names or acronyms to those correct or preferred ones. The appendixes discuss the composition of the social sciences and provide brief histories of each discipline. A list of index and abstract abbreviations with full titles and starting dates and a subject index are also included.

INDEXES, ABSTRACTS, AND DATABASES

Indexes and Abstracts

12. **Alternative Press Index.** Vol. 1- , No. 1- . Baltimore, Md.: Alternative Press Center, 1969- . quarterly with annual cumulation. $225.00/yr. (institutions). LC 76-24027. ISSN 0002-662X.

The *API* is a subject index to alternative, critical, or radical periodicals, both scholarly and popular. Arrangement of the entries is by subject headings (including proper names), then alphabetically by article title. Periodical titles are abbreviated in many of the bibliographic citations. A periodical list translates these abbreviations into full titles and includes addresses and subscription prices. It also lists the specific volume and issue numbers indexed in that issue of *API*. Book, film, theater, record, and television reviews are cited by author/artist or film/play/program title under headings for the type of review. Biographies, autobiographies, and obituaries are listed by name. The annual cumulation includes selective abstracts for a small percentage of the articles.

Like *The Left Index* (see entry #26), this index covers a broad range of sociological subjects from a critical perspective. These can include topics, such as gender, racism, inequality, feminist theory, postmodernism, crime, communities, social change, and the family. *API* indexes more periodicals than does *The Left Index*, but it provides only subject access. Though periodical titles overlap somewhat, both indexes have enough distinct titles to provide complementary access to critical literature. The *API* is also available on CD-ROM (*API CD-ROM*) from the National Information Services Corporation.

13. **American Statistics Index: A Comprehensive Guide and Index to the Statistical Publications of the U.S. Government.** Washington, D.C.: Congressional Information Service, 1973- . monthly, with quarterly and annual cumulations. LC 73-82599. ISSN 0091-1658.

Two related volumes comprise this index to government statistics. To locate a statistical publication, one must look in the index volume to find its code number. By looking up this number in the accompanying abstract volume, one finds a bibliographic citation and abstract of the document. The citation is usually accompanied by a government document number, which is used to retrieve the document that contains the data. Sociologically relevant data cited here include demographic data, population data, vital statistics, educational data, and more.

The index volume permits searching by a number of routes: subjects and names, categories (geographic, economic, and demographic), titles, and agency report numbers. This database is also available through online database services such as DIALOG (*ASI*, file #102).

14. **Bibliographic Index.** Vol. 1- . New York: H. W. Wilson, 1937- . semiannual, with annual cumulations. service basis. LC 46-41034. ISSN 0006-1255.

Included here are citations to book-length bibliographies, as well as bibliographies in books, articles, and pamphlets. The only criterion for inclusion is that the bibliography contain 50 or more citations. A substantial number of sociological topics are covered, such as equality, gerontology, social classes, sampling, the Frankfurt school of sociology, and much more. This index can also be searched online through the WILSONLINE database service. Like other Wilson indexes, this source may also be available as a database on many online library catalogs.

15. **Book Review Digest.** Vol. 2- , No. 1- . New York: H. W. Wilson, 1906- . monthly (except February and July), with annual cumulations. service basis. LC 6-24490. ISSN 0006-7326.

The *Book Review Digest* provides both an index to and brief excerpts from book reviews appearing in almost 100 periodicals. To be included, a title must have been reviewed two times (for nonfiction) or three times (for fiction) in journals covered by this source. A number of important sociology and sociology-related review sources are included, such as the *American Journal of Sociology*, *Contemporary Sociology*, *Journal of Marriage and the Family*, and *The New York Review of Books*, among others.

Arrangement of the entries is by author. The complete citation for the reviewed book includes the author, title, publisher, date, price, Dewey decimal number, LC number, ISBN, and subject headings. This information is complemented by a brief summary of the book. The accompanying excerpts from reviews are generally one paragraph long and include a complete reference to the review source. Subject and title indexes are appended. This index can also be searched online through the WILSONLINE database service, on CD-ROM, and on many online library catalogs.

16. **Book Review Index.** Vol. 1- , No. 1- . Detroit: Gale, 1965- . quarterly, with semiannual cumulations. $215.00/yr. ISSN 0524-0581.

Covering reviews in over 600 publications, the *Book Review Index* arranges citations to reviews alphabetically by the author of the reviewed book. These citations include the review's source, volume, date, and pages. Also included, in some cases, are abbreviations indicating whether the reviewed work is a reference book, periodical, children's book, or young adult book. A title index is also provided; it cites an author's name, which can be cross-referenced in the author index. Reviews of sociological works are traced not only through *Contemporary Sociology*, the American Sociological Association's reviewing journal, but also through related social science journals, such as *Families in Society*, *Society*, *Sociological Review*, *Policy Studies Journal*, and *Social Service Review*. A CD-ROM version of this index is also available.

17. **Combined Retrospective Index to Book Reviews in Scholarly Journals, 1886-1974.** Evan Ira Farber, executive ed. Woodbridge, Conn.: Research Publications, 1979. 15v. LC 79-89137. ISBN 0-8408-0157-2.

As a retrospective index to reviews, this is an invaluable source. Twelve of the 15 volumes comprise the alphabetical index of authors of reviewed books. Each reviewed title is listed separately, followed by the journal title, volume, year, and page(s). Volumes 13–15 comprise the alphabetical title index. The title is accompanied by a *see* reference to the author; by looking up the author's name in the author index, one can find the review citations. Reviews of many of the classic works in sociology can be found here, and therein lies its value for sociologists doing historical research.

18. **Comprehensive Dissertation Index, 1861-1972.** Ann Arbor, Mich.: University Microfilms International, 1973. 8v. LC 73-89046.

19. **Comprehensive Dissertation Index. Supplement.** Ann Arbor, Mich.: University Microfilms International, 1973- . annual. LC 76-642006. ISSN 0361-6657.

For locating dissertations by either author or subject, these sources are useful, though accessing information through electronic versions of *Dissertation Abstracts International* is much faster. To find dissertations by subject, one first must locate the volume for the discipline. The cumulative volumes for 1861–1972 and 1973–1977 are devoted to specific disciplines, whereas the supplements for 1978 and subsequent years are labeled either "Social Sciences and Humanities" or "Sciences." The latter supplements are subdivided by discipline. Within disciplines, dissertations are arranged by as many title keywords as apply. Thus, multiple subject access points for each dissertation should exist.

Citations include author, title, date completed, university awarding the degree, pages, order number, and a *Dissertation Abstracts International* citation. The last item allows one to locate the abstract in *DAI*. The author index includes the same citation information.

20. **Cumulative Subject Index to the Public Affairs Information Service Bulletins 1915-1974.** Ruth Matteson Blackmore, ed. Arlington, Va.: Carrollton Press, 1977. 15v. LC 76-50520. ISBN 0-8408-0200-5.

Given the number of years that the *PAIS Bulletin* (now the *PAIS International in Print*) has been issued, this index is quite a time saver for historical research. Sociologists interested in tracing the way social and policy issues were analyzed and addressed over time should find this useful. Subject headings are broken down into subheadings and sub-subheadings, making finding materials on one's specific topic relatively easy. The index uses *see* and *see also* references for used and related terms. Citations include the year, page, column (left or right), and numerical position of the article in the *PAIS Bulletin*.

21. **Current Contents: Social and Behavioral Sciences.** Vol. 1- , No. 1- . weekly, except last week of December. Philadelphia: Institute for Scientific Information, 1969- . $530.00/yr. ISSN 0092-6361.

Current Contents is a guide to the tables of contents of over 1,400 journals, including numerous sociological journals. As such, it is a great service for scholars interested in scanning social and behavioral science literature for relevant references. Of course, not all journals are covered in each issue. Those included are listed in the front of the index and subsequently grouped under broad social science headings (e.g., law, psychology, social work and social policy, and sociology and anthropology). Each issue of *Current Contents* has an author and address directory, a title word index, and a publisher's directory. A cumulative journal index is published triannually, and a complete publisher's address directory is issued twice yearly. Also included in each issue are the tables of contents of three or four multiauthored new books. This source is also available as *Current Contents Search* in the DIALOG database service (file #440).

22. **Directory of Published Proceedings: Series SSH-Social Sciences/Humanities.** Vol. 1- . Harrison, N.Y.: InterDok Corp., 1968- . quarterly, with annual and four year cumulations. $375.00/yr. ISSN 0012-3293.

Along with *Index to Social Sciences and Humanities Proceedings* (see entry #25), this directory provides access to published conference proceedings. Its main section includes descriptions of each proceeding, with information on the date of the conference, an access number, location, conference name or publication title, conference acronym, conference theme, conference sponsor, proceedings title, series or serial information, editor, publisher, distributor, acquisition information (i.e., cost, LC number, ISBN, number of pages and volumes, date of publication), and subject descriptor. Supplementary lists of country codes, publishers and their addresses, editors, and acronyms, as well as a subject/sponsor index are also available. Proceedings focus on such sociological topics as social movements, gerontology, sociology of education, policy studies, race relations, urban sociology, social psychology, and more.

23. **Dissertation Abstracts International.** Vol. 30- . Ann Arbor, Mich.: University Microfilms International, 1969- . monthly, with annual author index. ISSN 0419-4209(pt. A); 0419-4217(pt. B); 1042-7279(pt. C).

For those involved in advanced research or thesis and dissertation literature reviews, this is an essential source. The author-written abstracts are organized into volumes by broad topics: the humanities and social sciences (part A), the sciences and engineering (part B), and worldwide (part C). Within volumes, abstracts are classified by broad subject (e.g., sociology) and more specific subjects. Subcategories for sociology are: general, criminology and penology, demography, ethnic and racial studies, individual and family studies, industrial and labor relations, public and social welfare, social structure and development, and theory and methods. Abstracts are then arranged alphabetically by author.

Citations include author, title, date of completion, institution, pages, dissertation director, and order number. A keyword title index, which cites dissertations by every keyword in the title, provides further access. An author index, which is cumulated annually (except for part C, the worldwide abstracts volume), is also included. Part C, *Worldwide Abstracts*, is a sequel to the previous title, *European Abstracts*, which began in 1976. It includes titles in the original abstracts' languages, along with English translations; the abstracts, themselves, are usually translated into English.

Coverage back to 1938 is provided by *Dissertations Abstracts* and *Microfilm Abstracts*. *DAI* is also available through database vendors (such as DIALOG, file #35), on CD-ROM (e.g., from SilverPlatter), and through many library online catalogs. These electronic versions of *DAI* are much faster and less laborious to search than the print version but do not include abstracts of older dissertations.

24. **Human Resources Abstracts.** Vol. 1- , No. 1- . Thousand Oaks, Calif.: Sage, 1966- . quarterly. $330.00/yr.(institutions). ISSN 0099-2453.

Approximately 250 books and articles are abstracted in each issue. Topics covered span the social sciences, with many of interest to sociologists. These subjects include work life and environment, education, industrial and labor relations, workplace crime and violence, stress, organizations, aging, health, social services, and more. Entries are arranged alphabetically by author within the subject categories. The paragraph-long citations include subject headings so that one can find related articles through the subject index. An author index is also provided, as is a supplementary, unannotated list of related citations (arranged by the same subject categories used in the body of the volume).

25. **Index to Social Sciences and Humanities Proceedings.** Philadelphia: Institute for Scientific Information, 1979- . quarterly, with annual cumulations. $1,175.00/yr. ISSN 0191-0574.

This indexes published proceedings, with coverage including such subject areas as sociology, demography, criminology, urban studies, religion, and ethnic group studies, among others. Also available are the "most significant" (p. v) proceedings, which may be available as books, journal issues, preprints, or Institute for Scientific Information (ISI) reprints. The main body of the index is the conference proceedings section. Entries are arranged by proceeding number, and information is provided on the conference title, location, date, sponsor, title and availability of proceedings (in books or journals), ordering address, titles of papers, and more. Many papers are available through an ISI service called *The Genuine Article*.

Access to these proceedings is provided by a number of indexes: category (broad subject), permuterm subject (to papers/conferences and books), sponsor, author/editor, meeting location, and corporate (arranged by an author's geographic location and organizational affiliation).

A large number of sociology and related social science conference proceedings are cited. For tracking down additional conference papers, one should consult those listings in *Sociological Abstracts* (see entry #116) or the *Directory of Published Proceedings* (see entry #22).

26. **The Left Index: A Quarterly Index to Periodicals of the Left.** Santa Cruz, Calif.: The Left Index, 1982- . quarterly, with an annual subject cumulation. $70.00/yr(institutions). LC 82-5102. ISSN 0733-2998.

Sociology students and researchers interested in finding articles written from a critical or conflict perspective should find this index useful. It is valuable to cricial analyses of social issues and cites articles from approximately 100 Marxist, radical, and left periodicals that address topics relevant to all of the social sciences. Sociological topics are well represented, including social movements, social classes, social theory, work, criminology, race, sex roles, and more. One can also find subject index entries for specific theorists, such as Antonio Gramsci, Jürgen Habermas, Emile Durkheim, Hannah Arendt, and Louis Althusser. Access to entries is provided by author, subject, book review, and journal indexes, as well as an annual, cumulated subject index. Listings of selected documents and recent periodicals are also available.

27. **Monthly Catalog of United States Government Publications.** Washington, D.C.: GPO, 1895- . monthly, with semiannual and annual indexes. ISSN 0362-6830.

This is the most comprehensive and definitive print index to government publications. It offers a variety of access points in the cumulative indexes, including author, title, subject, keyword, series/report, contract number, and stock number. The indexes provide entry numbers, which are used to look up the citations. Further, these citations generally include a government document (SuDocs) number, by which the documents are arranged in library collections.

The U.S. government publishes a great deal of data of use to sociologists, including data on population, aging, health, crime, income, educational achievement, and more. This index is also available through online database services, such as DIALOG (file #66, *GPO Monthly Catalog*), on CD-ROM (*MOCAT, MARCIVE*) and, for new records, on the Internet (Available: http://www.access.gpo.gov/su_docs) (Accessed: October 2, 1996).

28. **PAIS International in Print.** Vol. 1- , No. 1- . New York: Public Affairs Information Service, Inc., 1991- . monthly, with cumulations every fourth issue and annually. $590.00/yr. ISSN 1051-4015.

PAIS International in Print indexes and briefly abstracts books, articles, government documents, agency reports, and other materials relating to public affairs and public policy. It has a subject arrangement and includes a number of topics of interest to sociologists, such as crime, poverty, group behavior, family, work, women, culture, race relations, social status, evaluation research, and policy sciences. Coverage of state and federal publications on these subjects facilitates social policy analysis. Comparative analysis is made possible by the selective inclusion of foreign language publications in French, German, Italian, Portuguese, and Spanish. This title continues the earlier *PAIS Bulletin*, retrospective searching of which can be accomplished by using the *Combined Retrospective Index to the Public Affairs Information Service Bulletins 1915-1974*.

PAIS is also available online through database services, such as OCLC and DIALOG (*PAIS International*, file #49), on CD-ROM (from SilverPlatter and Ebsco), and on many library online catalogs. A new selective, full-text version on CD-ROM, called *PAIS Select*, is also available.

29. **Social Sciences Citation Index.** Vol. 1- , No. 1- . Philadelphia: Institute for Scientific Information, 1973- . 3 issues/yr. with annual cumulations. $5,920.00/yr. ISSN 0091-3707.

This is an invaluable reference work in the social sciences, covering some 4,700 journals and selective monographic series. It is really four indexes in one: a citation index, a source index, a corporate index, and a subject index. The citation index may be used to find who has cited authors and their particular work. Then, one can look up that person's name in the source index and find a complete reference to their article. The corporate index is an alphabetical list of institutions accompanied by a list of authors affiliated with those institutions. Finally, the permuterm subject index is a sophisticated index to combinations of all significant terms in the title and subtitle of an article. This is useful if one remembers only parts of a title, or if one wants articles relating certain concepts.

This index is issued three times a year, with an annual cumulation. (The years 1976–1980 are cumulated as an index.) An online equivalent, *Social SciSearch*, is available through the DIALOG database service (file #7). CD-ROM versions, with or without abstracts, are also available from the Institute for Scientific Information.

30. **Social Sciences Index.** Vol. 1- , No. 1- . Bronx, N. Y.: H. W. Wilson, 1974- . quarterly, with annual cumulations. service basis. ISSN 0094-4920.

Like other Wilson indexes, this is an easy-to-use author and subject index to English language social science articles in over 400 periodicals published worldwide. Virtually any sociological specialty will show up as a subject here; *see* and *see also* references direct the user to preferred and additional subject terms. A separate section at the end of each issue cites book reviews alphabetically by book author or title.

The major sociological journals are indexed here, as are the journals representing the various specializations, making this a good source for representative, current articles on sociological topics. This source is also available in various versions on CD-ROM. A version citing bibliographic references, part of the Wilsondisc series, is available from H. W. Wilson and covers from 1983 to the present. A full-text version, covering 1989 to the present, is available from UMI (University Microfilms International). This source is also available from the DIALOG database service (*Wilson Social Sciences Abstracts*, file #142), from the WILSONLINE database service, and through many online library catalogs.

Databases

31. **ASI (American Statistics Index).** Washington, D.C.: Congressional Information Service, 1974- . monthly updates. DIALOG file #102.

This is the online equivalent of the printed index of the same name (see entry #13). It identifies statistics in publications issued by approximately 500 Federal and regional agencies. Like the print source, it includes an abstract of the publication and a description of its statistical data. Some of the subject areas covered include population and census data, employment and unemployment statistics, crime data, vital statistics, and educational data.

32. **ASSIA: Applied Social Sciences Index & Abstracts.** London: Library Association, 1987- . DataStar Label: ASSI.

Social science journal articles from the United Kingdom and North America are indexed on this online counterpart to the print source *Applied Social Sciences Index & Abstracts: ASSIA* (ISSN 0950-2238). The emphasis of the database is on applied aspects of the social sciences. DataStar is a collection of European-oriented databases, which are offered through Knight-Ridder Information, the provider of DIALOG and its databases.

33. **Current Contents Search.** Philadelphia: Institute for Scientific Information, 1990- . weekly updates. DIALOG file #440.

All of the seven print versions of *Current Contents*, including the social and behavioral sciences version (see entry #21), are covered by this DIALOG database. An advantage of this collective version of *Current Contents* is that it also includes the medical and life sciences journals, which may be of interest to medical sociologists. Approximately 1,400 social and behavioral science journals are indexed.

34. **Dissertation Abstracts Online.** Ann Arbor, Mich.: University Microfilms International, 1861- . monthly updates. DIALOG file #35.

The online equivalent of *Dissertation Abstracts International* (see entry #23), this cites doctoral dissertations and masters theses produced in the United States since 1861. British and European dissertations have been included since 1988. Some dissertations from other countries are included as well. Abstracts begin to accompany the dissertation citations in about 1980, though they accompany much older citations in the print version of the source. *Dissertation Abstracts* is also available on CD-ROM from SilverPlatter.

35. **Index to Social Sciences and Humanities Proceedings.** Philadelphia: Institute for Scientific Information, 1994- . quarterly.

A relatively new CD-ROM, this is the electronic version of the printed source of the same name. Included are bibliographic references to over 100,000 conference papers presented at some 18,000 conferences. Approximately 800 conferences and 6,000 papers are added every quarter.

36. **MARCIVE GPO/CAT PAC.** [CD-ROM]. San Antonio, Tex.: MARCIVE Inc., 1986- . monthly updates.

MARCIVE is a CD-ROM database that is advertised as the "enhanced *Monthly Catalog* on CD-ROM." Like its print equivalent, the *Monthly Catalog of United States Government Publications* (see entry #27), *MARCIVE* provides a variety of searching options for identifying government documents. One can search by title or series, author or agency, subject, number (e.g., SuDoc), or a combination of fields of information. Retrieved are detailed bibliographic citations to government publications, many of which may be available in depository library collections.

37. **PAIS International.** New York: Public Affairs Information Service, 1972- . monthly updates. DIALOG file #49.

This DIALOG database provides citations from the *PAIS International in Print* (since 1991), the superseded *PAIS Bulletin* (1976-1990), and the PAIS *Foreign Language Index* (1972-1990). Like the print equivalents, it provides international coverage on books, articles, and government documents in social policy and the social sciences.

38. **Public Opinion Online (POLL).** Storrs, Conn.: Roper Center for Public Opinion Research, 1936- . weekly updates. DIALOG file #468.

Included in this full-text database are public opinion surveys and results from major polling companies and news gathering organizations. Roper, Harris, Gallup, and Yankelovich polls are covered, as are surveys conducted by major newspapers and broadcast networks, among others. Coverage is 1936 to the present, though selective earlier coverage is available. A wide range of social policies and issues is treated.

39. **Social SciSearch.** Philadelphia: Institute for Scientific Information, 1972- . weekly updates. DIALOG file #7.

The online counterpart to the *Social Sciences Citation Index* (see entry #29), this indexes major social science journal articles and important monographs by numerous fields of information, including keyword in title, author, and journal. Furthermore, it allows the user to trace where particular scholarly works have been cited by other authors. In addition to scanning approximately 1,500 social science journals for articles, about 3,000 journals in the natural and biomedical sciences are scanned for social science articles as well.

40. **Wilson Social Sciences Abstracts.** [CD-ROM]. New York: H. W. Wilson, 1983- . quarterly updates.

This is a CD-ROM variation on Wilson's *Social Sciences Index* (see entry #30). It indexes articles from approximately 400 social science journals and, unlike the print source, includes abstracts. Major sociological journals are included, as are sociologically relevant journals from the other social sciences. This source is also available on the DIALOG database service (file #142).

HANDBOOKS AND YEARBOOKS

41. **American Reference Books Annual.** Vol. 1- . Englewood, Colo.: Libraries Unlimited, 1970- . annual. index. $95.00. ISSN 0065-9959.

With over 1,800 books reviewed in each volume, this is one of the major reviewing sources for new reference books. Broad subject headings include general reference works, the social sciences, the humanities, and science and technology. Each of these is extensively subdivided by subject area and type of reference source. Sociology, for example, regularly includes subsections on aging, the family, community, social welfare, and more. Other major social sciences covered in this source include anthropology, education, history, political science, psychology, and law/criminology.

While new scholarly books can be found in reviews and bibliographies, new reference books can prove to be more elusive. *ARBA*'s annual compilation of signed, evaluative reviews provides scholars and librarians with information on important new reference titles. Each volume includes thorough author/title and subject indexes.

42. **Books in Print.** New York: Bowker, 1948- . 9v. annual. index. $510.00/set. ISSN 0068-0214.

These volumes provide bibliographic and ordering information for new and old books in print. The set is made up of two related four-volume sets covering titles and authors, as well as a supplementary volume on publishers. For both sets, arrangement of entries is alphabetical. Bibliographic information includes not only the author(s) and title, but also number of pages, date of publication, publisher, price, edition, and ISBN.

The ninth volume provides lists of symbols and abbreviations, a name index, and a variety of information on and indexes to publishers, distributors, and wholesalers. Subject access is provided through the four-volume companion set, *Subject Guide to Books in Print* (see entry #43). All of the information in the print volumes of *Books in Print* is also available on CD-ROM (*Books in Print PLUS*), and online through database vendors, such as DIALOG (*Books in Print*, file #480) and LEXIS-NEXIS.

43. **Subject Guide to Books in Print.** New York: Bowker, 1957- . 5v. annual. $359.95/set. ISSN 0000-0159.

These are the companion volumes to *Books in Print* (see entry #42). They provide subject access to *BIP* using Library of Congress subject headings. Information included in the entries is the same as that included in *BIP* (i.e., author, title, publisher, ISBN, price, pages, date of publication, edition). The last volume also contains a key to publishers' and distributors' abbreviations, as well as a list of Library of Congress subject headings, which are used throughout these volumes.

DICTIONARIES AND ENCYCLOPEDIAS

44. Kuper, Adam, and Jessica Kuper, eds. **The Social Science Encyclopedia.** 2d ed. London: Routledge, 1996. 923p. $89.95. ISBN 0-415-10829-2.

Approximately 600 social scientific terms, fields, theories, and theorists receive fairly sophisticated descriptions in this encyclopedia. The signed entries, written by over 500 contributing experts, cover not only topics in the various social sciences, but also related topics in such disciplines as biology, business, media, and medicine. Major sociological fields and topics are treated. Sociological theorists are covered very selectively, with entries on major figures like Marx, Durkheim, and Weber.

Entries range in length from a few paragraphs to a few pages. Bibliographic references and suggested readings are appended to most articles, as are *see also* references to related terms. While the entries are generally well written, they are not for beginners, making this an excellent one-volume encyclopedia for the more advanced student or scholar. This edition is a major revision and update of the first edition, with half of the entries being "new or . . . completely rewritten" (p. vii). Consequently, many recent and important topics are included, such as postmodernism and cultural studies, among others.

45. Outhwaite, William, and Tom Bottomore, eds. **The Blackwell Dictionary of Twentieth-Century Social Thought.** Oxford: Blackwell, 1993. 864p. index. $49.95. LC 92-20837. ISBN 0-631-15262-8.

The topics covered in this source range across all of the social science disciplines, with a focus on those "bodies of thought that have been influential in this century" (Preface). Entries were written by experts and focus primarily on concepts, theories or schools of thought, and organizations and institutions. Overall, the essays are fairly lengthy for a dictionary, typically running to two double-column pages. Concepts that are mentioned in the entries and that are defined elsewhere in the dictionary are capitalized. *See* and *see also* references direct the user to preferred and related subjects. A short, though consistently excellent, suggested reading list accompanies each entry . Throughout, major sociological and sociology-related terms are included. No biographical entries on important figures are given; relevant information is bundled in with the essays on their theories. However, a "Biographical Appendix," with very brief biographies, is provided on approximately 80 individuals, including Emile Durkheim, Karl Marx, Antonio Gramsci, Jürgen Habermas, Theodor Adorno, Louis Althusser, Hannah Arendt, George Herbert Mead, Herbert Marcuse, Max Weber, Talcott Parsons, Herbert Spencer, Thorstein Veblen, Georg Simmel, Michel Foucault, Karl Mannheim, and others. This dictionary is not for beginning sociology students. However, it is well written and should be valuable for upper-level undergraduates, graduate students, and researchers exploring new subject areas.

46. Stearns, Peter N., ed. **Encyclopedia of Social History.** New York: Garland, 1994. 856p. index. (Garland Reference Library of Social Science; Vol. 780). $95.00. LC 93-29230. ISBN 0-8153-0342-4.

Social history, as the editor of this encyclopedia explains, is distinguished by both its frequent focus on non-elite social groups and its interest in the historical development of a broad range of social behaviors. This source's subjects and method make it of potential interest to sociologists, as important sociological concepts are treated, including alienation, bureaucracy, culture of poverty, gender socialization, mobility, and stratification and inequality. Likewise, essays on important social institutions, such as the family, mass media, education, religion, and the family are presented. Major concepts related to societal development, such as modernization or postindustrial society, are also included. The essays are one to four pages long, with a modest number of references for further reading. They also include *see also* references to related concepts found in the encyclopedia. A name/subject index is provided. If good social analysis is necessarily historical, as some argue, then this encyclopedia should help broaden the user's focus on familiar sociological topics.

STATISTICS

47. **County and City Data Book.** Washington, D.C.: Department of Commerce, Economic Statistics Administration, Bureau of the Census; distr., Washington, D.C., GPO, 1949- . irregular. ISSN 0082-9455.

Now in its 12th edition (1994), this data book continues to be a good source of basic statistics on states, counties, cities (25,000 or more), and places (2,500 or more). Data included cover such broad areas as population, health, social welfare programs, crime, housing, work, education, labor force, income, government, employment, business statistics, elections, and agriculture. The contents of the statistical tables and how they were compiled are explained in an introductory section of source notes and explanations. These data are drawn from both governmental agencies (e.g., Bureau of Census, Bureau of Labor Statistics, National Center for Health Statistics) and private agencies (e.g., American Hospital Association).

The appendixes include source notes and explanations for the different data tables, descriptions of the geographic and metropolitan statistical areas, county maps by state, and table outlines. Although the data book does not go into great depth, it can be excellent for comparative data on fundamental subjects. It is also available on diskette and CD-ROM in many libraries.

48. **Demographic Yearbook.** New York: Department for Economic and Social Information and Policy Analysis, United Nations, 1948- . annual. $125.00. ISSN 0082-8041.

For comparative research into population and demography, the *Demographic Yearbook* is an invaluable tool. It presents country-by-country data on such areas as population, birth and death rates, fetal mortality, legally induced abortions, and nuptiality. Each of these broad categories includes a handful of subcategories of data, with each table listing countries alphabetically within their world region. In addition to the recurring categories of data, every issue of the yearbook has a special topic section with data on a particular subject. Many of these should be of use to sociologists as they touch on key subjects, like fertility and mortality, population aging, marriage and divorce, international migration, and household composition. These special topics are revisited periodically. Extensive technical notes explaining the content and limitations of the data tables are available, with all notes and table headings in both English and French. Finally, a subject index identifies which volumes in this series contain data on a particular subject. Researchers should note the existence of an approximate two-year lag between the year of the data and the publication year of the volume.

49. **Historical Statistics of the United States: Colonial Times to 1970.** Washington, D.C.: Bureau of the Census; distr., Washington, D.C.: GPO, 1975. 2v. LC 75-38832. ISBN 0-318-11732-0.

These two volumes contain historical statistics arranged under 24 major topics, covering population, health, resources, business and economics, government, social statistics, and other areas. As in other census publications, introductory sections are available describing data collection criteria and data comparability for the various tables. How many years each table represents varies. Each volume has a time period index, a subject index, and a list of contributors.

50. **State and Metropolitan Area Data Book: A Statistical Abstract Supplement: Metropolitan Areas, Central Cities, States.** Washington, D.C.: U.S. Department of Commerce, Bureau of the Census; distr., Washington, D.C.: GPO, 1979- . irregular. ISSN 0276-6566.

This is an abstract of both governmental and nongovernmental data drawn from a variety of agencies and associations. Though billed as representing "some of the most up-to-date facts available" (4th ed, p. ix), the most recent edition was published in 1991. The data included are selective and cover such areas as population, crimes, health, income, labor force, school enrollment, and vital statistics. These are some of the same categories covered by the *County and City Data Book* (see entry #47), though, in this data book, they are broken down by different geographical areas.

The statistics are presented for four different areas: metropolitan areas (MSAs, CMSAs, and NECMAs); metropolitan areas and their component counties; central cities of SMSAs (broken down by central city and metropolitan area); and states. A section of source notes and explanations describes all of the data tables. Four appendixes help clarify some of the concepts and categories: geographic concepts and codes; an alphabetical listing of PMSA's with CMSA's; component counties of metropolitan areas, by state; and central cities of metropolitan areas, by state. Table outlines for all tables, and a subject index for the data on states are also included.

51. **Statistical Abstract of the United States.** Washington, D.C.: Bureau of the Census; distr., Washington, D.C., GPO, 1878- . annual. LC 4-18089. ISSN 0081-4741.

Supplemented by both the *State and Metropolitan Area Data Book* (see entry #50) and the *County and City Data Book* (see entry #47), this is a compendium of selective data on a wide range of subjects. Topics covered include population, vital statistics, immigration, health, education, law enforcement, environment, and elections. A section of comparative international statistics is also available. Though the data included throughout the volume are selective, source notes can lead to the original documents and, possibly, more extensive data on the subject.

Data presented in many of the tables are retrospective. This feature, combined with the number of years the abstract has been published, lends itself to the charting of historical trends. The appendixes include information on metropolitan statistical areas, methodology and limitations, sources of data, tables with historical statistics, tables deleted from the previous edition, and newly added tables. A thorough subject index in also included.

52. **Statistical Yearbook.** Lanham, Md.: UNESCO Publishing and Berman Press, 1963- . annual. $95.00. ISSN 0082-7541.

Included in this yearbook are comparative data, by country, in the areas of education, scientific manpower, research and development expenditures, culture and communication (e.g., number of book titles published, radio and television receiver per 1,000 inhabitants, and daily newspapers), printed materials (e.g., libraries and book production data), film and cinema, broadcasting, and international trade in printed matter. In all, data from over 200 countries are reflected in the tables. Because of variations in countries' record keeping, there are some gaps. Table headings and introductory sections are provided in English, Spanish, and French. Appendixes covering member states, school years, exchange rates, UNESCO statistical publications, and introductory texts in Russian and Arabic are included. Sociologists interested in sociology of education or comparative development issues may find this yearbook particularly relevant.

DIRECTORIES

53. **Encyclopedia of Associations, Vol. 1: National Organizations of the U.S.** Detroit: Gale, 1961- . 3v. annual. ISSN 0071-0202.

Included here are brief descriptions of approximately 23,000 national and international organizations and associations. Entries are organized by broad subject categories in the first two volumes, which are labeled Volume 1, Part 1 and Volume 1, Part 2. These include categories for educational, cultural, social welfare, health, public affairs, and other organizations. For effective searching, one needs to use the subject and keyword index found in the third volume, which is labeled Volume 1, Part 3. Citations include the address, phone number, director, purpose of the organization, publications, and annual conventions. Other volumes in the series include *Encyclopedia of Associations: International Organizations* (ISSN 1041-0023) and *Encyclopedia of Associations: Regional, State, and Local Organizations* (ISSN 0894-2846). This is an invaluable guide for identifying professional sociological and sociology-related organizations.

54. **Research Centers Directory.** Detroit: Gale, 1960- . 2v. annual. $485.00/set. LC 60-14807. ISSN 0800-1518.

Over 13,000 research centers are listed in this directory, including "centers, laboratories, institutes . . . research support facilities, technology transfer centers, think tanks . . . and more" (20th ed., 1996, p. viii). The entries are organized under 17 broad subject categories, where they are then arranged alphabetically by the center's name. Of particular interest to sociologists might be the categories for medical and health sciences (medical sociology), government and public affairs (policy studies), labor and industrial relations (industrial sociology and sociology of work), behavioral and social sciences (aging, family, ethnicity, conflict, and more), education (sociology of education), and humanities and religion (sociology of religion). For each research center the information includes such items as address, phone number, E-mail address, date founded, director, staff, source of support, research activities and fields, and publications and services. Subject, geographic, and personal name indexes are included. Additionally, a master index lists centers by name, keyword in the name, and college/university affiliation. This directory is supplemented by *New Research Centers* (1965-). An expanded version of this directory is available through the DIALOG database service (*Research Centers and Services Directory*, file #115); it also includes government centers, international centers, and research services.

55. Sykes, Wendy, Martin Bulmer, and Marleen Schwerzel, eds. **Directory of Social Research Organisations in the United Kingdom.** London: Mansell, 1993. 421p. index. $70.00. ISBN 0-7201-2165-5.

Over 1,000 British social research organizations are described in this directory. To be included, the organization had to either conduct or commission empirical social research. These organizations reflect a range of institutions and settings, including governmental research units, private research institutes, market research firms, higher education research centers, public companies, and more. The organizations are listed alphabetically in the main section of the directory. Each has a number of common categories of information: address, phone, fax, head (chair or director), sector (type of organization), number of researchers, fields of research, commission research (yes or no), recent projects, training opportunities, research services offered, main contact, and other contacts. When recent projects are described, the entry mentions their funding source and main output. The directory also provides some brief, introductory essays on conducting market research in various institutional settings. The supplementary material includes a list of freelance researchers, philanthropic foundations that fund social research, United Kingdom and international social research associations, and training courses. Additional indexes are available for other organizations (not listed in the main entry section) and for research fields. The latter, with sometimes hundreds of entry numbers under broad research areas, is minimally helpful.

56. **World Directory of Social Science Institutions.** 4th ed. Paris: UNESCO, 1985. 905p. index. (World Social Services Information Services). ISBN 92-3-002358-2.

Almost 2,000 social science institutions worldwide are described in this directory. It is arranged into three sections. The first section is an alphabetical list of organization names and acronyms, with a cross-reference to the entry number and complete description, which is located in the second section. Section two is an alphabetical list of official organization names, accompanied by the full description of the organization. This section lists institutions alphabetically within their country; it is preceded by a subsection of 289 international and regional organizations. The descriptions include such information as the address, organization creation date, staff, senior researchers, type of organization, parent organization, topical coverage, geographical coverage, activity, publications, and a brief annotation. Section three is an alphabetical list of institution heads, with a cross-reference to the entry number for the organization. Though somewhat dated, this is nonetheless useful for identifying relevant social science institutions in other countries.

57. **World List of Social Science Periodicals.** Paris: Unesco, 1991. 1,264p. index. (World Social Science Information Directories, 1). ISBN 92-3-002734-0.

Over 4,400 social science periodicals are described here, in four sections. Section one is an alphabetical title index with an entry number. Section two contains full entries for periodicals, arranged by country, then alphabetically by title. Section three is a subject index (including geographical coverage). Section four is an index of bibliographic and abstracting periodicals by field and geographical area. An annex (appendix) lists abbreviations of indexes and abstracts that are part of the periodical descriptions. The main entries include periodical title, starting date, frequency, ISSN, editor's name and address (usually), publisher (usually with address and phone), length and number of articles, and description. The introduction and headings are presented in English, French, and Spanish.

58. **The World of Learning.** London: Europa Publications Ltd., 1947- . annual. $415.00. ISSN 0084-2117.

Now in its 46th edition (1996), this is an excellent international directory of educational and cultural institutions, organizations, and centers. It is arranged alphabetically by country. Entries for various academies, learned societies, libraries, museums and art galleries, universities, colleges, and research institutes are provided on each country. The address, phone number, founding date, membership, director's name, and publications are listed for many of the institutions. Some entries are descriptively annotated. Many college and university entries, both for the United States and elsewhere, include faculty members listed by their departmental/faculty affiliation. An introductory section lists some international organizations and associations, with accompanying addresses, phone numbers, functions, and contact names. A thorough index to the cited institutions is available. This source should help those trying to locate international sociology and sociology-related departments, associations, or research centers.

BIOGRAPHIES

59. **The National Faculty Directory.** 26th ed. New York: Gale, 1996. 3v. $685.00. LC 76-14404. ISBN 0-8103-9069-8.

This is a straightforward alphabetical list of approximately 650,000 teaching faculty members at 3,600 U.S. and 240 Canadian institutions of higher education. Faculty with nonteaching responsibilities, or librarians with faculty rank, are not included. For faculty members who are included, a departmental affiliation, institutional affiliation, and mailing address are provided. Individuals' phone numbers and academic rank are not provided. An introductory "Roster of Colleges and Universities" lists institutions alphabetically within each state and provides an address and phone number.

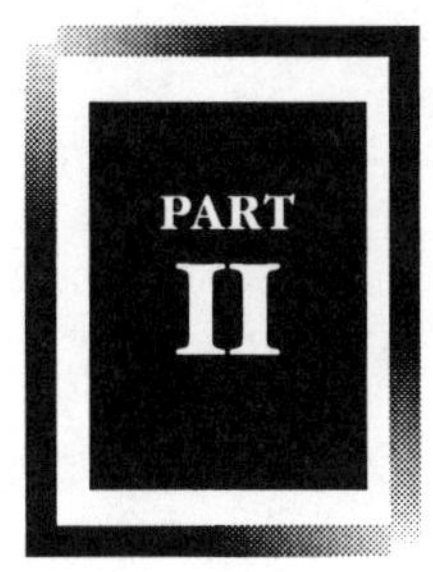

Social Science Disciplines

ANTHROPOLOGY

Guides

60. Kibee, Josephine Z. **Cultural Anthropology: A Guide to Reference and Information Sources.** Englewood, Colo.: Libraries Unlimited, 1991. 205p. index. (Reference Sources in the Social Sciences, No. 5). $47.50. LC 91-14042. ISBN 0-87287-739-6.

The overlap between the field of cultural anthropology and the various subdisciplines of sociology is significant and includes such areas as medical anthropology, urban anthropology, anthropology of education, political anthropology, research methods, religion, and anthropology of women, among others. This annotated guide describes reference sources in these and other areas of cultural anthropology, as well as sources from related disciplines. Its 668 entries are arranged into nine chapters: general and social science reference sources; general anthropology reference sources; anthropology bibliography; subfields of anthropology; anthropology and the humanities; additional topics in anthropology; area studies; periodicals; and supplemental resources. The chapters for subfields, the humanities, and additional topics are all subdivided by topic; "Area Studies" is comprised of sections on the world regions. Throughout the book, reference sources within sections are arranged by the type of source. Supplemental resources include directories and descriptions of anthropological organizations, libraries, archives, and publishers. One-to-two paragraph descriptive abstracts accompany virtually all entries. Author/title and subject indexes are also provided.

Indexes, Abstracts, and Databases

61. **Abstracts in Anthropology.** Vol. 1- , No. 1- . Amityville, N.Y.: Baywood Publishing, 1970- . quarterly. $277.00/yr. ISSN 0001-3455.

Over 700 articles from approximately 150 journals are abstracted in each issue. They are classified by subject under major subject categories: archaeology, physical anthropology, linguistics, and cultural anthropology. The section for cultural anthropology may be of most interest to sociologists. It has subheadings for social policy, family organization/marriage, medical anthropology, minorities, social organization, sociocultural change, symbol systems (e.g., religion), and urban studies, among others. A list of the indexed periodicals is in each issue, as well as subject and author indexes. Major topics and journals from sociology and the other social sciences are well represented here, making this much more than a tool just for anthropologists.

Dictionaries and Encyclopedias

62. Broude, Gwen J. **Marriage, Family, and Relationships: A Cross-Cultural Encyclopedia.** Santa Barbara, Calif.: ABC-CLIO, 1994. 372p. index. (Encyclopedias of the Human Experience). $49.50. LC 94-38979. ISBN 0-87436-736-0.

Anthropological and evolutionary approaches are used in this encyclopedia to explain many common features of marriage, family, and relationships. Over 100 terms are included, with essays ranging from two to eight pages. Entries are followed by *see also* references to related terms and by suggestions for further reading. The cross-cultural and anthropological nature of many of the entries is reflected in such concepts as bride price, descent rules and groups, kin selection, love magic, reproductive strategies, wife sharing, and residence rules, to mention but a few. However, more familiar sociology topics, such as marriage, divorce, rape, and spouse beating are also covered, albeit cross-culturally. The essays are well written and their cross-cultural focus should provide sociology students with useful background information. A supplementary bibliography and a detailed subject index are also included.

63. Levinson, David, and Melvin Ember, eds. **Encyclopedia of Cultural Anthropology.** New York: Henry Holt and Co., 1996. 4v. $395.00. LC 95-37237. ISBN 0-8050-2877-3.

By focusing on cultural anthropology in all its diversity, this encyclopedia has included many entries of interest to sociologists. The source includes 340 signed articles arranged alphabetically by title/topic across the four volumes. The articles generally fall within nine broad topical areas, including major subfields in anthropology (e.g., medical anthropology), major theoretical perspectives, research methods, and controversies (e.g., Margaret Mead vs. Derek Freeman), among others. Coverage includes not only subjects, but also regions of the world, specific countries, and major organizations. Among the sociology-related topics are aging, caste, crime, elite studies, culture, ethnicity, gender differences and roles, racism, functionalism, social stratification, Marxism, and religion. Throughout, the writing is very clear, and the routine focus on other cultures helps to clarify the concepts. All articles include *see also* references to related terms, as well as bibliographies of cited references. A list of anthropology periodicals is appended, as is a subject/name index.

ECONOMICS

Bibliographies

64. **International Bibliography of Economics.** Vol. 1- . London: Routledge, 1952- . annual. index. (International Bibliography of the Social Sciences). ISSN 0085-204X.

Thousands of articles and books taken from economics literature are cited in each volume, representing items from dozens of countries and in many languages. A detailed classification scheme for organizing the references is included. Among the sociologically relevant subject headings are those dealing with income and income distribution, the organization of production, social economics and policy, and public economy. Subheadings are included for topics, regions, and countries. Author and subject indexes are provided, with the latter being in both French and English.

Indexes, Abstracts, and Databases

65. **Business Periodicals Index.** Vol. 1- , No. 1- . New York: H. W. Wilson, 1959- . monthly, except August, with annual cumulations. service basis. ISSN 0007-6961.

This is a subject and name index to articles found in approximately 500 business and business-related periodicals. As with other Wilson indexes, its use is quite straightforward.

Article citations are arranged alphabetically by subject/name. Though the journal titles are often abbreviated, they are translated into full titles in a table at the front of the index. A broad range of sociologically interesting topics are covered, including work, health care, social class, power, social role and role conflict, sex role, socialization, organizational behavior, organizational structure, and more. A separate section is included for references to book reviews. This source is also available on CD-ROM and on the WILSONLINE database service.

66. **Journal of Economic Literature.** Vol. 1- , No. 1- . Nashville, Tenn.: American Economics Association, 1963- . quarterly. ISSN 0022-0515.

Formerly titled the *Journal of Economic Abstracts*, this serves as a major index to and review of economics books and articles. Each issue contains a few articles, numerous book reviews, an annotated listing of new books, and a section on current periodicals. This last section includes the tables of contents of current economics periodicals, a subject index of articles in current periodicals, and selected abstracts of some articles. Both the subject index and the selected abstracts are arranged according to the journal's classified system of subject headings. Of particular sociological interest are the headings for the sociology of economics, political economy, collective decision-making, health, education, welfare and poverty, organizations, and more.

An index of authors and articles in the subject index is also provided. Online database access to this journal's contents is available through DIALOG's *Economic Literature Index* (file #139). The database is also available on CD-ROM as *EconLit* (from SilverPlatter).

67. **Work Related Abstracts.** Warren, Mich.: Harmonie Park Press, 1973- . monthly updates (looseleaf). $490.00/yr. ISSN 0273-3234.

This continues the earlier *Employee Relations Abstracts* (1959-1972) and is an index to a broad range of articles on such areas as the labor market, labor-management relations, economics, management science, compensation and fringe benefits, human resource development, economics, education and training, and unions and employee organizations. The citations are arranged by entry number under these subject categories; an accompanying subject/name index provides more detailed access to the references. In addition to business, economics, and management journals, major sociology and behavioral sciences journals are also indexed. This includes such titles as *Gender and Society*, *Critical Sociology*, the *British Journal of Sociology*, the *American Journal of Economics and Sociology*, the *American Sociological Review*, *Administrative Science Quarterly*, and the *American Sociological Review*, among others. As a result, important topics in the sociology of work and organizations are covered.

EDUCATION

Guides

68. Buttlar, Lois J. **Education: A Guide to Reference and Information Sources.** Englewood, Colo.: Libraries Unlimited, 1989. 258p. index. (Reference Sources in the Social Sciences, No. 2). $35.00. LC 89-2651. ISBN 0-87287-619-5.

Major sources of information in education and its subfields are identified here, as are relevant sources from the related social and behavioral sciences. In all, 900 titles are covered in this book's 676 entries, which include research guides, directories, indexes, abstracts, bibliographies, statistics sources, and other reference works. Most entries were published after 1980, with the vast majority organized in 14 chapters for educational subfields. The most sociologically interesting of these include educational foundations (history, philosophy, and psychology of education), curriculum and instruction, evaluation in education, educational administration, international and comparative education, and women's studies and feminist education. All entries receive descriptive or evaluative annotations ranging from one to three paragraphs. Remaining chapters cover general education and social science reference sources, references works from other disciplines, educational research centers and organizations, and educational periodicals. A combined author/title/subject index is included.

Bibliographies

69. Stitt, Beverly A. **Gender Equity in Education: An Annotated Bibliography.** Carbondale, Ill.: Southern Illinois University Press, 1994. 168p. $24.95. LC 93-24315. ISBN 0-8903-1937-3.

As educational sociologists have increasingly documented, both the content and processes of schooling are implicated in the creation of gender inequalities. This bibliography is a guide to books, articles, research reports, curricula, and teaching materials intended to identify and address gender bias and stereotyping in education. These items are arranged into 22 topical chapters, including such sociologically rich areas as teaching, discrimination, gender role stereotyping, family and work issues, male focus, pregnant and parenting teens, science and mathematics, and more. Within chapters, references are arranged by title and are accompanied by paragraph-long annotations. Throughout the volume, a strong emphasis is placed on policies and practices that can promote more equitable outcomes. The broad topical index provides additional access points to those entries that touch on numerous topics.

Indexes, Abstracts, and Databases

70. **British Education Index.** Leeds, United Kingdom: British Education Index, 1976- . quarterly and annual updates. DIALOG file #121.

This is the electronic equivalent of the printed *British Education Index* and the *British Education Theses Index* (on microfiche). The first source is covered from 1976 to the present, while the second is covered from 1950 to the present. The database includes approximately 250 British education journals and contains any number of important topics in the sociology of education and educational policy. Education theses from United Kingdom and Irish universities and polytechnics are included.

71. **Current Index to Journals in Education.** Vol. 1- , No. 1- . Phoenix, Ariz.: Oryx Press, 1969- . monthly, with semiannual cumulations. $475.00/yr. ISSN 0011-3565.

Part of the ERIC "family" of reference publications, *Current Index to Journals in Education* (CIJE) and *Resources in Education* (RIE) index materials on a wide range of educational topics, including the sociology of education. For example, in these indexes one can find literature on the production of educational inequality, the sociology of school knowledge and the curriculum, and educational policy analysis. *CIJE* indexes articles from 830 journals, with the citations and abstracts arranged under the broad topical areas of the

16 ERIC clearinghouses. *RIE* focuses on the indexing of research reports, conference proceedings, books, manuscripts, etc. Both sources have a subject index, which uses subject headings from the *Thesaurus of ERIC Descriptors*, as well as an author index. They also provide descriptive abstracts, with those in *RIE* being substantially longer. *CIJE* includes a "journal contents" index that lists all of the indexed articles from each journal; *RIE* has supplementary "institution" and "publication type" indexes. The content of both indexes is available in the *ERIC* database, which can be searched on CD-ROM or through database vendors, such as DIALOG.

72. **Education Index.** Vol. 1- , No. 1- . New York: H. W. Wilson, 1929- . monthly, except July and August, with quarterly and annual cumulations. service basis. ISSN 0013-1385.

This straight, alphabetically arranged name/subject index identifies articles in over 400 education journals. It includes numerous articles and journals addressing issues in the sociology of education, and cites yearbooks and, as of late 1995, books in education. Ample *see* and *see also* references to preferred and related subject headings are included. Also, a separate section for book reviews is contained in the back of each issue; video, motion picture, and computer program reviews, as well as citations on law cases, are filed with their subjects. The book reviews are arranged alphabetically by the book's author or, when no author is available, by title. As is true of other Wilson indexes, this source is easy to use. It is also available on CD-ROM, online through the WILSONLINE database service, and on many computerized library systems.

73. **ERIC.** Washington, D.C.: U.S. Department of Education, OERI, 1966- . monthly updates. DIALOG file #1.

ERIC is the database equivalent of two printed indexes, the *Current Index to Journals in Education* (see entry #71) and *Resources in Education* (see entry #74). It includes all of the journal article and ERIC document references and abstracts from the beginning of the print indexes in 1966. Approximately 800 education journals are indexed and abstracted, including a number from Australia, England, and Canada. The database provides excellent coverage of topics in the sociology of education. Numerous companies provide CD-ROM versions of *ERIC*, including SilverPlatter, EBSCO, and Oryx. *ERIC* is also increasingly available on library online catalogs.

74. **Resources in Education.** Vol. 1- , No. 1- . Phoenix, Ariz.: Oryx Press, 1966- . monthly, with annual cumulations. $77.00/yr.(monthly issues); $365.00/yr.(annual cumulation). ISSN 0098-0897.

See *Current Index to Journals in Education* (entry #71).

Handbooks and Yearbooks

75. **The Condition of Education.** Washington, D.C.: National Center for Education Statistics; distr., Washington, D.C.: GPO, 1975- . annual. ISSN 0098-4752.

Begun in 1975, this annual provides a statistical overview of the current state of and trends in American education. Major topics covered include elementary/secondary education and higher education. Three other major topics receive special emphasis: elementary/secondary school teachers, educating handicapped students, and the transition from high school. Charts and tables of data are presented on various aspects of each major topic. Each of the five sections also has an introductory essay discussing the trends and data. Throughout, data of sociological interest relating to equity and achievement are included.

The subject index of each edition provides page references to subjects in both the current and earlier editions.

76. **Digest of Education Statistics.** Washington, D.C.: Department of Education, Office of Educational Research and Improvement, National Center for Education Statistics; distr., Washington, D.C.: GPO, 1975- . annual. index.

"Its primary purpose is to provide an abstract of statistical information covering the broad field of American education from kindergarten through graduate school" (1994 ed., p. iii). The 1994 edition includes 411 tables organized under seven headings: all levels of education, elementary and secondary education, postsecondary education, federal programs, outcomes of education, international comparisons, and learning resources and technology.

The statistics include "the number of schools and colleges, teachers, enrollments, and graduates, in addition to educational attainment, finances, federal funds for education, employment and income of graduates, libraries, and international comparisons of education" (1994 ed., p. iii). Appended are a guide to sources, a subject index to the tables, and definitions of key educational terms. This is arguably the single most important print source for educational data and very likely the first place an educational sociologist might check for data.

77. **Thesaurus of ERIC Descriptors.** 13th ed. Phoenix, Ariz.: Oryx Press, 1995. 704p. $69.50. ISBN 0-89774-788-7.

This thesaurus is essential for proper subject searching of articles and documents in ERIC's printed indexes, *Current Index to Journals in Education* and *Resources in Education* (entry #71), as well as its online and CD-ROM database version, *ERIC* (entry #73). The thesaurus is also available in electronic format in most of the electronic versions of the database. ERIC uses its own controlled vocabulary of subject headings to classify every article or document in its printed and electronic databases. Generally, one can retrieve more focused references by using ERIC's subject headings in a search. This thesaurus not only lists the subject headings alphabetically, but also indicates broader terms, related terms, and narrower terms, all of which are useful for expanding or narrowing searches.

Appended are a rotated display of descriptors (i.e., terms listed in context); a two-way hierarchical display listing all broader and narrower terms related to each subject heading; and a descriptor group display (i.e., terms listed under broad subject categories). Excellent and thorough explanatory material is presented in the front of the thesaurus.

78. **Encyclopedia of Educational Research.** 6th ed. Marvin C. Alkin, ed.-in-chief. New York: Macmillan, 1992. 4v. index. $360.00/set. LC 91-38682. ISBN 0-02-900431-4.

Sponsored by the American Educational Research Association, this encyclopedia provides an important overview of research in the field. It is intended for college students, researchers delving into new areas, parents, policymakers, and practitioners. Entries of sociological interest include class size, grouping students for instruction, the education of minorities, sexism and racism in educational research, textbooks and textbook publishing, urban education, the history of the curriculum, the education of African Americans, policy research, and women's education, among others. Many entries on research methods and statistics are also available, including case study design, ethnography, factor analysis, and structural equation modeling.

The entries are typically at least two pages long, with many being much longer. The essays, supplied by contributors from around the world, are well written and accompanied by a list of references and *see also* references to related headings. Appended is a guide to library research, as well as a thorough name/topic index. On any number of topics in educational sociology, these essays would provide a good overview of the key issues and research.

Dictionaries and Encyclopedias

79. **International Encyclopedia of Education.** 2d ed. Torsten Husen and T. Neville Postlethwaite, eds.-in-chief. White Plains, N.Y.: Pergamon Press, 1994. 12v. $3,795.00/set. LC 94-3059. ISBN 0-08-041046-4.

This second edition represents a considerable revision of the first edition. The 1,266 articles summarize international research on educational topics and national systems of education. Arrangement of the entries is alphabetical by subject. Articles are lengthy and include both cross-references and bibliographies of suggested readings. Coverage of topics in the sociology of education is excellent, including such subjects as educational inequality, the sociology of school knowledge and the curriculum, critical theory and education, social stratification, socialization, conflict and functionalist theories of schooling, sexism and gender roles, social class, and more.

The index volume includes a name index, a classified list of entries, a list of contributors and their entries, and a subject index. Lists for foreign terms, abbreviations and acronyms, and major education journals are also provided. This is an excellent and up-to-date source, with ample entries covering the range of topics in educational sociology.

80. Shafritz, Jay M., Richard P. Koeppe, and Elizabeth W. Soper. **The Facts on File Dictionary of Education.** New York: Facts on File, 1988. $40.00. LC 88-24554. ISBN 0-8160-1636-4.

Definitions included in this source cover key terms, theories, individuals, legislation, organizations, publications, and court cases in the field of education. Some of the terms are briefly defined, while others are defined at length and accompanied by suggestions for further reading. Those individuals not fully conversant with terminology in education or the sociology of education should find this a useful reference tool. It is not particularly strong at including terms from some of the critical sociological theories of schooling or the curriculum (e.g., cultural capital, selective tradition, resistance). However, the dictionary is solid in its coverage of more conventional concepts.

HISTORY

Guides

81. **The American Historical Association's Guide to Historical Literature.** 3d ed. Mary Beth Norton, general ed. New York: Oxford University Press, 1995. 2v. ISBN 0-19-505727-9.

Much social research is necessarily historical, and this guide can help sociologists and other social scientists find that relevant historical literature. Included here are almost 27,000 book, chapter, and article citations arranged by author under 48 subject chapters. These chapter headings correspond mainly to regional, national, and chronological periods. However, a few chapters are devoted to other topics, such as "Science, Technology, and Medicine" and "Theory and Practice in Historical Study." Within chapters, headings and subheadings delineate the subject matter; these are listed at the beginning of the chapter. Each chapter's sources and accompanying brief abstracts were compiled by contributors who specialize in that area. Detailed subject access to the references is provided by an extensive subject index, which includes numerous headings of sociological interest. In fact, the historical dimensions of virtually any sociological subject can be searched here. Though selective, this source is an excellent starting place for historical references. An author index is also provided, as is a list of journals from which some articles were drawn.

Indexes, Abstracts, and Databases

82. **America: History and Life.** Vol. 1- , No. 1- . Santa Barbara, Calif.: ABC-CLIO, 1964- . 5 issues/yr., including annual index. price varies. ISSN 0002-7065.

For historical research into the United States or Canada, this is the single best source to consult. It includes abstracts of articles and citations to book reviews and dissertations covering the prehistoric times to the present. Four issues are published each year, as well as a fifth issue, which is the cumulative annual index. Within each of the first four issues, references and abstracts are arranged by author under an extensive list of subject categories. These primarily focus on different geographical areas (e.g., regions, states, and provinces) and historical periods (e.g., United States of America—National History to 1945). Within these sections, references are further categorized as articles, reviews, or dissertations. Beyond the geographical breakdown are topical categories that may interest sociologists. The category "United States of America, 1945 to Present" includes categories for politics, crime, education, social groups, culture, health and medicine, and science and technology. The annual index includes author, subject, book/film/video/microfiche title (for reviews), and reviewer indexes. Five-year indexes are also published, with the most recent covering 1989–1993. This source is also available on CD-ROM and through the DIALOG database service (*America: History and Life*, file #38).

83. **The Combined Retrospective Index Set to Journals in History, 1838-1974.** Annadel N. Wile, exec. ed. Washington, D.C.: Carrollton Press, 1977. 11v. LC 77-70347. ISBN 0-8408-0175-0.

Part of the Combined Retrospective Index Series (C.R.I.S.), these 11 volumes provide subject and author access to articles in world history. The first nine volumes comprise the subject index. Under each major subject category, articles are located by keywords in the title. Each citation includes the abbreviated title, author, year, volume, journal number (translated in the front of the volume), and page. Volumes 10 and 11 comprise the author index; citations are identical in format to those in the subject index. Biographical information may be found in volume 6.

84. **Historical Abstracts.** Vol. 1- , No. 1- . Santa Barbara, Calif.: ABC-CLIO, 1955- . quarterly, including cumulative indexes. price varies. ISSN 0363-2717(pt. A); 0363-2725(pt. B).

The companion abstract to *America: History and Life*, this covers world history from 1450 to the present, excluding Canada and the United States. Abstracts of journal articles and citations for books and dissertations are included in two parts. Part A covers modern history from 1450 to 1914 and is organized by region, country, and historical period. A social science topical section is also included and covers such sociologically rich areas as social and cultural history, religions, and science and technology. Part B covers twentieth-century history from 1914 to the present. This, too, is organized primarily by region, country, and period, and a topical section is included here as well. The first two issues in each volume of both A and B include subject and author indexes; the third issue does not, and the fourth is the cumulative index for the entire volume. This source is international in coverage, drawing citations from sources in approximately 90 countries and 40 languages. However, titles are translated and abstracts are in English. Five-year indexes are available through 1989. Versions of this source are also available on CD-ROM and on the DIALOG database service (file #39).

POLITICAL SCIENCE

Guides

85. York, Henry E. **Political Science: A Guide to Reference and Information Sources.** Englewood, Colo.: Libraries Unlimited, 1990. 249p. index. (Reference Sources in the Social Sciences, No. 4). LC 90-41158. ISBN 0-87287-794-9.

Important reference works within political science and its specializations are identified here, as are relevant reference sources from the other social sciences. Most of the over 800 sources were published from 1980 through 1987, with the "vast majority" published in the United States or Great Britain. The guide is arranged into six chapters. The first two cover general social science sources and sources within other disciplines, respectively. The other disciplines include sociology, psychology, history, education, and economics. The remaining four chapters identify 1) general reference sources in political science; 2) sources by geographic fields (e.g., Asia and the Middle East, and Africa); 3) sources on topical fields; and 4) public policy sources. The "topical fields" covered include international relations, international organizations, human rights, communism and Marxism, peace and conflict, and terrorism. Some of these fields may interest sociologists in the areas of theory, social change, and social movements. Policy sociologists may find the public policy chapter interesting as well. Each of these chapters includes subsections for bibliographies, indexes, dictionaries, directories, and other categories of reference works. Separate chapters identify important databases, organizations, and journals. The reference book annotations range from 80 to 200 words and are thoroughly descriptive. Author/title and subject indexes are available for additional access to the entries.

Indexes, Abstracts, and Databases

86. **ABC Pol Sci: A Bibliography of Contents: Political Science & Government.** Santa Barbara, Calif.: ABC-CLIO, 1969- . 5 issues/yr., with annual index. service basis. ISSN 0001-0456.

Though ostensibly an index to journals in political science and government, *ABC Pol Sci* also indexes a significant number of journals in sociology, law, and economics. The tables of contents of approximately 300 international journals are listed in this source alphabetically by journal title, totaling about 1,800 references per issue. Among the journals covered are major sociological titles, such as *American Sociological Review*, *American Journal of Sociology*, and *Social Forces*. Also included are important journals in the area of social policy that should be of interest to policy sociologists. The coverage of these journals, along with related social science titles, makes this a valuable current awareness index. In addition to the tables of contents listings, access by the subject and author indexes is provided.

87. **International Political Science Abstracts. Documentation Politique Internationale.** Paris: International Political Science Association, 1951- . bimonthly, with cumulative subject index. $398.83/yr. ISSN 0020-8345.

Political science is broadly construed in this index and includes many references of interest to sociologists, particularly in the areas of policy sociology, political sociology, social groups, research methodology, and theory. Each issue abstracts about 1,200 articles from major international journals. While the articles may be in any number of languages, the titles are in both the original language and English. Abstracts are either in English or French, and source abstracts from the journal are used whenever possible. The citations and abstracts are arranged under broad categories: methods and theory, thinkers and ideas, institutions, political process, international relations, and national and area studies. A supplementary subject index is included, as is a list of indexed periodicals.

Dictionaries and Encyclopedias

88. Goodin, Robert E., and Philip Pettit, eds. **A Companion to Contemporary Political Philosophy.** Oxford: Blackwell, 1993. 679p. index. (Blackwell Companions to Philosophy). $24.95. LC 92-41450. ISBN 0-631-17993-3.

This book's value is in its historical and philosophical focus, as well as its discussion of some fundamental topics in sociology and the social sciences. It is a collection of 41 substantial essays on the social science disciplines, major ideologies, and a wide variety of special topics. Advanced sociology students should find useful the essays on sociology, community, democracy, Marxism, equality, power, the state, legitimacy, and sociobiology, among others. The essays, which run from 10 to 20 pages, are well written, though they do presume some background knowledge. They are accompanied by a list of references and suggestions for further reading.

89. Miller, David, ed. **The Blackwell Encyclopedia of Political Thought.** Oxford: Blackwell, 1991. 570p. index. $28.95. LC 86-29972. ISBN 0-631-17944-5.

Besides including entries on the history and theory of political thought, this encyclopedia has numerous essays on important sociological concepts, theories, and theorists. Major topics addressed include social class, alienation, community, elitism, equality, positivism, hegemony, and power, among others. A substantial number of biographical entries on contemporary and historical sociological figures is provided, including those on Auguste Comte, Emile Durkheim, Max Weber, Montesquieu, Georg Hegel, Georg Lukacs, Antonio Gramsci, Vilfredo Pareto, Louis de Bonald, Joseph de Maistre, Karl Marx, Jürgen Habermas, Herbert Marcuse, and many more. The entries are fairly lengthy, running from a few paragraphs to multiple, double-column pages. They are accompanied by suggestions for further reading. A detailed subject/name index is also included.

90. Nagel, Stuart S., ed. **Encyclopedia of Policy Studies.** 2d ed., rev. and expanded. New York: Marcel Dekker, 1994. 956p. index. (Public Administration and Public Policy, 53). $195.00. LC 93-44894. ISBN 0-8247-9142-8.

This is a collection of 35 overview essays arranged into two broad units: 1) general approaches to policy studies; and 2) specific policy problems. Essays in the first unit address various theories, methods, and techniques of policy analysis, as well as stages of policy formation and implementation. Essays on cross-national and interdisciplinary analysis are also included. The five essays in the second unit address specific problem areas, including "Problems with a Sociology or Psychology Emphasis." These essays touch on policy aspects of poverty and income maintenance programs, minority politics, criminal justice, education, and population. These chapters, along with the theoretical and methodological essays, should be most relevant for sociological researchers in policy analysis and program evaluation. Author and subject indexes are included.

PSYCHOLOGY

Guides

91. Baxter, Pam M. **Psychology: A Guide to Reference and Information Sources.** Englewood, Colo.: Libraries Unlimited, 1993. 219p. index. (Reference Sources in the Social Sciences Series, No. 6). $36.50. LC 93-13182. ISBN 0-87287-708-6.

This guide is comprised of 667 annotated citations to sources in psychology and related disciplines. The entries are arranged under four broad categories: general social science sources; related social science disciplines; general psychology sources; and special topics (subdisciplines) in psychology. Most chapters are subdivided by type of reference source, such as bibliographies, indexes, handbooks, dictionaries, and directories. Sources are listed alphabetically by author within these categories and are accompanied by well-written, descriptive, and evaluative annotations of approximately 100 words. The section on related social science disciplines does include sociology, though the sources cited are the usual indexes, abstracts, dictionaries, and handbooks. However, its 24 special topics in psychology should hold special interest for sociologists, as they include subsections on psychology of marriage and the family; psychosexual behavior and sex roles; and social, interpersonal, and environmental interaction, among others. Within some of these sections, more specific topics covered include family violence, death and dying, aging, suicide, drug/alcohol abuse, and social networks. The guide also provides a combined author/title index, as well as a subject index.

Bibliographies

92. Caton, Hiram, editor-in-chief. **The Bibliography of Human Behavior.** Westport, Conn.: Greenwood, 1993. 575p. index. (Bibliographies and Indexes in Anthropology, No. 7). $95.00. LC 93-3066. ISBN 0-313-27897-0.

The title of this bibliography is a bit misleading, as its focus is primarily on biological or evolutionary influences on human behavior. As such, it represents the nature or hereditarian perspective within the broader nature-nurture debate. Over 6,700 book and article references are cited alphabetically by author under 20 subject headings. Of particular interest to some sociologists may be the sections on cultural evolution, sociobiology, ethology, parenting, sexuality, social psychology, and politics. The chapter on politics, though brief, does address some policy issues. The emphasis throughout is on biological explanations for human behavior. While "the criteria for inclusion were the attributes of the good scientific article" (p. vii), these attributes are clearly more contentious and controversial than the editors acknowledge in their preface. Though literature reflecting alternative perspectives is selectively included (with some notable omissions), there is still no mistaking the bibliography's hereditarian focus. Some users may regret the absence of abstracts, but the compilers have opted for a larger number of citations.

Additional access to the entries is provided by author and subject indexes, though the latter occasionally makes insufficient use of subheadings.

Indexes, Abstracts, and Databases

93. **Child Development Abstracts and Bibliography.** Vol. 1- , No. 1- . Chicago: University of Chicago Press, 1927- . 3 issues/yr. $68.00/yr. ISSN 0009-3939.

These abstracts are published by the University of Chicago Press for the Society for Research in Child Development. Books and articles on a wide range of topics related to child development are included. They are alphabetized by author within one of six headings: biology, health, and medicine; cognition, learning, and perception; education; psychiatry and clinical psychology; social psychology and personality; theory, methodology, and reviews. Numerous citations relate to class, racial, and sexual inequalities and differences. These should be of particular interest to sociologists studying family systems, gender and socialization, differential educational achievement and performance, child abuse, and more. Book notices with page-long reviews are also included. Author and subject indexes are provided, as is a list of author addresses.

94. **Psychological Abstracts.** Vol. 1, No. 1- . Washington, D.C.: American Psychological Association, 1927- . monthly. $1,349.00/yr. ISSN 0033-2887.

This is not only the major guide to journal articles, books, book chapters, and dissertations in psychology, but also a useful source for sociologists and social psychologists. Articles are drawn from approximately 1,300 English-language journals, and about 4,000 article and book abstracts are included each month. The annotated entries are arranged alphabetically by author under any of 22 major subject categories and their subtopics. Of particular interest to sociologists might be the chapters on social processes and social issues, social psychology, health and mental health treatment and prevention, and industrial and organizational psychology.

Each issue includes both a brief subject index and an author index, as well as an index of book titles. An annual index can be found in the last issue of each volume. This source is also available on CD-ROM (*PsychLIT*), on online database services (e.g., *PsycINFO* on DIALOG, file #11), and on magnetic tape for loading on local computer systems and online library catalogs. For best searching results, one should consult the *Thesaurus of Psychological Index Terms*, which is used to label all items in the index/database. This thesaurus is periodically updated.

Handbooks and Yearbooks

95. **Diagnostic and Statistical Manual of Mental Disorders: DSM-IV.** 4th ed. Washington, D.C.: American Psychological Association, 1994. 886p. index. $45.00. LC 94-6304. ISBN 0-89042-062-9.

This is intended to give clinicians, researchers, and statisticians empirically supported, diagnostic criteria for mental illnesses and disorders. Descriptions of these disorders are arranged into chapters according to their type. These include substance-related disorders, anxiety disorders, sexual and gender disorders, disorders diagnosed in infancy/childhood/adolescence, personality disorders, and dissociative disorders, to name a few. Many more specific disorders are identified within these broad categories. For example, the category of disorders diagnosed in infancy, etc. includes learning disorders, mental retardations, and attention deficit/hyperactivity disorder. "Learning disorders" is broken down further to include reading, mathematics, and written expression. For most disorders, at the least, information on the diagnostic features, associated features and disorders, prevalence, specific culture/age/gender features, course, and differential diagnosis is provided. Extensive supplementary information is included in the manual, including a user's guide, a glossary, an annotated list of changes from the DSM-III R, an alphabetical listing of diagnoses, a subject index, and more. Sociologists studying health and mental illness, family systems, or social support/networks may find this source useful.

96. Hersen, Michel, and Alan S. Bellack, eds. **Dictionary of Behavioral Assessment Techniques.** New York: Pergamon, 1988. 519p. index. (Pergamon General Psychology Series). LC 86-25352. ISBN 0-08-031975-0.

Over 280 behavioral assessment techniques and research instruments are described in this volume. A broad range of techniques is covered, including teacher ratings, staff ratings, self-report instruments, behavioral observation, structured and semistructured interviews, parent ratings, therapist ratings, self-monitoring techniques, nurse's ratings, physiological measures, and more. These instruments and techniques are arranged alphabetically and are fully described, including their purpose, development, psychometric characteristics, clinical use, future directions, and references. Sociologists may be interested in the instruments and techniques relating to drug abuse and alcoholism, marital distress, social skills, and parent-child interactions/conflict, to name a few. A supplementary "User's Guide" provides alternative subject access to the instruments by alphabetically listing the focus of the assessment (e.g., alcoholism, depression), followed by its title and assessment modality. An author index is also available. This source should be most useful to social psychologists, medical sociologists, and sociologists of marriage and the family, as well as those studying support networks, mental health, and stress.

97. **Survey of Social Science: Psychology Series.** Frank N. Magill, ed. Pasadena, Calif.: Salem Press, 1993. 6v. $425.00/set. LC 93-34708. ISBN 0-89356-732-9.

These volumes present 410 short, well-written overviews of a variety of topics in psychology and related disciplines, including sociology and education. The essays are approximately six pages each and are arranged alphabetically by subject. Each essay includes an overview of the topic, a discussion of its practical uses or applications, and a discussion of its context within the broader field of psychology. An accompanying annotated bibliography is included, as well as a list of cross-references to other entries. As a convenience for the user, each entry begins by identifying the type of psychology and the broader field of study to which the term relates; brief definitions of principal terms are also available. Many articles here should interest sociologists, including such topics as gender identity, aging, divorce, alcoholism, stress, the family, and motivation. According to the editor, 42 articles relate to the area of social psychology, covering such topics as violence and the media, cognitive dissonance, self-esteem, racism, social identity theory, groups, religiosity, and more. Each volume includes an alphabetical list of all entries and a list arranged by subject and subtopic. Volume six contains a glossary and a cumulative subject/name index. These succinct overviews should prove excellent starting points for undergraduate students.

98. **Test Critiques.** Daniel J. Keyser and Richard C. Sweetland, general eds. Austin, Tex.: Pro-Ed, 1984- . $89.00/vol. LC 84-26895.

Now up to 10 volumes, this handbook provides descriptions and critical overviews of standardized tests and research instruments in psychology, education, business, and related disciplines. For most instruments, four categories of information are provided: an introduction to an instrument's development; an overview of its practical applications; a review of its technical aspects, including validity, reliability, and related data; and a critique. The entries also include a list of references and an indication of the tests' copyright holder. Test title, test author/reviewer, and subject indexes, available in each volume, are cumulative for all of the volumes to date; an index to test publishers is also provided. The subject index lists tests alphabetically by title under the three major subject categories (i.e., psychology, education, and business) and a handful of subheadings. Sociologists in social psychology, sociology of work and organizations, marriage and the family, and educational sociology may be particularly interested in the subtopics of "marriage and family" or "personality" (under "Psychology"); "academic achievement and aptitude" or "student attitudes and personality factors" (under "Education"); and "interpersonal skills and attitudes" (under "Business"). Along with sources like *Mental Measurements Yearbook* (entry #100) and *Tests in Print* (entry #99), this is an invaluable guide to existing research tools.

99. **Tests in Print IV: An Index to Tests, Test Reviews, and the Literature on Specific Tests.** Linda L. Murphy, Jane Close Conoley, and James C. Impara, eds. Lincoln, Nebr.: Buros Institute of Mental Measurements, University of Nebraska; distr., Lincoln, Nebr., University of Nebraska Press, 1994. 2v. index. $325.00/set. LC 83-18866. ISBN 0-910674-53-1.

This work indexes all previously published volumes of *Mental Measurements Yearbook* (MMY) and *Tests in Print* (TIP), and is a cumulative listing of and index to 3,009 tests that are still in print. Tests included in this index are a broad range of achievement, aptitude, attitudinal, and other instruments. Entries for tests identify their purpose, population, publication date, scores, administration, price data, time, author, and publisher. In many cases, one is referred to references and reviews in earlier editions of *MMY* and *TIP*. A list of recent references where the test has been used or evaluated may also be available.

The test entries are arranged alphabetically by title. Further access is provided by the reviewer, publisher, acronym, title, name, score, and classified subject indexes. Nineteen subjects are presented in the classified subject index, with the most sociologically interesting categories being behavior assessment, education, and personality. Also, the "miscellaneous" category includes such sociological topics as marriage and the family and alcohol and substance abuse.

100. **The Twelfth Mental Measurements Yearbook.** James C. Impara and Jane Close Conoley, eds. Lincoln, Nebr.: Buros Institute of Mental Measurements, University of Nebraska-Lincoln; distr., University of Nebraska Press, 1995. 1,259p. index. $150.00. LC 39-3422. ISBN 0-910674-40-X.

The *Mental Measurements Yearbook* provides "users with descriptive information, references, and critical reviews of tests" that are "commercially available" and "in the English language" (p. xi). This latest edition includes tests that are new or revised since the last edition. Along with the earlier editions, this title constitutes a major source of reviews of tests and research instruments in education, psychology, and the social and behavioral sciences. Many subjects are covered, including achievement, behavior assessment, developmental tests, education, intelligence, personality, vocations, and more. Tests are grouped according to these categories.

Citations for particular tests include the appropriate grade or age level of the subjects, scores, administration, author, publisher, price, and other details. They are often accompanied by relevant references and test reviews; if not, one is usually directed to a review in an earlier edition.Test title, name, acronym, classified subject, score, and publisher indexes are also provided.

Dictionaries and Encyclopedias

101. **Companion Encyclopedia of Psychology.** Andrew M. Colman, ed. London: Routledge, 1994. 2v. index. $250.00/set. ISBN 0-415-06446-5.

Covering "all major branches of psychological research and professional practice" (p.xi), this encyclopedia has 63 chapters providing overviews of major topics and subtopics in psychology. These chapters, each written by an expert in the area, are arranged under 13 section headings reflecting major topical areas: introduction, biological aspects of behavior, sensation and perception, cognition, learning and skills, emotion and motivation, individual differences and personality, developmental psychology, social psychology, abnormal psychology, special topics (e.g., gender issues), research methods and statistics, and the professions of psychology. All of the chapters under "Social Psychology" should be of sociological interest, particularly those on attitudes and persuasion, social influence processes, and prejudice and intergroup conflict. Social psychologists, gerontologists, and educational sociologists, among others, may be interested in the additional chapters on aging, stress and coping, social motivation, adolescence, and intelligence and cognitive styles. Each chapter is accompanied by a list of references and suggestions for further reading. Charts, pictures, and diagrams are included in some chapters. Overall, the encyclopedia is well written for its intended audience of students, faculty, and interested general readers. A glossary and subject/name index is appended.

102. **Encyclopedia of Human Behavior.** V. S. Ramachandran, Editor-in-Chief. San Diego: Academic Press, 1994. 4v. index. $595.00/set. LC 93-34371. ISBN 0-12-226920-9.

This provides a state-of-the-art overview of psychology, with over 200 articles addressing the major topics and subtopics in the field. The articles, which were written by experts, are arranged alphabetically by subject. Each article is preceded by an outline of its content and a glossary of key terms (with definitions). Sociology students and researchers will find clear overviews of a number of key topics, including aging, social support, attitude formation and change, birth order effects, suicide, divorce, authoritarianism, stress, peer relationships, sex roles, and more. The articles are well written and include references to other terms in the encyclopedia. The last volume includes a list of contributors and their articles, as well as a subject/name index.

103. **Encyclopedia of Psychology.** 2d ed. Raymond J. Corsini, ed. New York: John Wiley & Sons, 1994. 4v. $475.00/set. LC 93-22638. ISBN 0-471-55819-2.

While this encyclopedia is aimed at informing students and researchers in psychology and the behavioral sciences, it may also prove valuable to sociologists, particularly those with interests related to social psychology. It includes such topics as birth order, behaviorism, attitude measurement, socialization, gerontology, institutions, marriage and the family, and more. The entries range from a few paragraphs to a few pages and are written by scholars with expertise in the area on which they are writing. Essays are accompanied by references to further reading and a list of related subjects. The first three volumes include entries arranged alphabetically by subject, while the fourth volume includes biographies, a cumulative bibliography, name and subject indexes, an appended APA code of conduct and ethical principles, and guidelines for written contracts.

104. Sutherland, Stuart. **The International Dictionary of Psychology.** New York: Continuum, 1989. 491p. LC 88-39340. ISBN 0-8264-0440-5.

As the author of this book notes, current psychological research and writing is likely to include terms from many other disciplines, such as mathematics, neurology, artificial intelligence, philosophy, sociology, and others. This dictionary's strength, and its benefit for the user, is its inclusion of such terms, thus minimizing the need to consult multiple dictionaries. The definitions, though brief, do include cross-references to other terms. Furthermore, if concepts defined elsewhere are used in a definition, they appear in boldface print. Appended are a number of diagrams of the brain.

SOCIAL WORK

Indexes, Abstracts, and Databases

105. **Social Work Abstracts.** Vol. 1- , No. 1- . Washington, D.C.: NASW Press, 1965- . quarterly. $97.00/yr.(institutions). ISSN 0148-0847.

This continues *Social Work Research & Abstracts* and annually abstracts articles from approximately 450 social work and related journals. Each particular issue contains over 400 article abstracts that are arranged under some 30 subject categories. Those of most interest to sociologists may include children and families, addictions, aging, criminal justice, health care, mental health, and social policy. Within these categories, references are arranged by author and accompanied by paragraph-long abstracts and an address for the author. *See also* references to related abstracts appear at the end of each subject section. Each issue includes author and subject indexes, which are cumulated in the last issue of each volume. This source is also available on CD-ROM as *Social Work Abstracts Plus* (from SilverPlatter), which is updated semiannually.

Dictionaries and Encyclopedias

106. Barker, Robert L. **The Social Work Dictionary.** 3d ed. Washington, D.C.: NASW Press, 1995. 447p. $34.95. ISBN 0-87101-253-7.

The field of social work is much broader in its areas of concern than the non-social worker may suspect, covering such subjects as family therapy, counseling and group work, cognitive and moral development, educational equity, social theory, criminal justice, health care, and more. This breadth of responsibility necessitates familiarity with terminology from many subjects and disciplines. Theories, theorists, key concepts, organizations, court cases, and various pieces of legislation may need to be understood for a social worker to most effectively practice. All of these kinds of terms are included in this dictionary, which is intended both for social workers and related human service professionals, including sociologists.

Definitions range in length from a sentence to a long paragraph; italicized words in definitions are defined elsewhere in the dictionary. Cross-references direct the user from unused words, phrases, or acronyms to the preferred terms. Supplementary information includes a chronology of milestones in the history of social work, the National Association of Social Workers (NASW) Code of Ethics, and lists of state regulatory boards and NASW chapter offices.

This source has been regularly updated and expanded, which should ensure that the terminology is current. The definitions are well written and cover a broad range of topics, making this a valuable complement to sociology and social science dictionaries.

107. **Encyclopedia of Social Work.** 19th ed. Washington, D.C.: NASW Press, 1995. 3v. index. $150.00. LC 30-30948. ISBN 0-87101-255-3.

This encyclopedia is composed of 290 articles and 142 biographies central to the theory and practice of social work in the United States. Articles are arranged alphabetically by subject, with plenty of cross-references from unused to used subject headings. Many topics of sociological interest are addressed, including racial and ethnic groups, aging, teen pregnancy, child and elder abuse, families, criminal behavior, health care, HIV/AIDS, policy analysis, communities, program evaluation, qualitative research, suicide, and more. Each article is written by an expert in the field and is accompanied by bibliographic references, suggestions for further reading, cross-references to related subjects, and important keywords. Many of the articles include charts, tables, and graphs, though the editors suggest consulting Leon Ginsburg's *Social Work Almanac* for additional statistical data. Throughout the encyclopedia 80 *Reader's Guide* entries list all of the encyclopedia articles related to a particular major subject. The biographies, located in Volume Three, are three or four paragraphs in length and are cover figures in social work who are no longer living. The appendixes list various codes of ethics, policy statements, and organization executive directors, among others. Each volume contains a complete subject index including people, places, organizations, and legislation. This encyclopedia is also available on CD-ROM.

108. Ginsberg, Leon. **Social Work Almanac.** 2d ed. Washington, D.C.: NASW Press, 1995. 390p. maps. index. $34.95. ISBN 0-87101-248-0.

Social workers and social service professionals have a recurring need for statistical data on issues affecting their profession, including health care, crime, educational attainment, poverty levels, homelessness, and mental illness, among other topics. The *Social Work Almanac* meets this need by drawing data from government and private sources to present a statistical portrait of some of the country's most important social issues.

The data, which are as recent as 1993, are organized into nine chapters dealing with population and demography, children, crime, education, health, mental illness and disabilities, older adults, social welfare, and the social work profession. Within these chapters subsections are included that address more specific topics. For example, the chapter on older adults covers population trends, living arrangements, poverty, public expenditures, abuse, and criminal victimization. The data are well laid out in charts, graphs, and tables; source documents are cited. One of the nicest features of this book is its discussion of the various tables and figures. These brief discussions are often fairly educational, providing a context for the value of the data. A supplementary list of references is provided, as well as a subject index that includes institutions and program names. Major social issues of interest to sociologists are covered.

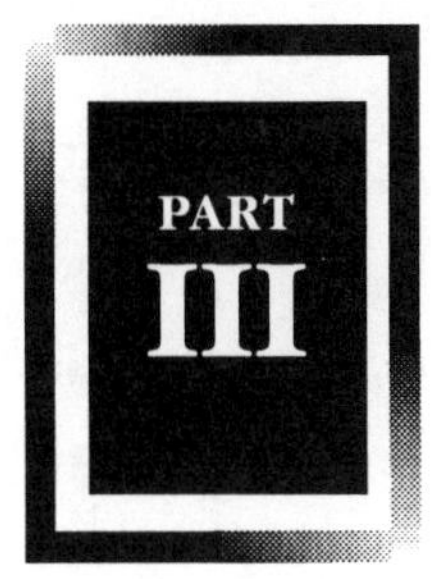

Sociology—General Reference Sources

GUIDES

109. Bottomore, T. B. **Sociology: A Guide to Problems and Literature.** 3d ed. London: Allen & Unwin, 1987. 372p. index. $39.95. LC 86-17278. ISBN 0-043-00108-4.

This latest edition of Bottomore's work remains a classic introduction to the field of sociology and some of its major works. Bottomore has broadened his consideration and treatment of theoretical approaches in sociology in this edition, and he has expanded his discussion of Third World countries. However, as a broad overview of the field, its specializations, and its classic literature, much of the book remains the same. It includes 20 chapters arranged into six parts: the scope and methods of sociology, population and social groupings, social institutions, the regulation of behavior, social change, and sociology and social practice. The chapters within each part roughly correspond to the standard subdivisions within the field. Each treats the historical development of the subject and discusses some of the classic and more recent works that contributed to that development. References within chapters are listed in the supplementary bibliography. Also, suggestions for further reading appear at the end of each of the book's six parts. Additional access to the book's content is provided by a combined name/subject index.

While the book is a well written and fascinating overview of the field, it is probably too sophisticated and encyclopedic for most beginning sociology students.

110. Brown, Samuel R. **Finding the Source in Sociology and Anthropology: A Thesaurus-Index to the Reference Collection.** New York: Greenwood, 1987. 269p. index. (Finding the Source, Number 1). $49.95. LC 86-31879. ISBN 0-313-25263-7.

This is a listing of 586 "core" reference sources for sociology and anthropology. The citations are arranged by title under various subject categories in the first part of the book. The four major categories include general sources, social sciences, anthropology, and sociology. Sociology is the largest section, and is subdivided further by general topics, statistics, subfields, and criminology. Six more specific sections follow these sections: population and life cycle; racial, ethnic and social groups; sexuality; social issues; social forces; and social welfare. These also include subtopics corresponding to more specific areas in sociology. The categorization of the citations is quirky and not particularly intuitive: Why are some topics buried under "subfields"? Why is "criminology" not listed with the six other specific headings? Furthermore, the unannotated citations comprise only 50 pages, yet more than 200 pages of thesaurus/subject index are included. Finally, the thesaurus layout for the index is unnecessarily clumsy; a thorough subject index, with plenty of *see* and *see also* references, would be as thorough and more user-friendly. Layout problems aside, this source covers many sociological reference sources through the mid-1980s. Title/subtitle and author indexes are also included.

111. Giarusso, Roseann, et al. **A Guide to Writing Sociology Papers.** 3d ed. New York: St. Martin's Press, 1994. 180p. index. $11.00. LC 92-62761. ISBN 0-312-08429-3.

Becoming a polished academic writer requires clear instruction and detailed feedback, accompanied by plenty of practice. This guide can help with the first two items. It provides excellent instruction about the writing process, particularly as applied to the field of sociology. The first five chapters explain how to get started on writing a paper, organizing your time, the writing process, acknowledging sources, and polishing your paper. These are general features of good writing in any discipline. However, where appropriate, the book includes examples and explanations relating to sociology. This is particularly evident in the discussion of selecting a topic and framing a question. The four chapters comprising the second part of the book address various types of sociology writing assignments: the textual analysis paper, the library research paper, the ethnographic field research paper, and the quantitative research paper. Each chapter includes valuable information on identifying the task or forming a question, gathering information and collecting data, organizing information, and writing the paper. The chapter on the library research paper discusses the use of specific library resources for sociological research. Each chapter also includes a sample student paper with accompanying annotations and feedback indicating its strengths and weaknesses. A final chapter contains a checklist for evaluating papers before they are submitted. A subject index is also included.

BIBLIOGRAPHIES

112. **International Bibliography of Sociology.** Vol. 1- . London: Routledge, 1952- . annual. index. (International Bibliography of the Social Sciences). $230.00. ISSN 0085-2066.

This is part of a series of annual volumes called the *International Bibliography of the Social Sciences*. Other volumes cover economics, political science, and social and cultural anthropology. Over 6,000 articles and books are cited in the current sociology volumes, representing items published in over 60 countries and in more than 70 languages. An extensive classification scheme for the arrangement of entries is available. This includes 11 major subject headings: general studies; theory and methodology; individuals, groups, and organizations; culture; social structure; population, family, gender, and ethnic group; environment, community, rural, and urban; economic life; labor; politics, state, and international relations; and social problems, social services, and social work. Each of these subject sections contains many more subheadings. All headings are in English and French. Both an author index and English/French versions of an extensive subject index are available. Also included are lists of over 2,500 periodicals consulted and their abbreviations, which are used in article citations. The international coverage of this bibliography is a major strength. Also, the turnaround time for publication of the annual bibliographies is less than a year after publication of the cited sources; this is impressive for a wide-ranging and international source. The *International Bibliography of the Social Sciences*, in its entirety, is also available on CD-ROM.

113. Smith, Tom W., Bradley J. Arnold, and Jennifer K. Wesley. **Annotated Bibliography of Papers Using the General Social Surveys.** 10th ed. Ann Arbor, Mich.: Inter-university Consortium for Political and Social Research, 1995. 779p. index. $36.00. ISBN 0-932132-52-9.

The General Social Survey (GSS) is an ongoing research program and dataset that collects demographic, behavioral, and attitudinal data spanning the social sciences. Data can touch on important sociological topics, such as race relations, job satisfaction, political participation, or group membership, not to mention a host of demographic variables. These data are used extensively in social science research. Books, journal articles, conference papers, reports, theses, and dissertations using GSS data are cited here alphabetically by author. Each entry includes not only a full reference and an abstract of findings, but also an indication of the GSS years, GSS mnemonics (variables), and other datasets employed in the research. A complete description of the GSS mnemonics and questions, as well as other details, can be found in the periodically updated GSS cumulative codebook. A mnemonic index is included, as is a supplementary list of a few hundred references that have not yet been abstracted or indexed. Colleges and universities that are members of the Inter-university Consortium for Political and Social Research (ICPSR) will probably have the GSS dataset, this bibliography, and the accompanying codebook.

INDEXES, ABSTRACTS, AND DATABASES

Indexes and Abstracts

114. **The Combined Retrospective Index Set to Journals in Sociology, 1895-1975.** Annadel N. Wile, exec. ed. Washington, D.C.: Carrollton Press, 1978. 6v. LC 77-70347. ISBN 0-8408-0194-7.

Part of the Combined Retrospective Index Series (C.R.I.S.), these volumes provide subject and author access to sociological articles in journals spanning an 80-year period. Over 100 sociology journals are indexed. The first five volumes comprise the subject indexes, with each covering different major headings (e.g., culture, family, and group interactions). A modest number of subheadings are included as well. Citations are then filed alphabetically by the keyword in the title. This is followed by a short title, author, journal number, year, volume, and page number. Journal titles corresponding to the numbers are found inside the front and back covers. The author index (volume 6) is arranged alphabetically, and accompanied by citations identical to those in the subject index. Overall, this may provide valuable historical coverage of sociological journal literature.

115. Lantz, Judith C., comp. **Cumulative Index of Sociology Journals, 1971-1985.** Washington, D.C.: American Sociological Association, 1987. 763p. index.

This source allows the user to search the contents of 10 major sociology journals, which include *American Journal of Sociology*, the *American Sociological Review*, *The American Sociologist*, *Contemporary Sociology*, the *Journal of Health and Social Behavior*, *Social Forces*, *Social Psychology Quarterly* (a.k.a. *Sociometry*), *Sociological Methodology*, *Sociological Theory*, and *Sociology of Education*. All but two of these titles, the *American Journal of Sociology* and *Social Forces*, are American Sociological Association journals. Both author and subject indexes are available; in each, article references include the abbreviated journal title, the month, the publication year, and the pages of the article. While this index does help in identifying some older articles in key journals, the entries may not be sufficiently detailed for interlibrary loan requests (titles and volume numbers are omitted). Though the coverage is somewhat dated, this index covers three years (1971-1973) that are not treated by the *Sociofile* database, which contains journal contents from 1974 to the present.

116. **Sociological Abstracts.** Vol. 1- , No. 1- . San Diego, Calif., Sociological Abstracts, Inc., 1953- . 7 issues/yr. $430.00/yr. ISSN 0038-0202.

This is one of the most important guides to the broad range of literature in sociology and its subdisciplines. It not only abstracts journal articles, books, and conference papers, but also indexes book reviews. Sources from around the world are cited, including some in foreign languages (though abstracts are in English). Entries are arranged by author under a detailed classification scheme of 29 subject headings and many more subheadings. Major headings reflect sociology's subdisciplines, with such categories as history and theory, social psychology, urban sociology, social differentiation, family and socialization, and mass phenomena, among others. The subheadings further detail the field. Social differentiation, for example, contains subheadings for social stratification/mobility, sociology of occupations and professions, and generations/intergenerational relations. A modest number of book abstracts and a more substantial listing of book reviews are found in a separate section. Author, subject, and reviewer indexes are included, as well as a source index listing all journal articles indexed in this source. An annual "Conference Abstracts Supplement" abstracts and indexes, by author and subject, presentations made at major international sociology conferences.

Sociological Abstracts is also available in computer searchable formats from commercial database vendors such as DIALOG (file #37) and on CD-ROM, as *Sociofile* (see entry #117).

Databases

117. **Sociofile.** [CD-ROM]. Norwood, Mass.: SilverPlatter Information Inc., 1986- . 3 updates/yr., with disk being cumulative. $1,995.00/yr.; $2,995.00/yr.(site license).

The CD-ROM equivalent of *Sociological Abstracts* (see entries #116 and #118), this includes references and abstracts for articles appearing in about 2,000 worldwide journals since 1974. Also included are citations to dissertations completed since 1986, and the 1980-to-present day contents of *Social Planning/Policy and Development Abstracts.*

118. **Sociological Abstracts.** San Diego, Calif.: Sociological Abstracts, Inc., 1963- . irregular updates. DIALOG file #37.

This is the DIALOG database equivalent to the print *Sociological Abstracts* (see entry #116) and to the CD-ROM *Sociofile* (see entry #117). It indexes and abstracts articles in over 1,600 journals, and includes references to book reviews, conference papers, dissertations, and more. Though indexing of articles extends back to 1963, abstracts are only available for items cited after 1973.

HANDBOOKS AND YEARBOOKS

119. **Annual Review of Sociology.** Vol. 1- . Palo Alto, Calif.: Annual Reviews, Inc., 1975- . annual. $52.00. ISSN 0360-0572.

Each volume contains up to 20 articles organized under broad subject categories, each containing a number of articles. Categories include theory and methods, social processes, institutions and culture, formal organizations, differentiation and stratification, demography, political and economic sociology, individual and society, and more. Of late, issues have also included a prefatory section of memoirs by or biographical essays on distinguished sociologists, such as Peter Blau, Seymour Martin Lipset, and Judith Blake. A subject index and cumulative indexes of authors and titles are included. This source is now available on the World Wide Web (http://www/annurev.org/soc/home.htm) with full text for 1993–1996 and abstracts for 12 years back. Articles must be ordered and downloaded.

120. Bart, Pauline, and Linda Frankel. **The Student Sociologist's Handbook.** 4th ed. New York: Random House, 1986. 291p. index. LC 85-19399. ISBN 0-394-35109-6.

This is a "do-it-yourself" guide to learning sociology. After a rather personalized, wide-ranging, and sophisticated introductory chapter, "Perspectives in Sociology," the authors discuss essential tools and techniques for library research and paper writing. Subsequent chapters cover the sociology paper, the mechanics of library research, periodical literature, guides to research and resource materials, governmental and non-governmental sources of data, and computers in sociological work. A number of reference and information sources are discussed, as is their utility for sociological study. In addition, two appendixes that outline the Dewey Decimal and Library of Congress classification systems are included.

Although the introductory chapter is thought-provoking and compelling, it is hard to see its appropriateness; its focus and sophistication do not seem to correspond to the rest of the book. Still, the remaining chapters, though a bit out of date, are quite well done and are nicely tailored to the field of sociology.

121. Caplow, Theodore, et al. **Recent Social Trends in the United States: 1960-1990.** Frankfurt am Main: Campus Verlag; Montreal, Buffalo: McGill-Queen's University Press, 1991. 590p. index. (Comparative Charting of Social Change). $70.00. ISBN 0-7735-0872-4.

The ultimate purpose of this statistical handbook is to provide "for the cross-national comparison of recent social trends" (p. ix). Toward that end, retrospective statistics have been collected on a variety of social institutions, attitudes, behaviors, and groups. These 78 tables of data are arranged under 17 subject categories representing such major sociological topics as age groups, stratification, social relations, ideologies, mobilizing institutions, integration and marginalization, attitudes and values, educational attainment, lifestyle, institutionalization of social forces, microsocial, women, and more. Each of the 78 trend reports includes an abstract, an overview of the trends and data, statistical tables, and a bibliography of references and sources. The appendixes include a list of members of the International Research Group, which produced this work, and a list of all of the research trends and their authors. A subject index is also available. Comparable books on other countries, such as France and the Federal Republic of Germany, are also available.

122. Davis, James A., and Tom W. Smith. **The NORC General Social Survey: A User's Guide.** Newbury Park, Calif.: Sage, 1992. 95p. (Guides to Major Social Science Data Bases, 1). $24.00. ISBN 0-8039-4367-9.

The General Social Survey is an ongoing research project and dataset that surveys U.S. households on variables of social scientific interest. Its database of responses constitutes an invaluable source for data analysis by sociologists and other researchers. This user's guide provides detailed explanations of this ongoing research's important aspects, such as its content, study design, sample design and weighting, field procedures, data preparation and distribution, and data analysis. Along with the introduction, these topics comprise the main chapters of the book and are important information for secondary users of the data. Many colleges and universities, particularly those that are members of the Inter-university Consortium for Political and Social Research (ICPSR), may have both the General Social Survey and its accompanying codebook.

123. Gans, Herbert J., ed. **Sociology in America.** Newbury Park, Calif.: Sage, 1990. 333p. index. (American Sociological Association Presidential Series). $52.00. LC 90-8218. ISBN 0-8039-3826-8.

This volume is a compilation of some of the papers from the 1988 American Sociological Association "Sociology in America" conference, all of which reflect on and analyze of the state of American sociology and its roles in our society. The 21 papers are organized into eight parts or sections on particular themes: sociology's effects on America; America's effects on sociology; sociology and public policy; sociology and critical issues (e.g., civil rights, gender, and the underclass); sociology's constituencies; sociology and social criticism; foreign sociologists' views of U.S. sociology; and sociology's relationship to some of the other social sciences. The papers' authors are notable figures in sociology, such as Dennis Wrong, Neil Smelser, Lewis Coser, Peter Rossi, Alain Touraine, Niklas Luhmann, and R. W. Connell, among others. Taken as a whole, their papers constitute a single useful overview of the state of the discipline as of 1988. Appended is a complete list of conference sessions, as well as the 1988 ASA Presidential Address given by Herbert Gans.

124. Hill, Martha S. **The Panel Study of Income Dynamics: A User's Guide.** Newbury Park, Calif.: Sage, 1992. 89p. (Guides to Major Social Science Data Bases, 2). $24.00. ISBN 0-8039-4609-0.

The Panel Study of Income Dynamics (PSID) is an ongoing research project collecting data for demographers, sociologists, and economists. Its data are particularly useful for to researching the areas of "income, employment, family health, wealth, and retirement" (back cover). This guide provides fairly detailed overviews of the content, methodology, and data analysis involved in the PSID. After an introductory chapter, subsequent chapters address the study design, field procedures, data preparation, data quality, content, data files, data analysis, and the process of getting started. The Inter-university Consortium for Political and Social Research (ICPSR) is the major source through which these data may be obtained.

125. Mohan, Raj P., and Arthur S. Wilke, eds. **International Handbook of Contemporary Developments in Sociology.** Westport, Conn.: Greenwood, 1994. 837p. index. $145.00. LC 93-37504. ISBN 0-313-26719-7.

This collection provides 34 chapter overviews of recent developments in sociology in various countries or, in some cases, regions (e.g., Latin America). The chapters are arranged under six broad geographic categories: Western and Northern Europe, the Western Hemisphere, Eastern Europe, Southern Europe, Africa and the Middle East, and the East. The essays discuss the major sociological theories, methods, and research findings from the last 20 years, as well as the development of sociology in each country. While uneven in their breadth and depth, these essays are fascinating and very informative on the international state of sociology. An interesting chapter on "Sociology's Academic Development as Reflected in Journal Debates" is also included. Three chapters are solely devoted to sociology in the United States, reflecting its predominant influence on sociology around the world. These chapters focus on methodological, metatheoretical, and research features of U.S. sociology. A selected bibliography, is included arranged by country, to complement the notes at the end of each chapter. Name and subject indexes are also provided.

126. Smelser, Neil J., ed. **Handbook of Sociology.** Newbury Park, Calif.: Sage, 1988. 824p. index. $89.95. LC 87-36762. ISBN 0-8039-2665-0.

"The volume is . . . predominantly a book on sociology as it stands in the United States" (p. 15). Its essays "make as objective an effort as possible to select out the most important theoretical themes and empirical research in their purview" (p. 17). The 22 chapters are arranged under four categories: "Theoretical and Methodological Issues"; "Bases of Inequality in Society"; "Major Institutional and Organizational Settings"; and "Social Process and Change." Specific chapter topics include social structure, inequality and labor, sociology of aging, gender/sex roles, family, religion, education, political sociology, deviance, social movements, and more. While many subtopics within sociology (e.g., demography and social psychology) do not receive chapter-level treatment, they are often discussed in other chapters. Each chapter is intended to cover both the historical development and current state of the subject area. The latter focus, according to the editor, should include discussion of competing paradigms and theoretical perspectives—points highlighted in the introduction. However, the theoretical breadth of current literature is not handled consistently well, as indicated by the chapter on "Sociology of Education." Overall, this handbook can serve an encyclopedia-like function in providing overviews of major topics in sociology.

127. Stratford, Jean Slemmons, and Juri Stratford. **Major U.S. Statistical Series: Definitions, Publications, Limitations.** Chicago: American Library Association, 1992. 147p. index. $35.00. LC 92-16746. ISBN 0-8389-0600-1.

The U.S. government is a major collector and disseminator of socioeconomic data, and this guide identifies and describes some of its specific producers, recurring statistical programs, and publications. The first seven chapters address major subject areas: population statistics; labor force statistics; economic indicators; price indexes and inflation measures; gross national product and other measures of production; foreign trade; and federal government finance. The chapters on population and the labor force may be particularly valuable for sociologists, as they specifically discuss the Census, the Current Population Survey and its *Current Population Reports*, Bureau of Labor Statistics data, and more. In all of the chapters, the content and scope of different statistical measures and programs are described. The last chapter discusses some key concepts in data compilation and presentation, such as estimated data, sampling error, questionnaire design, and more. An appendix identifies the availability of machine-readable versions of some data sources identified in the text. A name/title/subject index is provided.

128. **Survey of Social Science: Sociology Series.** Frank N. Magill, ed. Pasadena, Calif.: Salem Press, 1994. 5v. $375.00. LC 94-31770. ISBN 0-89356-739-6.

These volumes contain over 300 entries that describe various topics in sociology. The entries are more detailed than those in an encyclopedia, and are presented well for readers new to the topics. Each entry includes a list of key terms and their brief definitions, followed by an overview of the topic and its applications, and context. Entries conclude with a bibliography and some cross-references to related entries found elsewhere in the volumes. Appended is a glossary of key terms, as well as an alphabetical index of topics, a categorical index, and a subject index.

129. Wood, Floris W., ed. **An American Profile - Opinions and Behavior, 1972-1989.** Detroit: Gale, 1990. 1,065p. index. $89.50. ISBN 0-8103-7723-3.

Conducted since 1972, the General Social Survey is an ongoing survey of some of the demographic characteristics, opinions, and behaviors of the American population. It is an important data collection for social scientists, but is usually accessible only through the manipulation of large datasets by statistical analysis programs. However, this volume has extracted some of the more interesting questions, answers, and demographic variables from the General Social Survey and presented them in a readable format for interested social science students or researchers. The responses to over 300 questions are broken down into three categories: demography, opinions, and behavior. Four tables representing responses for the total population, by sex, race, and age, accompany each question. The questions relate to any number of important sociological topics, such as religious beliefs, social mobility, racial attitudes, attitudes toward family life, and more. An introduction explains how items were selected and describes the limitations on how the data are presented. A chronology of world events that may provide a useful connection to attitudes about social issues is included. Supplementary information includes a number of appendixes and a keyword index to all questions.

DICTIONARIES AND ENCYCLOPEDIAS

130. Abercrombie, Nicholas, Stephen Hill, and Bryan S. Turner. **The Penguin Dictionary of Sociology.** 3d ed. London: Penguin, 1994. 511p. $12.95. ISBN 0-14-051292-6.

New terms have been added and bibliographic references updated in this latest edition, which retains many of the other features that make it an excellent sociological dictionary. The definitions are clearly written and are relatively jargon-free, though some of the more theoretically sophisticated entries (e.g., Foucault) would be challenging for a beginning sociology student. The definitions refer the reader to terms defined elsewhere in the dictionary. *See* references to related concepts are also included, as well as references to further reading cited in the appended bibliography. Another nice feature is the inclusion of biographies on key theorists. To its credit, the dictionary defines key terms from a variety of theoretical perspectives, including radical ones. This new edition includes important concepts not previously included, such as "postmodernism," "deconstruction," and "post-structuralism." Where appropriate, it also makes distinctions between British and U.S. sociological approaches to a particular topic (e.g., class). Overall, this dictionary provides excellent definitions of both traditional and contemporary sociological concepts and theorists.

131. Bardis, Panos D. **Dictionary of Quotations in Sociology.** Westport, Conn.: Greenwood, 1985. 356p. index. $69.50. LC 85-943. ISBN 0-313-23778-6.

Bardis has compiled a historical assortment of quotes from sociologists, social philosophers, and others on some of the major concepts in sociology. For each concept or term, quotes are listed chronologically from the earliest to the most recent source. The sources of the quotes, which range from a few sentences to a long paragraph, are cited with an author, title, and publication year. A selected bibliography is also provided, as are helpful subject and name indexes. The subject index permits searching more specific topics than are found in the broad subject categories. The name index allows one to assemble a variety of quotes by a specific individual across a range of topics. The comparative nature of the quotes, both historically and culturally, makes for interesting reading. Also, the quotes could provide a useful key to further reading.

132. Booth, Barbara. **Thesaurus of Sociological Indexing Terms.** 4th ed. San Diego, Calif.: Sociological Abstracts, 1996. 344p. $70.00. LC 96-68558. ISBN 0-930710-13-4.

This lists all of the official subject terms used to classify entries in the print or electronic versions of the *Sociological Abstracts* database and *Social Planning/Policy & Development Abstracts*. Sociological concepts, geographic place names, and some personal names are included in this source. The main section of the thesaurus is an alphabetical list of subject headings (descriptors). These subject headings are typically accompanied by a list of broader, narrower, and related terms, all of which are headings that can be found elsewhere in the thesaurus. These other terms are often useful in broadening or focusing one's search. Entries for terms may also include a scope note (SN), which defines the term, and a historical note (HN), which indicates when a term was added or what term(s) it superseded. An entry may also include a list of "used for" (UF) terms. Throughout the thesaurus, these unused terms are listed with a "use" cross-reference to the preferred term. A "Rotated Descriptor Display" is appended that lists all keywords, including words in phrases, in alphabetical order and in the context of their keyword phrase. A final section lists six broad concepts and, in alphabetical order, all of the subject terms that relate to them. This thesaurus is invaluable for thorough subject searching in *Sociological Abstracts* in its various print and electronic formats.

133. Boudon, Raymond, and Francois Bourricaud. **A Critical Dictionary of Sociology.** Chicago: University of Chicago Press, 1989. 438p. index. $60.00. ISBN 0-226-06728-9.

Rather than providing conventional definitions on a comprehensive set of terms, the authors have written more personal essays on 73 sociological concepts, theories, and theorists. Furthermore, the terms discussed are not narrowly sociological, but instead reflect the more cosmopolitan approach of these two French sociologists. Consequently, the essays are probing and thought-provoking, features that help to explain the term "critical" in the title. The authors point out that their focus is on the more enduring questions in sociology, rather than on a discrete number of terms with fixed meanings. Despite these idiosyncrasies, many expected terms are included in this dictionary, such as alienation, anomie, functionalism, structuralism, ideologies, capitalism, authority, bureaucracy, suicide, and rationality. Similarly, some major sociologists are covered, including Auguste Comte, Karl Marx, Emile Durkheim, Herbert Spencer, and Max Weber.

Surprisingly, in such a selective list, one also finds entries on Jean-Jacques Rousseau, Niccolo Machiavelli, and Joseph Schumpeter. Throughout, the essays are well written and presume a certain amount of knowledge; a beginning student may be better off with one of the more conventional dictionaries, at least initially. Entries contain cross-references to related terms, as well as bibliographies of recommended readings. A thematic (subject/name) index is also included.

134. **Encyclopedia of Sociology.** Edgar F. Borgatta, editor-in-chief. New York: Macmillan Publishing Company, 1991. 4v. $375.00. LC 91-37827. ISBN 0-02-897051-9.

This four-volume set includes substantial, two- to nine-page entries on 370 key subject areas in the field of sociology. Though 370 may seem a scant number of topics, it is in fact a synthesis and consolidation of over 1,700 original, potential entries. Major sociological topics, theories, research methods, schools of thought, and subdisciplines are represented. The essays are written by experts on the various subjects and they provide an excellent introduction to and overview of their topics. Each entry is accompanied by a substantial list of references for further reading. Liberal use of *see* and *see also* references is also made to direct the user to preferred or related subject categories. Though no biographical entries are available for theorists, their ideas are often discussed at length within the relevant topics. More specific access to the terms, theories, and theorists within the entries is provided by a detailed subject index, though "ideology" is strangely absent. These essays provide valuable and relatively current overviews of fundamental topics in the field. A supplemental, alphabetical list of the encyclopedia's authors, their institutional affiliations, and the entries they wrote is included.

135. **Encyclopedic Dictionary of Sociology.** 4th ed. Richard Lachmann, editorial adviser. Guilford, Conn.: Dushkin, 1991. 321p. $12.95. ISBN 0-87967-886-0.

Included here are "more than 1,350 entries, each prepared by one of 120 authorities . . . Rather than provide exhaustive information on particular topics, the goal of this encyclopedia is to answer specific questions on the interrelationship among sociological concepts . . . Entries are arranged alphabetically, with some containing cross-references to either connect interrelated items or to deepen comprehension of the subject" (Oleg Zinan, *American Reference Books Annual, 1993*, pp. 355-356).

136. **International Encyclopedia of Sociology.** Frank N. Magill, ed. London, Chicago: Fitzroy Dearborn, 1995. 2v. $275.00. ISBN 1-884964-54-0.

Written for general readers, this encyclopedia includes 338 articles on the major topics, theories, institutions, and research techniques in the field of sociology. Articles are approximately four pages in length and are arranged alphabetically by topic. Each article includes a number of components to help clarify its meaning and importance. Both the type of sociology (e.g., major social institutions) and the specific field of study (e.g., education) are indicated and are accompanied by brief definitions of the topic and its principle terms. The text of the article itself is divided into three sections: the overview, which introduces the topic; an applications section, which explains how the topic relates to daily life and how it has been studied by sociologists; and the context, which explains the sociological relevance of the topic and its historical and cultural roots. Articles are also accompanied by brief, annotated bibliographies and cross-references to related concepts found elsewhere in the encyclopedia. A glossary, bibliography, and subject index are also included, as is an initial list 20 subject categories and their constituent articles.

137. Jary, David, and Julia Jary. **The Harper Collins Dictionary of Sociology.** New York: Harper Collins, 1991. 601p. LC 91-55446. ISBN 0-06-271543-7.

Intended primarily as a study aid, this dictionary has a broad scope, including not only key sociological terms and theorists, but also terms from the other social sciences that "have achieved wide use within sociology" (p. iii). For quick reference, all of the entries begin with a brief definition. Most of these definitions are followed by longer descriptions ranging from a paragraph to three or four pages. Methodological and statistical terms are included as well. In all of the definitions, terms defined elsewhere in the dictionary are indicated in capital letters. Key sociological works are cited within the definitions and listed in the appended bibliography. Although the brief definitions are convenient, the lengthier descriptions of many terms are also well done, giving this dictionary a well-rounded appeal to a variety of users.

138. Johnson, Allan G. **The Blackwell Dictionary of Sociology: A User's Guide to Sociological Language.** Cambridge, Mass.: Blackwell, 1995. 378p. $49.95. LC 95-1302. ISBN 1-55786-116-1.

Intended for the "average intelligent reader," this dictionary provides extremely well-written and concise definitions of fundamental concepts in sociology. The definitions range from a paragraph to a page and are notable for their clarity and avoidance of jargon, even for theoretically difficult concepts. The author's intent was to emphasize understandability, as opposed to depth or sophistication. All definitions are accompanied by a few references for further reading and *see also* references to related terms. The dictionary also makes extensive use of *see* references to direct the user to the correct term. Throughout the dictionary, terms defined elsewhere are indicated by capital letters. A final section includes brief biographical sketches of major sociological figures, along with a short list of their important works. The subject index is a nice addition, given that important concepts not elsewhere defined can be buried within the entries.

139. Marshall, Gordon, ed. **The Concise Oxford Dictionary of Sociology.** Oxford: Oxford University Press, 1994. 573p. LC 93-37140. ISBN 0-19-211670-3.

The strengths of this dictionary are its breadth of coverage and the conversational tone of many of its entries. The definitions range from a paragraph to a few pages in length and are surprisingly clear on some of the most difficult concepts (e.g., postmodernism). They include references to suggested readings and *see also* references to related terms defined elsewhere in the dictionary. Also, a liberal amount of cross-references from unused to used terms is included. Biographies are included, though only on deceased sociologists. Good writing and the inclusion of many recent important theoretical developments make this dictionary particularly valuable.

140. Thompson, Kenneth. **Key Quotations in Sociology.** London: Routledge, 1996. 207p. index. $15.95. ISBN 0-415-05761-2.

Students looking for quotes to use in papers, or faculty, to use in their teaching and writing, are the intended audience for this compilation. The quotations are arranged into two sections: by subject, and by theorist. The subject section includes major sociological concepts, usually with multiple quotations taken from a variety of sociological works. The source of each quote is fully cited. The section on sociological theorists is arranged alphabetically by theorist, with subsections for some specific topics. A number of quotes may be contained within these subtopics. Durkheim, for example, has subsections for sociological method, the division of labor, religion, politics, and moral education, each with multiple quotations. Both current and historical theorists are included, ranging from

Auguste Comte to Pierre Bourdieu and Anthony Giddens. Throughout the book, cross-references to related terms or relevant theorists are included. The number and variety of quotations on particular topics gives this book the feel of a dictionary or one-volume encyclopedia. In many cases, a reader could get a good grasp of a concept by reading the various quotes, as exemplified by the entries on "ideology." Name and subject indexes are included, with references to the page and the specific, numbered quote on that page.

JOURNALS

141. **Administrative Science Quarterly.** Vol. 1- , No. 1- . Ithaca, N.Y.: Johnson Graduate School of Management, Cornell University, 1956- . quarterly. $90.00/yr.(institutions). ISSN 0001-8392.

Specialists in the sociology of organizations consider this a fundamentally important journal. Issues include both empirical and theoretical articles, as well as book reviews and, occasionally, a review symposium. Indexed in: *ABC Pol Sci*, *Social Sciences Index*, *Sociological Abstracts*, *Social Sciences Citation Index*.

142. **American Journal of Community Psychology.** Vol. 1- , No. 1- . New York: Plenum Press, 1973- . bimonthly. $395.00/yr.(institutions). ISSN 0091-0562.

Sociologists in the areas of medical sociology, mental health service organizations, community and social support services, and family caregiving should find this useful. Approximately six articles per issue have, primarily, an applied focus. The journal is published in association with the Society for Community Research and Action (the Division of Community Psychology of the American Psychological Association). Indexed in: *Current Contents*, *Social Work Abstracts*, *Social Sciences Citation Index*, *Psychological Abstracts*, *Sociological Abstracts*.

143. **American Journal of Sociology.** Vol. 1- , No. 1- . Chicago: University of Chicago Press, 1895- . bimonthly. $96.00/yr.(institutions). ISSN 0002-9602.

Each issue includes as many as 10 research articles, review essays, and two to three dozen book reviews. The research articles cover a wide range of topics and methodologies. Indexed in: *Sociological Abstracts*, *Social Sciences Citation Index*, *Social Sciences Index*, and *Sociology of Education Abstracts*.

144. **American Sociological Review.** Vol. 1- , No. 1- . Washington, D.C.: American Sociological Association, 1936- . bimonthly. $120.00/yr.(institutions). ISSN 0003-1224.

Issues of this American Sociological Association (ASA) journal include approximately a dozen articles. While most of the articles use quantitative methodologies, some use other techniques (e.g., historical and ethnographic) or focus on theoretical issues. Topics covered span the subject specializations within sociology. Indexed in: *Social Sciences Index*, *Social Work Abstracts*, *Sociological Abstracts*, *Social Sciences Citation Index*, *Population Index*.

145. **The Australian and New Zealand Journal of Sociology.** Vol. 1- , No. 1- . Melbourne: Longman Australia, 1965- . 3 issues/yr. Aus.$85/yr.(institutions). ISSN 0004-8690.

Both articles and book reviews are included in this source, with articles covering a range of specializations, methodologies, and theoretical perspectives. This was formerly the journal of the Sociological Association of Australia and New Zealand, which has now split into the Australian Sociological Association (see entry #230) and the Sociology Association of AOTEAROA (New Zealand) (see entry #278). Indexed in: *Sociological Abstracts, Psychological Abstracts, Social Sciences Citation Index.*

146. **Berkeley Journal of Sociology.** Vol. 1- . Berkeley, Calif.: Sociology Department, University of California at Berkeley, 1955- . annual. $15.00/yr.(institutions). ISSN 0067-5830.

Recent articles in this journal have covered such topics as violent crime, record-keeping as a technology of power, congressional intelligence committees, peasant gains in rural Colombia, social movements, and Students for a Democratic Society. Indexed in: *Sociological Abstracts, Alternative Press Index.*

147. **British Journal of Sociology.** Vol. 1- , No. 1- . London: Routledge, 1950- . quarterly. $135.00/yr.(institutions). ISSN 0007-1315.

Published on behalf of the London School of Economics, this journal presents approximately 10 articles and as many reviews per issue. Subject coverage is broad, with recent articles on class analysis, women's employment, the political beliefs of the British electorate, a theory of modern superstition, and more. Though often quantitative, articles also engage in historical or theoretical analysis. Indexed in: *Sociology of Education Abstracts, Sociological Abstracts, Social Sciences Index, Social Sciences Citation Index.*

148. **British Journal of Sociology of Education.** Vol. 1- , No. 1- . Abingdon, Oxfordshire, England: Carfax, 1980- . quarterly. £212/yr.(institutions). ISSN 0142-5692.

From six to nine articles are published per issue of this journal, spanning a range of topics and, to some extent, countries. Recent articles have addressed racism, neo-Marxist theories of education, women teachers, Basil Bernstein's code theory, women in the academy, Canadian school reform, feminist post-structuralism, parental choice, self-managing schools, and more. Review symposia are also included in some issues. Indexed in: *Sociological Abstracts, Sociology of Education Abstracts, Social Sciences Citation Index.*

149. **Canadian Journal of Sociology Online.**
Available: http://gpu.srv.ualberta.ca/~ cjscopy/cjs.html
(Accessed: January 2, 1997).

The print version of the *Canadian Journal of Sociology* was founded in 1975. This electronic version offers samples of articles and book reviews, as well as announcements regarding upcoming events, conferences, special issues, etc. An e-mail subscription function and employment listings, as well as a forum for students, faculty, and departments is included. The journal covers the range of topics, theoretical perspectives and methodologies of sociology. Links to other Web sites of interest are also provided.

150. **Canadian Review of Sociology and Anthropology.** Vol. 1- , No. 1- . Montreal: Canadian Sociology and Anthropology Association, 1964- . quarterly. $98.00/yr.(institutions). ISSN 0008-4948.

Published by the Canadian Sociology and Anthropology Association, this journal provides broad coverage of the field. Recent articles have focused on such specializations as political sociology, educational sociology, sociological practice, methodology, theory, and sociology of the family, among others. Articles may be in either English or French, though the abstracts are in both languages. Many of the articles focus on Canadian society.

Issues also include book reviews. Indexed in: *Sociological Abstracts*, *Social Sciences Index*.

151. **Clinical Sociology Review.** Vol. 1- . Jacksonville, Ala.: Sociological Practice Association, c/o Hugh McCain, Jacksonville State University, 1982- . annual. $25.50/yr.(institutions). ISSN 0730-840X.

This covers a wide range of subject areas in applied sociology, including such recent article and book review topics as welfare, family violence, marital quarrels, income inequality, and a hospice model for bereaved children. Issues may also include teaching notes and book reviews. Indexed in: *Sociological Abstracts*, *Social Work Abstracts*, *Psychological Abstracts*.

152. **Contemporary Sociology: A Journal of Reviews.** Vol. 1- , No. 1- . Washington, D.C.: American Sociological Association, 1972- . bimonthly. $105.00/yr.(institutions). ISSN 0094-3061.

The reviews in this ASA journal are divided into two sections: featured essays (review essays) and reviews. The featured essays, which sometimes focus on a common theme, review new books at some length; it is common for particular essays to review a number of new books on the same topic. These essays can run to three double-column pages in length and may include references. The second section contains the vast majority of the reviews, which are shorter than the review essays and are organized under broad subject categories for the major specializations in sociology (e.g., theory and methods, social hierarchies, urban, life course, and criminology). Each issue also includes a list of publications received for review, as well as a section for commentary.

153. **Criminology: An Interdisciplinary Journal.** Vol. 1- , No. 1- . Columbus, Ohio: American Society of Criminology, 1963- . quarterly. $90.00/yr.(institutions). ISSN 0011-1384.

Drawing on the social and behavioral sciences, law, criminal justice, and history, articles here focus on theory, research, policy, and "current controversies." Issues typically include six or more articles and exchanges over particular articles. Occasional research notes and a presidential address from the annual conference of the American Society of Criminology, the journal's sponsor, is included. Indexed in: *Sociological Abstracts*, *Sage Urban Studies Abstracts*, *PAIS International in Print*, *Current Contents*, *Social Sciences Citation Index*, *Criminal Justice Abstracts*, *Criminal Justice Periodical Index*.

154. **Critical Sociology.** Vol. 15- , No. 1- . Eugene, Oreg.: Department of Sociology, University of Oregon, 1988- . 3 issues/yr. $40.00/yr.(institutions). ISSN 0896-9205.

Formerly the *Insurgent Sociologist*, each issue of the journal publishes approximately six articles, an essay review, and six book reviews. The articles are written from what may be loosely considered a critical sociological perspective, or at least they deal with issues raised from such a perspective. Furthermore, the articles span quantitative and qualitative methodological approaches and may also focus exclusively on theory. Indexed in: *Left Index*, *Alternative Press Index*, *Sociological Abstracts*.

155. **Current Research in Social Psychology.** irregular. free. ISSN 1088-7423.
Available: http://www.uiowa.edu/~ grpproc/cris/cris.html
(Accessed: January 25, 1997).

This is a new electronic, refereed journal published out of the Center for the Study of Group Processes at the University of Iowa. At this point, its publication is irregular, though there were seven issues published in the first volume, with each issue comprised of one article. The journal's editorial policy suggests it will publish both short and long pieces, as well as fairly narrow and technical articles. The electronic format permits this breadth of editorial focus. Recent articles have addressed group processes in standardized test performance (part of the IQ debate), feminine speech in homogeneous gender groups, and the coalition structure of the four-person family, among others.

156. **Current Sociology.** Vol. 1- , No. 1- . London: Sage, 1952- . 3 issues/yr. £99/yr.(institutions). ISSN 0011-3921.

Published for the International Sociological Association, this journal often focuses on particular themes (e.g., the military and society; biography, autobiography, socialization, and identity). Overviews of some of these themes, as well as annotated bibliographies, sometimes accompany the research articles, making the journal an excellent current literature review. Indexed in: *Social Sciences Index, Sociological Abstracts, Social Sciences Citation Index.*

157. **Demography.** Vol. 1 , No. 1- . Silver Spring, Md.: Population Association of America, 1964- . quarterly. $85.00/yr. ISSN 0070-3370.

Published by the Population Association of America, this journal includes articles drawn from the social sciences, statistics, public health, and epidemiology. Articles on theory, methods, or policy are welcome, as are comparative and historical works. Studies on developed and developing countries are also represented. Within issues, articles are grouped under such categories as migration, outcomes for children, labor force, population forecasting, fertility and contraception, mortality, and family and household. Indexed in: *Social Sciences Index, Population Index, Social Sciences Citation Index.*

158. **Discourse: Studies in the Cultural Politics of Education.** Vol. 1- , No. 1- . Abingdon, Oxfordshire, England: Carfax, 1980- . 3 issues/yr. $138.00/yr.(institutions). ISSN 0159-6306.

Broadly critical and multidisciplinary in orientation, this journal nonetheless has a distinctly sociological and policy focus. Issues typically contain approximately eight articles, one or two essay reviews, and some shorter book reviews. Throughout, issues of class, gender, race, educational inequality, and the creation of social identity are prominent. The journal is also international in scope. Indexed in: *Sociological Abstracts, Sociology of Education Abstracts.*

159. **Electronic Journal of Sociology.** 1994- . 3 issues/yr. free.
Available: http://olympus.lang.arts.ualberta.ca:8010/
(Accessed: December 10, 1996).

The *Electronic Journal of Sociology* is a refereed, electronic journal available on the Internet in both html and ASCII formats. Begun in 1994, it publishes three issues per year with two to three articles per issue. As yet, no discernible editorial focus to the articles published has been made. The editors note the availability of "optional interactive peer review" and "reader comments." The turnaround time for considering submissions is claimed to be much briefer than for print journals.

160. **Gender & Society.** Vol. 1- , No. 1- . Thousand Oaks, Calif.: Sage, 1987- . bimonthly. $165.00/yr.(institutions). ISSN 0891-2432.

Issues contain approximately six articles and as many reviews dealing with such topics as gender stratification, sexism in educational institutions, gender and ethnicity, work, family, and the range of sociological subdisciplines. Indexed in: *Sociological Abstracts*, *Psychological Abstracts*, *Women Studies Abstracts*.

161. **The Gerontologist.** Vol. 1- , No. 1- . Washington, D.C.: Gerontological Society of America, 1960- . bimonthly. $94.00/yr.(institutions). ISSN 0016-9013.

In this journal, aging is dealt with in a variety of social and psychological contexts, including work, caregiving and social support, self-esteem, health, gerontological practice, long-term care, demographic trends, policy, and more. Each issue contains more than a dozen articles grouped around a handful of themes; a symposium section usually contains four or five articles on an issue. Book and audiovisual reviews are also available. A special issue each year is devoted to abstracts from the annual meeting of the Gerontological Society of America, the journal's sponsor and publisher. Indexed in: *Social Sciences Index*, *Social Work Abstracts*, *Social Sciences Citation Index*, *Psychological Abstracts*, *Sage Family Studies Abstracts*, *Sage Urban Studies Abstracts*.

162. **Human Organization.** Vol. 1- , No. 1- . Oklahoma City, Okla.: Society for Applied Anthropology, 1941- . quarterly. $60.00/yr. ISSN 0018-7259.

Though primarily an anthropology journal, this nonetheless publishes articles in social organization and the anthropology of urban life, both of which should interest sociologists. Articles are often international in scope. Recent articles have been on such topics as homelessness, AIDS in ethnic communities, and the social construction of whiteness, among others. Indexed in: *Sociological Abstracts*, *Social Sciences Index*, *Urban Studies Abstracts*, *Social Sciences Citation Index*.

163. **Humanity and Society.** Vol. 1- , No. 1- . New York: Association for Humanist Sociology, 1977- . quarterly. $50.00/yr. ISSN 0160-5976.

The journal of the Association for Humanist Sociology (see entry #228), recent articles have covered a range of interesting topics, such as imperialism and class struggle, baseball, worker participation, official corruption in developing countries, loss of clerical work autonomy, and more. Indexed in: *Sociological Abstracts*, *Criminal Justice Abstracts*.

164. **International Journal of the Sociology of Law.** Vol. 1- , No. 1- . London: Academic Press, 1972- . quarterly. £110/yr. ISSN 0194-6596.

Issues can include up to six articles, as well as some book reviews. The articles are often international or comparative in scope, and an occasional journal issue is devoted to a special topic (e.g., Law and Popular Culture). Indexed in: *Current Contents*, *Sociological Abstracts*.

165. **International Migration Review.** Vol. 1- , No. 1- . New York: Center for Migration Studies, 1966- . quarterly. $64.00/yr.(institutions). ISSN 0197-9183.

Each issue includes a substantial number of articles and reviews, as well as research notes and conference reports. Articles are often international, comparative, or multidisciplinary, and they relate migration to such issues as neighborhood change, women's labor, trade unions, immigration politics, national identity, and more. Indexed in: *Population Index*, *Sociological Abstracts*, *Social Sciences Index*, *Social Sciences Citation Index*, *Current Contents*.

166. **International Studies in Sociology of Education.** Vol. 1- . Wallingford, Oxfordshire: Triangle Books Ltd., 1991- . semiannual. £64.00/yr. ISSN 0962-0214.

Though a relatively new journal, this deals with important sociological topics in an international context. Plenty of policy analysis may be found here, as well as a focus on qualitative methodologies (case studies and historical analysis) and theory. Recent articles have addressed racism, masculinity, critical students, student voice in school reform, the cultural practices of assertive girls, antiracist education, and policy production in Australian education, among others. Theme issues (e.g., on the market ideology in education) are included. Both mainstream and more critical theoretical perspectives are represented. Indexed in: *Sociology of Education Abstracts*, *Multicultural Education Abstracts*.

167. **Journal of Health and Social Behavior.** Vol. 1- , No. 1- . Washington, D.C.: American Sociological Association, 1960- . quarterly. $80.00/yr.(institutions). ISSN 0022-1465.

Formerly the *Journal of Health and Human Behavior*, this ASA journal covers a broad range of topics within medical sociology. Recent articles have focused on such topics as Asian immigrants and stress, poverty and children's mental health, social support, religion and subjective health, parental divorce and adolescent depression, and gender differences in response to marital dissolution, among others. Indexed in: *Sociological Abstracts*, *Social Sciences Index*, *Sage Public Administration Abstracts*, *Psychological Abstracts*, *Social Sciences Citation Index*.

168. **Journal of Marriage and the Family.** Vol. 1- , No. 1- . Minneapolis, Minn.: National Council on Family Relations, 1938- . quarterly. $95.00/yr.(institutions). ISSN 0022-2445.

Approximately 20 articles and 10 reviews are included per issue, with articles arranged under broad subject categories (e.g., divorce; eldercare; theory and methods; gender and household labor; work and family; and children, unwed motherhood, and child care). Comments on earlier articles, as well as an occasional symposium or group of articles on a particular theme are also included. Indexed in: *Sage Family Studies Abstracts*, *Sociological Abstracts*, *Social Work Abstracts*, *Social Sciences Index*, *Social Sciences Citation Index*.

169. **Journal of Social Policy.** Vol. 1- , No. 1- . Cambridge: Cambridge University Press, 1972- . $149.00/yr.(institutions). ISSN 0047-2794.

Though primarily British in focus, this journal's international and comparative coverage should be of interest to policy sociologists. Included are theoretical and empirical research articles on a range of policy issues, such as postmodern social policy, welfare policy, housing debt crises, researching living standards, feminism and child daycare, women and health in China, and work and care in the life course, among others. Issues also include a social policy digest that summarizes recent policy developments in the United Kingdom. A large section of book reviews is also available. This is the journal of the Social Policy Association. Indexed in: *Social Sciences Index*, *Sociological Abstracts*, *Social Sciences Citation Index*.

170. **Journal of Social Psychology.** Vol. 1- , No. 1- . Washington, D.C.: Heldref, 1930- . bimonthly. $116.00/yr. ISSN 0022-4545.

The emphasis here is on "experimental, empirical, and field studies of groups, cultural effects, cross-national problems, language, and ethnicity" (back cover). In addition to the approximately 12 articles per issue, shorter articles are included in sections titled "Current Problems and Resolutions," "Replications and Refinements," and "Cross-Cultural Notes." Indexed in: *Current Contents, Social Sciences Citation Index, Psychological Abstracts, Sociological Abstracts, Sociology of Education Abstracts.*

171. **Journal of Sport and Social Issues.** Vol. 1- , No. 1- . Thousand Oaks, Calif.: Sage, 1976- . quarterly. $128.00/yr.(institutions). ISSN 0193-7325.

The official journal of the Center for the Study of Sport in Society (see entry #210) at Northeastern University, this includes editorial commentaries and a modest number of articles on mostly topical social issues in sports. A recent issue included articles on the Olympics, men coaches in women's sports, and retention factors in coaching and athletic management. Articles are frequently, though not exclusively qualitative in methodology, and a variety of disciplines and theoretical perspectives is represented.

172. **Journals of Gerontology. Series B, Psychological Sciences and Social Sciences.** Vol. 50B- , No. 1- . Washington, D.C.: Gerontological Society of America, 1995- . bimonthly. $95.00/yr.(institutions). ISSN 1079-5014.

Formerly the *Journal of Gerontology*, this is now two journals focusing on gerontology published in one bound issue. One journal is for the psychological sciences and one is for the social sciences, with each journal occupying half of the issue and having its own title page, table of contents, and editorial statements. Approximately six articles are included in each of these two journals. Throughout, articles use quantitative methodologies while focusing on a variety of topics, such as stress, poverty and inequality, social networks, self-efficacy, health inequality, mental health, social roles, and more. Indexed in: *Social Sciences Index, Social Work Abstracts, Social Sciences Citation Index, Sage Family Studies Abstracts, Sage Urban Studies Abstracts, Psychological Abstracts.*

173. **Population Studies.** Vol. 1- , No. 1- . London: Population Investigation Committee, 1947- . 3 issues/yr. $110.00/yr. ISSN 0032-4728.

Published by the Population Investigation Committee at the London School of Economics, this is an important source of research in demography and population. Each issue contains approximately seven or eight articles, many with an international focus. A substantial number of book reviews are included as well. Indexed in: *Population Index, Sociological Abstracts, Current Contents.*

174. **Public Opinion Quarterly.** Vol. 1- , No. 1- . Chicago: University of Chicago Press, 1937- . quarterly. $55.00/yr.(institutions). ISSN 0033-362X.

This is the journal of the American Association of Public Opinion Research (see entry #225) and is a major source of research on survey research methods and techniques. Issues include research articles, articles on polls, review essays, and book reviews. Indexed in: *Social Sciences Index, Public Affairs Information Service.*

175. **Race & Class.** Vol. 16- , No. 2- . London: Institute of Race Relations, 1974- . quarterly. $75.00/yr.(institutions, via airmail). ISSN 0306-3968.

The journal's subtitle ("A Journal for Black and Third World Liberation") suggests its critical and international orientation. Issues can include a half dozen articles, a few commentaries, and some book reviews. Over and above the topics of race and class, issues of decolonialization and development are prominent. Indexed in: *Alternative Press Index, The Left Index, Social Sciences Citation Index.*

176. **Rural Sociology.** Vol. 1- , No. 1- . Urbana, Ill.: Rural Sociological Society, 1936- . quarterly. $87.00/yr.(institutions). ISSN 0036-0112.

While falling within the purview of rural sociology, this journal's articles still cover a range of subtopics. These can include such subjects as globalization, environmental sociology, social class, poverty, race and ethnicity, social identity, women and gender issues, rural-urban contrasts, and more. Typically, more than six articles are included per issue, and these are occasionally grouped around themes. Book reviews are also included. Indexed in: *Sociological Index, Social Sciences Index, Social Sciences Citation Index.*

177. **Social Forces.** Vol. 1- , No. 1- . Chapel Hill, N.C.: University of North Carolina Press, 1922- . quarterly. $56.00/yr.(institutions). ISSN 0037-7732.

Associated with the Southern Sociological Society (see entry #251), *Social Forces* publishes approximately a dozen articles and four dozen reviews per issue. Topics span the subject specializations in sociology, including work, social groups and movements, gender, family, crime, social inequality, social mobility, social support/networks, and more. Articles employ both quantitative and qualitative/historical methodologies. Indexed in: *Sociological Abstracts*, *Social Sciences Index*, and *Social Sciences Citation Index.*

178. **Social Identities.** Vol. 1- , No. 1- . Abingdon, Oxfordshire, England: Carfax, 1995- . semiannual. $98.00/yr.(institutions). ISSN 1350-4630.

As stated by the editors in the first issue, the journal's intent is "to serve as a forum for contesting ideas and debates pertaining to the formations of, and transformations in, socially significant identities such as race, nation, ethnicity, gender and class, their attendant forms of material exclusion and power, as well as the political and cultural possibilities these identifications open up" (Vol. 1, No. 1, p. 3). The journal is international and multidisciplinary, and sociological concerns, broadly construed, are clearly central. Issues include six or more articles and a few book reviews. Indexed in: *Sociological Abstracts*, *Social Planning/Policy & Development Abstracts.*

179. **Social Indicators Research.** Vol. 1- , No. 1- . Dordrecht, Netherlands: Kluwer, 1974- . monthly, except April, September, & November. $235.00/volume. ISSN 0303-8300.

Approximately six articles per issue focus on quality-of-life measurement from an international and interdisciplinary perspective. The research may be philosophical, empirical, or methodological in nature and its focus can range from the individual to international systems. Topics covered span many of the sociological specializations, including health, religion, welfare, poverty, stratification, population, mental health, social customs and morality, and more. Indexed in: *Sociological Abstracts*, *Current Contents*, *Social Sciences Citation Index*, *Sage Urban Studies Abstracts*, *Sage Family Studies Abstracts*, *Social Work Abstracts.*

180. **Social Networks.** Vol. 1- , No. 1- . Amsterdam: Elsevier, 1978- . quarterly. $259.00/yr.(institutions). ISSN 0378-8733.

The journal of the International Network for Social Network Analysis (INSNA) (see entry #235), this publishes three or four articles per issue in the area of structural analysis. Indexed in: *Anthropological Index*, *Social Sciences Citation Index*, *Current Contents*, *Sociological Abstracts.*

181. **Social Problems.** Vol. 1- , No. 1- . Berkeley, Calif.: University of California Press, 1953- . quarterly. $85.00/yr.(institutions). ISSN 0037-7791.

This is the official journal of the Society for the Study of Social Problems (see entry #246). Each issue contains approximately seven articles, often arranged under broad themes (e.g., race and immigration; state, economy, and work; studies in violence and welfare; global economy and labor). Also included is the presidential address given at the SSSP annual conference. Indexed in: *Current Contents, Sociological Abstracts, Social Sciences Index, Social Sciences Citation Index, Social Work Abstracts, Psychological Abstracts.*

182. **Social Psychology Quarterly.** Vol. 1- , No. 1- . Washington, D.C.: American Sociological Association, 1937- . quarterly. $95.00/yr.(institutions). ISSN 0190-2725.

Formerly titled *Sociometry* and *Social Psychology*, this ASA journal includes up to six articles and a few research notes per issue. Articles employ a variety of methodologies and theoretical perspectives, including symbolic interactionism and ethnomethodology. Article topics are varied, though occasional theme issues (e.g., gender and social interaction) are available. Indexed in: *Social Sciences Index, Psychological Abstracts.*

183. **Social Science and Medicine.** Vol. 1- , No. 1- . Oxford: Elsevier Science; Pergamon, 1982- . semimonthly in two volumes. $2,139.00/yr.(institutions). ISSN 0277-9536.

International and interdisciplinary in scope, this journal is important for medical sociologists and medical anthropologists interested in theory, policy, or practice. A range of social factors in the provision and outcome of health care are addressed, and both physical and mental health issues are represented. Journal issues also include book reviews, and specific issues have been devoted to conference papers (e.g., the International Conference on the Social Sciences and Medicine).

184. **Social Science Quarterly.** Vol. 49- , No. 1- . Austin, Tex.: University of Texas Press, 1968- . quarterly. $59.00/yr.(institutions). ISSN 0038-4941.

Published on behalf of the Southwestern Social Science Association, this is an interdisciplinary journal with plenty of sociology contributors and topics. Issues typically include a symposium of articles on a special topic, as well as approximately 10 articles on a range of social science subjects. Sociologically interesting topics from recent issues have included women's occupations; family structure, schooling, and adult poverty; education and employment effects on pregnancy; generational differences in educational attainment among Mexican Americans; and gender and authority, among others. Also included are book reviews, review essays, and research notes. Indexed in: *Current Contents, Sociological Abstracts, Public Affairs Information Service, Social Sciences Index.*

185. **Social Science Research.** Vol. 1- , No. 1- . Orlando, Fl.: Academic Press, 1972- . quarterly. $210.00/yr. ISSN 0049-089X.

Spanning a range of social science topics, articles here nonetheless share the journal's focus on methodology and quantitative research. Recent articles have been written on occupational status, women's wages, welfare and migration, race and residential segregation, old-age economic activity in 1910, and detecting discrimination in public contracting, to name a few. Indexed in: *Social Sciences Index, Social Sciences Citation Index.*

186. **Sociological Focus.** Vol. 1- , No. 1- . Columbus, Oh.: Department of Sociology, Ohio State University, 1967- . four issues/yr. $45.00/yr.(institutions). ISSN 0038-0237.

The journal of the North Central Sociological Association (NCSA) (see entry #241), this includes both articles and, annually, the text of the presidential address at the NCSA conference. Reports of research on the region are included, as well as briefer research notes. Articles span the sociological subdisciplines and employ primarily quantitative methodologies. Indexed in: *Current Contents*, *Sociological Abstracts*, *Social Sciences Citation Index*.

187. **Sociological Inquiry.** Vol. 1- , No. 1- . Austin, Tex.: University of Texas Press, 1930- . quarterly. $43.00/yr.(institutions). ISSN 0038-0245.

This is the journal of Alpha Kappa Delta, the International Sociology Honor Society. Articles and book reviews are included, with recent articles addressing such topics as racial prejudice and criminal victimization, attitudes towards the welfare state, the sociology of religion, students' peer friendship groups, and Erving Goffman. Special (theme) sections are occasionally included. Indexed in: *Social Sciences Index*, *Sociological Abstracts*, *Social Sciences Citation Index*.

188. **Sociological Methods & Research.** Vol. 1- , No. 1- . Thousand Oaks, Calif.: Sage, 1972- . quarterly. $205.00/yr.(institutions). ISSN 0049-1241.

Also known by its acronym, SMR, this journal is devoted to clarifying methodological problems and advancing understanding in the areas of research methodology and statistics. About five articles are provided per issue, and review articles may be included. Indexed in: *Current Contents*, *Sociological Abstracts*, *Social Sciences Citation Index*, *Sociology of Education Abstracts*.

189. **Sociological Perspectives.** Vol. 1- , No. 1- . Greenwich, Conn.: JAI Press, 1958- . quarterly. $170.00/yr.(institutions). ISSN 0731-1214.

As the Pacific Sociological Association's (see entry #242) official journal, this publishes about six to eight articles per issue. The address given by the association's president at the annual conference is also included. A wide range of topics are treated, as reflected in a recent issue's articles on postmodernism; gender-role attitudes; social identities; caregiving and depression; and gender, sex and reproduction in outer space. A variety of theoretical approaches and methodologies are employed. Special theme issues are available, such as those recently published on inequality and environmental conflict. Indexed in: *Sociological Abstracts*, *Social Sciences Index*, *Social Sciences Citation Index*.

190. **The Sociological Quarterly.** Vol. 1- , No. 1- . Berkeley, Calif.: University of California Press, 1960- . quarterly. $135.00/yr.(institutions). ISSN 0038-0253.

The "Official Journal of the Midwest Sociological Society" (see entry #237), this contains up to 10 articles per issue. Articles are grouped under broad subject categories spanning the sociological specializations, including "Race, Economy, and Family"; "Poverty, Inequality and Gender"; "Theoretical and Methodological Developments"; "Community, Democracy, and Social Control"; and "Politics, Media, and Postindustrialism," among others. A range of methodologies and theoretical perspectives is represented. Indexed in: *Social Sciences Index*, *Sociological Abstracts*, *Social Sciences Citation Index*, *Social Work Abstracts*, *Psychological Abstracts*.

191. **Sociological Research Online.** London: Sage, 1996- . irregular. free. ISSN 1360-7804. Available: http://www.soc.surrey.ac.uk/socresonline/ (Accessed: December 10, 1996).

Published out of the United Kingdom, this electronic journal focuses on applied sociology dealing "with current political, cultural and intellectual topics and debates." Each issue has anywhere from three to six feature articles, a review article, and numerous book reviews. Additional information includes editorial information, the composition of the editorial board, information on submitting manuscripts, authors' guides to nonbiased language and ethical writing, notices of workshops, a noticeboard, and additional Internet links of interest to sociologists.

192. **The Sociological Review.** Vol. 1- , No. 1- . Oxford: Blackwell, 1953- . quarterly. $192.00/yr.(institutions). ISSN 0038-0261.

This is a British sociology journal published on behalf of Keele University. Its articles reflect primarily qualitative, interpretive, or social constructionist approaches to social analysis, with some other articles focusing on issues or debates within sociological theory. From six to ten articles are included per issue, and these span the subdisciplines within the field. A substantial book review section is included. Indexed in: *Social Sciences Index*, *Sociological Abstracts*, *Current Contents*, *Social Sciences Citation Index*.

193. **Sociological Spectrum.** Vol. 1- , No. 1- . London: Taylor and Francis, 1981- . quarterly. $143.00/yr.(institutions). ISSN 0273-2173.

The official journal of the Mid-South Sociological Association (see entry #236), *Sociological Spectrum* publishes five or six articles per issue and covers a range of methodologies and subject specializations. Recent article topics include environmental sociology, social support/networks, elites and the Social Register, institutional racism, academic achievement among Vietnamese American adolescents, subjective class identification among men and women, and more. Occasional issues are devoted to special topics (e.g., "Society, Culture, and the Environment"). Indexed in: *Sociological Abstracts*, *Social Sciences Citation Index*.

194. **Sociological Theory.** Vol. 1- , No. 1- . Cambridge, Mass.: Blackwell, 1983- . 3 issues/yr. $79.00/yr.(institutions). ISSN 0735-2751.

Another of the American Sociological Association journals, articles here predictably focus on sociological theorists, theories, and schools of thought. Recent articles have covered Max Weber, Karl Mannheim, and Everett Hughes and the Chicago Tradition. Indexed in: *Sociological Abstracts*.

195. **Sociology.** Vol. 1- , No. 1- . Cambridge: Cambridge University Press, 1967- . quarterly. $137.00/yr. ISSN 0038-0385.

This is a journal of the British Sociological Association (see entry #231). Issues include both articles and numerous reviews on the range of specializations and theoretical perspectives in the field. Indexed in: *Sociological Abstracts*, *Social Sciences Index*, *Social Sciences Citation Index*.

196. **Sociology of Education.** Vol. 1- , No. 1- . Washington, D.C.: American Sociological Association, 1927- . quarterly. $95.00/yr.(institutions). ISSN 0038-0407.

An American Sociological Association (ASA) journal, *Sociology of Education* publishes primarily quantitative research and policy-related articles. It addresses a wide range of topics in the field using a variety of theoretical perspectives, including conflict theory and social constructionism. Approximately four to six articles are contained in each issue, with an occasional issue devoted to a special topic (e.g., sociology and educational policy). Indexed in: *Sociological Abstracts*, *Social Sciences Index*, *Sociology of Education Abstracts*, *Social Sciences Citation Index*.

197. **Sociology of Health & Illness.** Vol. 1- , No. 1- . Oxford: Blackwell, 1979- . six issues/yr. $297.00/yr.(institutions). ISSN 0141-9889.

A medical sociology journal, this has a noticeable British and European focus, in regard to the articles' authors and research settings. Issues include approximately six articles and cover a wide range of topics. For example, recent articles have addressed anorexia nervosa, British national health service reforms, socioeconomic inequalities in health, the interplay between doctors and nurses, doctor-patient relationships, and AIDS, to name a few. As many as a dozen book reviews are also included, as are occasional rejoinders to earlier articles. Indexed in: *Sociological Abstracts*, *Social Sciences Citation Index*, *Psychological Abstracts*.

198. **Sociology of Sport Journal.** Vol. 1- , No. 1- . Champaign, Ill.: Human Kinetics, 1984- . quarterly. $90.00/yr.(institutions). ISSN 0741-1235.

International in scope and varied in subject focus, a typical issue includes four or five articles and occasional research notes and book reviews. Recent articles have addressed the subjects of racism; sports participation; gender, age, and sport involvement; sports medicine; and the sociocultural context of sport and health, among others. Also included is the presidential address from the annual conference of the North American Society for the Sociology of Sport, the journal's sponsor. Indexed in: *Sociological Abstracts*, *Current Contents*, *Social Sciences Citation Index*, *Physical Education Index*.

199. **Symbolic Interaction.** Vol. 1- , No. 1- . Greenwich, Conn.: JAI Press, 1977- . quarterly. $185.00/yr.(institutions). ISSN 0195-6086.

The official journal of the Society for the Study of Symbolic Interaction (SSSI) (see entry #247), this is a major outlet for work in interactionism, phenomenology, and related perspectives. Issues can include up to six articles, sometimes on a central theme, and a few book reviews. An author/title index is located at the end of each volume. Indexed in: *Sociological Abstracts*, *Psychological Abstracts*.

200. **Teaching Sociology.** Vol. 1- , No. 1- . Washington, D.C.: American Sociological Association, 1973- . quarterly. $95.00/yr.(institutions). ISSN 0092-055X.

The focus of this journal is not only on the theory and practice of teaching sociology, but also on curricular matters. Included are sections for articles, notes, issues, comments and replies, review essays, and book reviews. While a range of teaching topics may be covered, occasional theme issues are also included. The book reviews focus on works that could serve as texts or supplemental texts in courses, and the reviewers' comments emphasize the teaching-related strengths and weaknesses of the book. Indexed in: *Sociological Abstracts*, *Social Sciences Citation Index*, *Current Index to Journals in Education* (ERIC), *Current Contents*.

201. **Theory and Society.** Vol. 1- , No. 1- . Dordrecht, The Netherlands: Kluwer Academic Publishers, 1974- . bimonthly. $319.00/yr.(institutions). ISSN 0304-2421.

Subject areas emphasized in this journal include political sociology and political economy, global development, social change, and sociological theory (particularly as applied to development issues and change). Articles are often theoretical, historical, or comparative, and are less likely to make use of quantitative methodologies. A typical journal issue contains three or four articles and some book reviews. Indexed in: *Sociological Abstracts, Current Contents, Social Sciences Citation Index.*

202. **Theory, Culture, and Society.** Vol. 1- , No. 1- . London: Sage, 1982- . quarterly. £120/yr.(institutions). ISSN 0263-2764.

Recent issues have covered such topics as identity formation, globalization, Islamic fundamentalism, urban sociology, ideology in the information society, and the family, among others. Occasionally, a theme issue (e.g., on Japan) may be published, or an issue may contain an interview with a well-known theorist (e.g., Jürgen Habermas). Indexed in: *Sociological Abstracts, Alternative Press Index.*

203. **Urban Affairs Review.** Vol. 30- , No. 1- . Thousand Oaks, Calif.: Sage, 1995- . bimonthly. $250.00/yr.(institutions). ISSN 1078-0874.

Formerly the *Urban Affairs Quarterly*, this includes articles falling within such areas as political socialization, power structure research, organizational sociology, economic development, public policy, social movements, social change, and more. Despite the breadth of topics covered, the contexts remain urban and metropolitan areas. Issues typically include about five articles, a comparable number of reviews, and an occasional research note. Indexed in: *Sage Urban Studies Abstracts, Sociological Abstracts, Social Sciences Index, Social Sciences Citation Index.*

204. **Work and Occupations.** Vol. 1- , No. 1- . Thousand Oaks, Calif.: Sage, 1974- . quarterly. $167.00/yr.(institutions). ISSN 0730-8884.

International in coverage, this journal typically includes four or more articles and as many book reviews. Recent articles have focused on comparable worth and earnings inequality, occupational sex segregation in Sweden, Black men's employment problems, and assaultive violence in U.S. post offices, to name a few. Special issues devoted to a single theme (e.g., work and family) are also occasionally published. Indexed in: *Sociological Abstracts, Current Contents, Sage Family Studies Abstracts, Sage Public Administration Abstracts.*

205. **Work, Employment and Society.** Vol. 1- , No. 1- . Cambridge: Cambridge University Press, 1987- . quarterly. $137.00/yr. ISSN 0950-0170.

Recent articles have covered such topics as women's work, homeworking women, ethnic entrepreneurs, part-time workers, French unions, employee participation, and sexual harassment, among others. Book reviews are also included. This is a journal of the British Sociological Association (see entry #231). Indexed in: *Sociological Abstracts, Social Sciences Citation Index.*

RESEARCH CENTERS

206. **A.E. Havens Center for the Study of Social Structure and Social Change.** Department of Sociology, 8128 Social Science Bldg., University of Wisconsin - Madison, Madison, WI 53706, USA. (608)262-1420.

Directed by Erik Olin Wright, this center focuses on the study of social change and social movements, from critical theoretical perspectives. It receives both university and private support, and assists in organizing conferences, workshops, etc.

207. **Carolina Population Center.** University Sq., CB 8120, University of North Carolina, Chapel Hill, NC 27516-3997, USA. (919)966-1710.

The center conducts research on population and related interdisciplinary topics, and is supported by its parent institution, various levels of government, and foundations. Additional services include postdoctoral training and the maintenance of an electronic database of citations to population literature.

208. **Center for Migration Studies.** 209 Flagg Pl., Staten Island, NY 10304-1199, USA. (718)351-8800. (E-mail: lftoc@csiunx.it.csi.cuny.edu).

Besides being an important center for research and policy in the areas of migration and immigration, the center also publishes the quarterly journal *International Migration Review* (see entry #165).

209. **Center for the Study of Group Processes.** Professor Barry Markovsky, Director, Center for the Study of Group Processes, Department of Sociology, University of Iowa, Iowa City, IA 52242-1401, USA. (319)335-2490.

Established in 1992, the center not only supports multidisciplinary research in group processes, but also maintains a research laboratory and Web site (see entry #497), attracts visiting scholars, promotes conferences and workshops, and more. It also publishes the electronic journal *Current Research in Social Psychology* (see entry #155).

210. **Center for the Study of Sport in Society.** 360 Huntington Ave., 161CP, Northeastern University, Boston, MA 02115, USA. (617)437-4025.

Part of Northeastern University, this is one of the most important centers focusing on the sociology of sport. It also supports research into other aspects of sports, such as business and journalism. Among its other activities, the center publishes the *Journal of Sport and Social Issues* (see entry #171).

211. **Economic and Social Research Council (ESRC).** University of Essex, Colchester C04 3SQ, United Kingdom. 44(0)1206-872001.

ESRC is the British equivalent of the Inter-university Consortium for Political and Social Research (see entry #215). It not only collects and distributes research datasets, but also conducts summer workshops in research methods and statistics, provides electronic World Wide Web access to its archive (see entry #264), and publishes the *ESRC Data Archive Bulletin.*

212. **Ethel Percy Andrus Gerontology Center.** University Park, MC 0191, University of Southern California, Los Angeles, CA 90089-0191, USA. (213)740-6060. (E-mail: eschneid@mizar.usc.edu).

Part of the University of Southern California, this center supports research, training, and graduate education in gerontology and its related disciplines.

213. **Institute for Social Research.** P.O. Box 1248, Ann Arbor, MI 48106, USA. (313)764-8363.

The institute conducts research and provides training and services in a variety of areas of social science. It is the institutional host for the Inter-university Consortium for Political and Social Research (ICPSR), as well as such studies as the *Panel Study of Income Dynamics* (PSID), the *National Study of Black Americans*, and *Monitoring the Future.*

214. **Institute of Gerontology.** 226 Knapp Bldg., 87 E. Ferry, Wayne State University, Detroit, MI 48202, USA. (313)577-2297.

Part of Wayne State University, the institute supports teaching and research in gerontology and its various areas of focus (e.g., work, family relations, caregiving, health care, policy). Its graduate student organization also maintains a Web site (see entry #334) that is an excellent guide to other Web sites on gerontology.

215. **Inter-university Consortium for Political and Social Research.** P.O. Box 1248, Ann Arbor, MI 48106-1248, USA. (313)764-2570. (E-mail: netmail@icpsr.umich.edu).

ICPSR is a consortium of over 300 U.S. and Canadian colleges and universities, as well as a few hundred more institutions from around the world. It collects and distributes, to consortium members, datasets of research on a variety of topics primarily in the social and behavioral sciences. Many universities own some of these datasets and make them available to campus researchers; datasets not owned may be ordered from ICPSR by the campus Official Representative. The list of available datasets and services can be found in ICPSR's *Guide to Resources and Services* (see entry #4) and at ICPSR's Website (http://www.icpsr.umich.edu) (see entry #267). ICPSR also conducts summer workshops in advanced research methods and statistical techniques.

216. **National Council on Family Relations.** 3989 Central Avenue Northeast, Suite 550, Minneapolis, MN 55421, USA. (612)781-9331. (E-mail: ncfr3989@ncfr.com).

Founded in 1938, NCFR provides support and services for researchers, educators, and practitioners working with the family. It includes thousands of members and regional, state, and local groups. Besides publishing the *Journal of Marriage and the Family*, the NCFR also hosts 10 interest group sections for its members: family therapy, family policy, international, family and health, family science, education and enrichment, research and theory, ethnic minorities, religion and family life, and feminism and family studies.

217. **National Council on the Aging.** 409 Third St. SW, Washington, DC 20024, USA.

Established in 1950, NCOA provides information, training, and research on issues related to aging. It also publishes an important guide to the literature on aging, *Abstracts in Social Gerontology* (see entry #318).

218. **National Institute on Aging.** 9000 Rockville Pike, Bethesda, MD 20892, USA. (301)496-1752.

Part of the National Institutes of Health, the National Institute on Aging "conducts and supports biomedical and behavioral research to increase knowledge of the aging process and the physical, psychological, and social factors associated with aging" (*The United States Government Manual, 1996/97*, p. 289).

219. **National Opinion Research Center.** 1155 E. 60th St., Chicago, IL 60637, USA. (312)753-7500. (E-mail: bovapatr@norcmail.uchicago.edu).

Affiliated with the University of Chicago, the National Opinion Research Center conducts important research in the social sciences, education, and health services. Its most notable ongoing research is probably the General Social Survey (GSS). The center also supports a Web site (see entry #266) that describes its research projects and available services.

220. **Office of Population Research.** 21 Prospect Ave., Princeton, NJ 08544, USA. (609)258-4946. (E-mail: opr.@opr.princeton.edu).

Part of Princeton University, this center not only promotes research in population and demography, but also publishes the *Population Index* (see entry #381), an important tool in searching the field's literature. The center also offers graduate certificates and Ph.D. training in population and demography.

221. **Ontario Institute for Studies in Education.** 252 Bloor St. W., Toronto, Ontario, M5S 1V6, Canada. (416)923-6641.

OISE is a major research center devoted to a broad spectrum of educational studies, including the sociology of education, critical pedagogy, critical curriculum studies, and women's studies. It is affiliated with the University of Toronto, publishes the journal *Curriculum Inquiry*, and is the University's graduate department of education.

222. **Research Information Center (AARP).** 601 E St. NW, A-2, Washington, DC 20049, USA. (202)434-6240.

Part of the American Association of Retired Persons, the center supports research in social gerontology, among other areas. It also provides the *AgeLine* database (see entry #319), a major source for finding literature in the field.

223. **The Roper Center for Public Opinion Research.** P.O. Box 440, Storrs, CT 06268, USA. (203)486-4440. (E-mail: testsfs@uconnvm.uconn.edu).

The Roper Center not only conducts polls on a variety of social and public policy issues, but also maintains a collection of about 12,500 machine-readable datasets of surveys conducted in the United States and over 70 foreign countries. Some questions extend back as far as 1936. The Center has its own retrieval system, the Public Opinion Location Library (POLL), for searching these datasets. This information is also available through DIALOG and NEXIS databases.

224. **Sport Information Resource Centre (SIRC).** 1600 James Naismith Dr., Ste. 107, Gloucester, Ontario K1B 5N4, Canada. (613)748-5658.

This is very likely the major provider of bibliographic information on sports, whether it be through its online DIALOG database, *SPORT* (file #48), or through its CD-ROM product, *SPORT Discus*. These databases provide access to articles, dissertations, and theses on many aspects of sports, including sport psychology and sport sociology.

ORGANIZATIONS

Details on organizations were drawn from the **Encyclopedia of Associations** (see entry #53), **The World of Learning** (see entry #58), journals published by the organizations, and World Wide Web sites.

225. **American Association of Public Opinion Research.** P.O. Box 1248, Ann Arbor, MI 48106, USA. (313)764-1555.

Publishers of *Public Opinion Quarterly*, AAPOR also holds an annual conference and generally addresses the research interests of public opinion and social researchers.

226. **American Society of Criminology.** 1314 Kinnear Rd., Ste. 212, Columbus, OH 43212, USA. (614)292-9207.

Dedicated to developing criminology in both academic and applied settings, the organization publishes *Criminology: An Interdisciplinary Journal*, holds an annual conference, and gives research awards, among its many activities. It has three interest group sections: critical, international, and women. It also supports a World Wide Web site (see entry #304).

227. **American Sociological Association.** 1722 N St. NW, Washington, DC 20036, USA. (202)833-3410.

With some 12,000 members, this is the largest sociological organization in the United States. It has approximately two dozen interest group sections and publishes major journals in the field, such as *American Sociological Review*, *Contemporary Sociology* (a journal of reviews), *Journal of Health and Social Behavior*, *Sociology of Education*, *Social Psychology Quarterly*, *Sociological Theory*, and *Teaching Sociology*. ASA also holds an annual conference and maintains a World Wide Web site (ASANet, see entry #256).

228. **Association for Humanist Sociology.** c/o Donald Goodman, John Jay College, 899 10th Ave., New York, NY 10019, USA. (212)237-8461.

AHS publishes both *The Humanist Sociologist* and *Humanity and Society* (see entry #163), sponsors an annual conference, and maintains a World Wide Web site (see entry #257). Its goals include promoting a more humanistic and value-centered sociology, and pursuing those interests with other disciplines.

229. **Association of Black Sociologists.** c/o Robert G. Newby, Department of Sociology, Central Michigan University, Mount Pleasant, MI 48859, USA. (517)774-3160.

This organization supports and encourages the interests, perspectives, and research agendas of Black sociologists. It also works to improve the general level of sociological research and teaching. It publishes the monthly *ABS Newsletter*, holds an annual conference, and provides a discussion list (ABSLST-L) (Available: listserv@cmuvm.csv.cmich.edu).

230. **The Australian Sociological Association.** School of Social Inquiry, Deakin University, 662 Blackburn Rd., Clayton, Victoria 3168, Australia. (03)9244-7177.

With over 500 members, TASA's goal is to promote sociology in Australia. Its members receive a journal, *The Australian and New Zealand Journal of Sociology* (see entry #145), and a newsletter. TASA also holds an annual conference and maintains a World Wide Web site (see entry #258) and related electronic discussion list. It also has three special interest sections: health, women, and postgraduate.

231. **British Sociological Association.** Unit 3G, Mountjoy Research Centre, Stockton Rd., Durham, England DH1 3UR. (191)383-0839.

Dedicated to promoting sociological study in Britain, the British Sociological Association publishes two journals, *Sociology* (see entry #195) and *Work, Employment and Society* (see entry #205).

232. **Canadian Sociology and Anthropology Association.** Canadian Sociology and Anthropology Association, Concordia University, LB 615, 1400 boul de Maisonneuve O., Montreal, QC H3G 1M8, Canada. (514)848-8780.

Founded in 1966, the Canadian Sociology and Anthropology Association publishes a quarterly journal, the *Canadian Review of Sociology and Anthropology* (see entry #150), and broadly supports research and publication in these disciplines. It also holds an annual conference and maintains a World Wide Web site (see entry #260).

233. **European Sociological Association.** c/o SISWO, Pantage Muidergracht 4, NL-1018 TV, Amsterdam, Netherlands. 31 20 5270600.

Though a fairly new association (founded in 1992), the ESA has over 500 members and holds a biennial conference, publishes a newsletter (*European Sociologist*), and maintains an E-mail discussion list (*european-sociologist*) and World Wide Web site (see entry #265).

234. **Gerontological Society of America.** 1275 K St. NW, Ste. 350, Washington, DC 20005, USA. (202)842-1275. (E-mail: geron@geron.org) (http://www.geron.org).

With both a multinational and interdisciplinary membership, this association is involved in promoting study of and research on aging. Toward this end, it holds an annual conference, publishes *The Gerontologist* (see entry #161) and the *Journals of Gerontology* (see entry #172), provides fellowships and awards, and maintains a Web site (see entry #333).

235. **International Network for Social Network Analysis.** Department of Sociology, University of South Carolina, Columbia, SC 29208, USA. (803)777-3140.

This organization has an international membership, publishes a quarterly journal, *Social Networks* (see entry #180), and sponsors an annual conference.

236. **Mid-South Sociological Association.** c/o Thomas J. Durant (President-Elect), Department of Sociology, 126 Stubbs Hall, Louisiana State University, Baton Rouge, LA 70803, USA. (503)388-1645.

MSSA sponsors an annual conference, publishes a journal, *Sociological Spectrum* (see entry #193), and has a World Wide Web site (see entry #268).

237. **Midwest Sociological Society.** c/o Barbara Heyl, President, Department of Sociology and Anthropology, 4660 Illinois State University, Normal, IL 61790-4660, USA. (309)438-2820.

Among other activities, it publishes *The Sociological Quarterly* (see entry #190).

238. **National Council on Family Relations.** 3989 Central Ave. NE, Ste. 550, Minneapolis, MN 55421, USA. (612)781-9331.

A multidisciplinary research and information organization, NCFR supports family life through its annual conference, journals (*Family Relations* and *Journal of Marriage and the Family*, see entry #168), various awards, *Family Studies Database* (see entry #351), and the *Inventory of Marriage and Family Literature* (see entry #352).

239. **National Council on the Aging.** 409 3rd St. SW, Ste. 200, Washington, DC 20024, USA. (202)479-1200.

NCOA is an interdisciplinary research and information organization. It works with numerous other organizations, presents awards, holds an annual conference, and publishes an important guide to research, *Abstracts in Social Gerontology* (see entry #318).

240. **North American Society for the Sociology of Sport.** c/o Mary Duquin, Department of Physical Education, University of Pittsburgh, Pittsburgh, PA 15261, USA. (412)648-8274.

Sociologists of sport and leisure may find this a useful organization. It publishes the *Sociology of Sport Journal* (see entry #198) and holds an annual conference.

241. **North Central Sociological Association.** c/o Dean Purdy, Executive Officer, Office of Student Life, Bowling Green State University, Bowling Green, OH 43403, USA. (419)372-2843.

This is a regional sociology association of over 400 members from Ohio, Indiana, Kentucky, Michigan, Ontario, West Virginia, southern and eastern Illinois, and western Pennsylvania. It publishes the journal *Sociological Focus* (see entry #186), sponsors an annual conference, and maintains a Web site (see entry #272) describing the organization's activities.

242. **Pacific Sociological Association.** c/o Dean S. Dorn, Pacific Sociological Association, Department of Sociology, California State University, Sacramento, CA 95819-6005, USA. (916)278-5254.

Founded in 1929, PSA publishes the journal *Sociological Perspectives* (see entry #189), holds an annual conference, and provides a World Wide Web site (see entry #273) describing its organization and services. Membership includes students and faculty primarily from the western region of the United States and Canada. The PSA also publishes a newsletter, *The Pacific Sociologist.*

243. **Population Association of America.** 1722 N Street NW, Washington, DC 20036, USA.

The Population Association of America publishes an important index to the literature, the *Population Index*, and maintains a World Wide Web site (see entry #381).

244. **Rural Sociological Society.** Institute for Environmental Studies, University of Illinois, 1101 W. Peabody Dr., Urbana, IL 61801-4723, USA. (E-mail: burdge@ux1.cso.uiuc.edu).

Supporting research and teaching in rural sociology, the organization holds an annual conference and publishes two important journals in the field, *Rural Sociology* (see entry #176) and *The Rural Sociologist.*

245. **Society for Applied Sociology.** c/o Anne Arundel Community College, Division of Social Sciences, 101 College Parkway, Arnold, MD 21012-1895, USA. (410)541-2835.

Founded in 1978, the society is interested in the application of sociological knowledge in a variety of settings. The organization publishes the *Journal of Applied Sociology*, holds an annual conference, and conducts a student paper competition, among its other activities. It also provides a World Wide Web site (see entry #286) that describes the organization, its structure, and its services and membership benefits.

246. **Society for the Study of Social Problems.** Department of Sociology, 906 McClung Tower, University of Tennessee, Knoxville, TN 37996-0490, USA. (615)974-3620.

Interested in promoting research and policy on important social problems, SSSP holds an annual conference and publishes the quarterly journal *Social Problems* (see entry #181). It has a number of subject divisions for those interested in specific social problems, including family, crime, inequality and class, education, community research, health, environment, and more. SSSP also annually presents the prestigious C. Wright Mills Award for what it deems the best book on social problems.

247. **Society for the Study of Symbolic Interaction.** Tennessee Tech University, Cookeville, TN 38505, USA. (615)372-3437.

SSSI promotes research in symbolic interaction through its annual conference, newsletter, and journal, *Symbolic Interaction*. It also maintains a World Wide Web site (see entry #555).

248. **Sociological Practice Association.** c/o David J. Kallen, Department of Pediatrics/ Human Development, Michigan State University, B140 Life Sciences, East Lansing, MI 48824, USA. (517)353-0709.

Formerly the Clinical Sociology Association, this organization supports both research and training in sociological practice or applied sociology. Among its activities, it gives awards, conducts certification, holds sessions at conferences, and publishes the *Clinical Sociology Review* (see entry #151).

249. **Sociologists for Women in Society.** Department of Sociology, North Carolina State University, Raleigh, NC 27965, USA. (513)873-4950.

Supporting the professional development of women sociologists, this organization is involved in not only providing placement services and aid to individuals involved in sex discrimination cases, but also supporting the networking of women sociologists. It also publishes the quarterly journal *Gender & Society* (see entry #160) and meets annually at the American Sociological Association conference.

250. **Sociology Association of AOTEAROA (New Zealand).**
See entry #278.

251. **Southern Sociological Society.** P.O. Drawer 6245, Mississippi State, Mississippi 39762, USA.

The society's objectives include encouraging quality teaching and research, and disseminating sociological knowledge. Cooperation with other groups, as well as the development of future sociologists and research programs, are also objectives. The society publishes the journal *Social Forces* (see entry #177), maintains a Web site (see entry #281), and holds an annual conference.

DIRECTORIES

252. **Biographical Directory of Members.** Washington, D.C.: American Sociological Association, 1990. 518p.

This is a straightforward directory of American Sociological Association members, totaling over 13,000 in 1990. Members are listed alphabetically, and for each, many basic categories of information are provided. The entry indicates the type of membership, mailing address, degrees, E-mail address (if provided), current position, areas of interest, and section memberships within the association. The E-mail addresses are listed separately in the supplementary "Directory of Electronic Addresses." The indexing also includes a geographical listing of members by state and city/town (including foreign countries) and an index of members listed by "Areas of Competence." Faculty are mobile, so the biennial updating of this source, as advertised by ASA, is essential. This work is valuable both for locating other scholars and for researching potential graduate programs. In many respects, it is comparable to the association's *Directory of Members* (see entry #254).

253. **Directory of Departments.** Washington, D.C.: American Sociological Association, 1995. $20.00(institutions).

Included here are descriptions of 2,183 institutions in the United States, Canada, and other countries. Information includes institution name, a code number for the highest degree offered, the chairperson, department title, address, phone/extension, fax number, E-mail address, and number of sociology faculty. It also contains indexes for state/country and departmental code.

254. **Directory of Members.** Washington, D.C.: American Sociological Association, 1992- . biennial. $50.00(institutions).

This directory is similar to the *Biographical Directory of Members*. It lists approximately 13,000 ASA members alphabetically and includes some fundamental information about them, such as type of membership, mailing address, E-mail address (if provided), phone number, and ASA section memberships. Supplementary E-mail and geographic indexes (by state or foreign country) are included, as well as a list of E-mail addresses for ASA offices and programs. However, unlike the *Biographical Directory*, no index for section memberships/areas of interest is available. Nor does this volume list one's current position if it varies from the member's preferred mailing address.

255. **Guide to Graduate Departments of Sociology.** Washington, D.C.: American Sociological Association, 1995. 399p. $50.00(institutions). ISSN 0091-7052.

This, now annual, publication gives fairly detailed information on graduate sociology programs in the United States (207) and some foreign countries (39). Programs in the United States are listed alphabetically by the name of the institution. For each program, common categories of information are provided. These include the expected directory information, such as phone, address, E-mail, fax, department chair, director of graduate studies, application deadline, tuition, financial aid, numbers of graduate students (full- and part-time), and number of graduate degrees awarded in a recent year. Some indication of whether teacher training is available for graduate students is also available. Another section lists the department's special programs and areas of expertise. A list of full- and part-time faculty members with their degree date, appointment level, and specializations is included. Some departmental entries also include the authors and titles of some recently completed Ph.D.s in the program. The international programs are listed at the end of the volume alphabetically by country, then by institution. The information they provide is comparable to that supplied for U.S. programs. Special programs, Ph.D.s awarded, and faculty are also indexed.

WORLD WIDE WEB/ INTERNET SITES

256. **American Sociological Association (ASANet).**

Available: http://www.asanet.org/
(Accessed: December 10, 1996).

ASANet provides a guide to the association's upcoming annual conference program highlights, as well as information on other conferences and meetings. It also includes an employment bulletin, a description of new and existing publications (including ASA journals), membership information, descriptions of the 35 ASA interest group sections, and governance and committee information. See also entry #227.

257. **Association for Humanist Sociology.**

Available: http://www.kutztown.edu/~ehrensal/ahshome.html
(Accessed: December 31, 1996).

AHS was founded in 1976 with the goal of more actively addressing problems of equality, peace, and social justice. It constitutes a support network for sociologists desiring to make their discipline more relevant to people's needs. This site discusses membership in the association (see entry #228), its journal, *Humanity and Society* (see entry #163), the annual conference, the AHS Internet discussion list, and links to Web sites of interest.

258. **The Australian Sociological Association (TASA).**

Available: http://www.faass.newcastle.edu.au/tasa/tasa.htm
(Accessed: October 29, 1996).

This home page has information on TASA's E-mail discussion list, membership procedures, executive board and membership, journal and newsletter, awards and conferences, and constitution and ethical guidelines. Links to numerous other sociology sites on the Internet and World Wide Web are also provided. See also entry #230.

259. **California Sociological Association (CSA).**

Available: http://www-rohan.scsu.edu/dept/sdsusoci/csahmp.html
(Accessed: December 16, 1996).

Included here are news items related to the organization, information about the annual conference, membership costs and procedures, and details on subscribing to the association's discussion list (*csatalk*). Information on the organization's officers and history, other conferences and symposia, publishing opportunities, and related Web sites (including sociology organizations) is also available.

260. **Canadian Sociology and Anthropology Association/La Societé canadienne de sociologie et d'anthropologie.**

Available: http://artsci-ccwin.concordia.ca/SocAnth/CSAA/csaa_hm.html
(Accessed: December 31, 1996).

This CSAA/SCSA Web site describes the organization (see entry #232), its journal (*The Canadian Review of Sociology and Anthropology*, see entry #150), conferences, the organization's E-mail network, awards, membership information, the status of women, student concerns, and more. Lists of and links to other sociology and anthropology departments in Canada, as well as other sociology Web sites, are included.

261. **Council for European Social Science Data Archives (CESSDA).**
Available: http://www.nsd.uib.no/cessda/
(Accessed: December 10, 1996).

A consortium of data archives in Europe, CESSDA promotes the acquiring, archiving, distributing, and searching of social science datasets. It is comprised of data archives from Denmark, Norway, Sweden, the United Kingdom, Holland, Germany, France, Australia, and Hungary. Among its features is an integrated data catalog that can search for relevant datasets in any or all of the members' data archives. It also provides electronic links to the Web sites for data archives in Canada, the United States, Switzerland, and Israel.

262. **Culture Section.**
Available: http://pantheon.cis.yale.edu/~ melende/culture.online.html
(Accessed: December 31, 1996).

One of the American Sociological Association's (ASA) interest groups, the Culture Section maintains a Web site that describes the section's officers, subcommittees, and services. It also includes selective items from the newsletter, *Culture*, which is also available online. Announcements about prizes, conference sessions, and section news are also available. This site can also be accessed through the ASA's Web site, *ASANet* (see entry #256).

263. **Discussion Groups of Interest to Sociology.**
Available: http://www.shu.edu/~ brownsam/vl/listserv.html
(Accessed: December 10, 1996).

This site lists discussion groups, directories, and discussion group archives worldwide that relate to sociology. It provides Internet addresses for these listservs, as well as instructions on how to subscribe.

264. **ESRC Data Archive.**
Available: http://dawww.essex.ac.uk/
(Accessed: December 10, 1996).

Located at the University of Essex, ESRC (Economic and Social Research Council) Data Archive acquires, houses, and distributes approximately 7,000 datasets in the social sciences. The datasets' primary focus is on post-war Britain, though the related History Data Unit includes pre-war data. Broad topics addressed by these datasets include education, elites, race relations, ethnic minorities, crime, population studies, health, politics, social stratification, social welfare, and religion. An online retrieval system, BIRON, is used for locating topics and variables in the datasets. ESRC also publishes a couple of newsletters for users of the General Household Survey and the Labour Force Survey, as well as *ESRC Data Archive Bulletin,* which is distributed three times a year. Information on ordering datasets and on a visiting fellowship/internship program is available, as well as links to other data archives worldwide. See also entry #211.

265. **The European Sociological Association.**
Available: http://www.qub.ac.uk/socsci/miller/esaintro.html
(Accessed: December 10, 1996).

A relatively new association, ESA (see entry #233), held its first conference in 1992. Its purpose is "to facilitate sociological research, teaching and communication on European issues" ("Aims" section on Web homepage). Information on the Web site includes a brief history of the association, its aims, conferences, newsletter, and research groups, as well as membership and governance information. In addition, a description of how to submit material to the association's newsletter, *European Sociologist*, and how to join the discussion list of the same name, **european-sociologist** (available: mailbase@mailbase.ac.uk), is provided. To join the list at this address, type the message *join european-sociology firstname(s) lastname*.

266. **General Social Survey Data and Information Retrieval System (GSSDIRS).**
Available: http://www.icpsr.umich.edu/gss/
(Accessed: December 10, 1996).

Researchers interested in the General Social Survey and its cumulative dataset should find this Web site useful. It has an introduction that includes a site map, news and announcements, and credits and project information. A "Main Applications" section includes information on GSS search engines, main codebook pages, codebook appendixes, GSS publications, trends in GSS variables, and data applications. An updated and searchable bibliography of works citing the General Social Survey is also available. This is an online and current version of the periodically updated print bibliography (see entry #113).

267. **ICPSR (Inter-university Consortium for Political and Social Research).**
Available: http://www.icpsr.umich.edu/index.html
(Accessed: October 29, 1996).

The site provides overviews of ICPSR's many resources and services, its membership, and its governance. One can also access the descriptions of all of the datasets in its archive, as well as the related data collections in the areas of aging and criminal justice. Among the specific resources and services covered are the Summer Training Program in quantitative methods, datasets available on CD-ROM (e.g., the American National Election Study, and the Panel Study of Income Dynamics), the Eurobarometer E-mail list, and the General Social Survey Web site (see entry #266).

268. **Mid-South Sociological Association (MSSA).**
Available: http://www.uakron.edu/hefe/mssapage.html
(Accessed: December 10, 1996).

Included here is an announcement of the upcoming annual meeting, a list of executive council members and past presidents, a membership form, a membership listing with accompanying World Wide Web homepage addresses, and information on the MSSA journal, *Sociological Spectrum* (see entry #193). Numerous links to other social science Web sites are available.

269. **Midwest Sociological Society.**
Available: http://osiris.colorado.edu/SOC/ORGS/mss.html
(Accessed: December 17, 1996).

This site identifies and provides contact addresses, phone numbers, and E-mail addresses for both the organization president and the person in charge of membership and registration information. Links to the Department of Sociology at the University of Colorado at Boulder (home of this Web site) and to other professional organizations are also provided.

270. **National Opinion Research Center (NORC).**
Available: http://www.norc.uchicago.edu
(Accessed: December 10, 1996).

Affiliated with the University of Chicago, NORC specializes in survey research and conducts some of the most prominent studies in the social sciences, education, and health services. This site provides a history and overview of NORC, a description of its resources and research capabilities, an overview of the General Social Survey (which it conducts), a description of NORC's publications, and educational and employment opportunities. Descriptions of key studies in its various areas of research, as well as descriptions of recent (1995) studies are also included. See also entry #219.

271. **New Zealand Social Research Data Archives (NZSRDA).**
Available: http://www.massey.ac.nz/~NZSRDA/nzsrda/archive.htm
Started in 1992, this archive is a collection of machine-readable datasets in the social sciences. It has 32 social and economic issue datasets on such topics as religion and social inequality; all datasets are thoroughly described. This site includes information on depositing and acquiring data, as well NZSRDA and international contact addresses.

272. **North Central Sociological Association.**
Available: http://miavx1.muohio.edu/~ajjipson/NCSA.HTMLx
(Accessed: November 27, 1996).
Included here is information about the organization (see entry #241), its officers and members, and its activities, including the annual conference. A description of the association's journal, *Sociological Focus* (entry #186), and its listserv/discussion list is also included. Other sociology World Wide Web links are also provided.

273. **Pacific Sociological Association (PSA).**
Available: http://www/csus.edu/psa/body.html
(Accessed: December 16, 1996).
The PSA site includes information on becoming a member of the organization and on attending the annual conference. Lists of the officers and committees, a position paper of the Committee on the Status of Racial and Ethnic Minorities, and articles from the Committee on Freedom of Research and Teaching are also included. In addition, links to the Web sites for other sociology associations are provided.

274. **Progressive Sociology Network (PSN).**
Available: http://csf.colorado.edu/psn/
(Accessed: December 10, 1996).
Information here revolves around concerns with civil rights, women's rights, racial and ethnic minorities' rights, social justice, and related progressive issues. It includes archives of the PSN discussion list, the Progressive Population Network (see entry #393) discussion list, the SOCGRAD discussion list, the Racial-Religious-Ethno-Nationalist Violence Studies (REVS) list, and a Homeless list. A link to a full-text archive of titles by Marx and Engels (the *Marx/Engels Archive*, see entry #553) and links to related sites are available.

275. **QUALIDATA - ESRC Qualitative Data Archival Resource Centre.**
Available: http://www.essex.ac.uk/qualidata/
(Accessed: December 10, 1996).
As part of ESRC (Economic and Social Research Council), this archive focuses on locating, evaluating, cataloging, and finding a suitable archival home for qualitative data. The site includes recent news, guidelines for depositing qualitative data, descriptions of outreach activities and workshops, links to other relevant Web sites, and descriptions of

recent data deposits. Also included are full-text issues of *Social Research Update*, which contains news and information related to ESRC. It is published by the University of Essex's Sociology department, which runs QUALIDATA.

276. **The Roper Center for Public Opinion Research.**
Available: http://www.lib.uconn.edu/RoperCenter/resource.htm
(Accessed: December 10, 1996).

The Roper Center (see entry #223) specializes in public opinion polling data. Its resources include 12,500 machine-readable datasets from public opinion polls conducted in the United States and about 75 foreign countries. Besides Roper polls, its collection routinely includes polls conducted by *The Los Angeles Times*, CBS News/*The New York Times*, ABC News/*The Washington Post*, and NBC News/*The Wall Street Journal*. The Center's Public Opinion Location Library (POLL) retrieval system is also described. This is an online service that allows a user to search for specific questions posed as far back as 1936; over a quarter of a million questions are in the database. Access is available through the Lexis-Nexis and DIALOG database services, as well as through the University of Connecticut computer center. The Roper Center survey and data analysis services are also reviewed, as is its bimonthly magazine, *The Public Perspective*. Information on the University of Connecticut master's degree in survey research and the International Survey Library Association is also provided.

277. **Social Science Data Archive (SSDA).**
Available: http://ssda.anu.edu.au
(Accessed: December 9, 1996).

An agent for the Australian Consortium for Political and Social Research, Inc., this archive has 720 machine-readable datasets available for researchers. Most data are on the social sciences. Included are Australian Census data from 1966, 1971, 1976, 1981, and 1986. The archive also includes some datasets acquired from overseas sources, such as the Inter-university Consortium for Political and Social Research (see entry #267), the Economic and Social Research Council (see entry #264) in Britain, and the Roper Center for Public Opinion Research (see entry #276).

278. **Sociology Association of AOTEAROA (New Zealand).**
Available: http://www.massey.ac.nz/~NZSRDA/nzssorgs/saanz/saanz.htm
(Accessed: December 16, 1996).

The association is a member of the International Sociological Association and the Federation of New Zealand Social Science Organizations. This site includes membership information, details on subscribing to the listserv, a noticeboard, a code of ethics, descriptions of annual meetings and conferences, descriptions of and guides to other New Zealand social science organizations and sociology sites, a list of the organization's officers/representatives/committee members, and a guide to the New Zealand Social Research Data Archive (a collection of machine-readable social science data on New Zealand). The organization also publishes *New Zealand Sociology*.

279. **SocioSite: Going Dutch Sociology.**
Available: http://www.pcsw.uva.nl/sociosite/
(Accessed: February 3, 1997).

Maintained by the Sociological Institute of the University of Amsterdam, this Web site provides links to sociological subjects, sociologists, journals, archives, departments, research centers, news groups, and more. It is worldwide in coverage and its subject guide includes virtually any specialization in the field of sociology.

280. **The SocioWeb.**
Available: http://www.sonic.net/~markbl/socioweb/
(Accessed: December 31, 1996).
This is one of the major guides to the wide variety of sociological information on the World Wide Web. It is organized into subsections for new information, university departments, a calendar of events, general research, topical research, hot resources, sociological associations, calls for papers, sociological discourse (a guide to listervs), and SocioWeb 101, an undergraduate journal (under development).

281. **Southern Sociological Society.**
Available: http://www/msstate.edu/Org/SSS/sss.html
(Accessed: December 17, 1996).
Included here is information on the society's annual conference, its bylaws and constitution, and the ballot for and biographies of candidates for office. The conference information includes a description of the program, as well as a means of electronically submitting one's proposal. The organization's newsletter, *The Southern Sociologist Newsletter*, is also described.

282. **Teaching Sociology.**
Available: http://www.orat.ilstu.edu/students/mbgraham/teachsoc2/TS.html
(Accessed: December 10, 1996).
The American Sociological Association publishes a journal by the same name (see entry #200). This site is its offshoot and includes information on joining and sending messages to the Teaching Sociology listserv/discussion list. Also included here is a list of the editors and editorial board for the journal, a description of the procedures for submitting and processing manuscripts, and information on subscribing to the journal (which is only available in print form). A link to the American Sociological Association (ASA) homepage (see entry #256) is also available.

283. **WWW Virtual Library: Sociology.**
Available: http://www.w3.org/vl/Sociology/Overview.html
(Accessed: December 10, 1996).
This provides links to a wide range of sociology-related sources on the World Wide Web. Included are links to institutions (including departments of sociology) and to information in related disciplines and fields. An Internet resources category provides links to research centers, resource directories, discussion groups, electronic journals and newsletters, organizations, and more.

284. **Yahoo!-Social Sciences: Sociology.**
Available: http://www.yahoo.com/Social_Science/Sociology
(Accessed: December 31, 1996).
Another of the major guides to World Wide Web sociology sites, this provides links to courses, organizations, journals, institutes, and papers, as well as to more specific sites, such as criminal justice, social psychology, and urban studies.

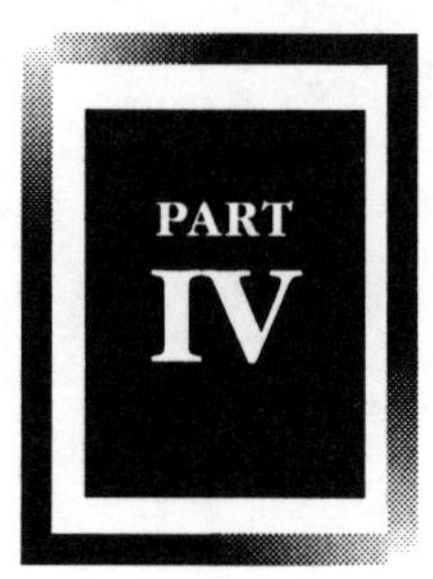

Sociological Fields

CLINICAL AND APPLIED SOCIOLOGY

Bibliographies

285. Fritz, Jan M. **The Clinical Sociology Handbook.** New York: Garland, 1985. 292p. index. (Garland Bibliographies in Sociology, Vol. 7; Garland Reference Library of the Social Sciences, Vol. 134). LC 82-49133. ISBN 0-8240-9203-1.

"Clinical sociology is social intervention" (p. xviii) intended to bring about social change, whether at the individual, institutional, or societal level. The approximately 600 entries included here cover clinical sociological literature from 1931 through 1981. Books, articles, dissertations, unpublished papers, and other sources are included.

Entries are arranged into 113 broad subject chapters, such as aging/gerontology, criminology/deviance, health and illness, small group dynamics, and policy analysis. Within chapters, the entries are arranged alphabetically by author. Descriptive annotations are provided. Also, entries that span a number of areas are cited in each, though the annotation is included only once. A cross-reference directs one to the location of the annotated entry.

An introductory chapter providing a history of clinical sociology is included. Additional chapters provide information about the Clinical Sociological Association, professional affiliations of clinical sociologists, and education and training in this field.

World Wide Web/Internet Sites

286. **Society for Applied Sociology.**
Available: http://www.indiana.edu/~appsoc
(Accessed: December 16, 1996).

This is an international organization, founded in 1978, for those "interested in applying sociological knowledge" (homepage) and exploring the relationship between theory and practice. The site includes statements on bylaws, ethics, and membership procedures, as well information on the annual meeting and related conferences. Descriptive information on the society's publications, the *Journal of Applied Sociology* and *Social Insight*, is also included. Links to other Web sites are also listed.

CRIMINOLOGY, LAW, AND DEVIANCE

Guides

287. **Data Resources of the National Institute of Justice.** 8th ed. Washington, D.C.: U.S. Department of Justice, Office of Justice Programs, National Institute of Justice, 1995. 336p. index.

This is a guide to 230 research datasets sponsored by the National Institute of Justice. The study descriptions are arranged alphabetically by the name of the principal investigator. For each study, information is provided on its principal investigators, purpose, methodology, contents, geographic coverage, file structure, and related reports and publications. The datasets and codebooks are obtainable in a variety of electronic formats (i.e. diskette, CD-ROM, ftp) from the Inter-university Consortium for Political and Social Research (ICPSR); free printed codebooks are also available from the National Archive of Criminal Justice Data (NACJD). Additional access to the entries is provided by indexes of topics and principal investigators. Supplementary information includes a list of forthcoming datasets, as well as a list of studies available on diskette and CD-ROM.

288. O'Block, Robert L. **Criminal Justice Research Sources.** 3d ed. Cincinnati, Ohio: Anderson Publishing, 1992. 189p. $24.95. ISBN 0-87084-665-5.

Targeted at the criminal justice or criminology student, this new edition continues to provide a guide to the variety of sources of information available in libraries. In particular, discussion of indexes and abstracts, journals, bibliographies, computerized literature searches, general reference sources, historical research sources, legal research, sources of international data, audiovisual material, and government documents is included. Both criminal justice sources and more general sources are cited. Many works are annotated, and discussions on using particular tools are included. A glossary is also provided.

Bibliographies

289. Abel, Ernest, comp. **Homicide: A Bibliography.** New York: Greenwood, 1987. 169p. index. (Bibliographies and Indexes in Sociology, No. 11). $55.00. LC 87-7553. ISBN 0-313-25901-1.

Though now a bit dated, this bibliography does include over 1,600 scholarly references published prior to 1985, with some historical references extending as far back as the 1920s. The historical coverage may be of most value. Books, book chapters, and journal articles are cited. The predominant disciplines represented include sociology (criminology, population, demography, and marriage and family), psychology, and law. Issues of family violence, substance abuse, and suicide are most prominent. References are listed alphabetically by author, with a subject index to aid accessing the references. However, the index is not detailed enough, especially given the lack of annotations. Furthermore, journal article titles are abbreviated, with no list translating these into full titles. This could create some difficulties for novice users. Overall, the bibliography's strength is its retrospective coverage of twentieth-century literature.

290. Beirne, Piers, and Joan Hill, comps. **Comparative Criminology: An Annotated Bibliography.** New York: Greenwood, 1991. 144p. index. (Research and Bibliographical Guides in Criminal Justice, No. 3). $45.00. LC 91-27306. ISBN 0-313-26572-0.

The focus here is on the "systematic study of crime, law, and social control in two or more cultures" (p. viii). Such comparisons can help to broaden the scope and, possibly, the explanatory power of criminological theory and research. The 500 entries were published since the 1960s and include books, book chapters, journal articles, and conference papers. Most entries are in English. They are arranged by author under three broad categories and 14 chapters, with the latter addressing general issues, cross-national data, perceptions of crime, violent crime, property crimes, economic/political crime, transnational corporate crime, correlates of crime (i.e., age, class, gender, and race), underdevelopment and modernization, social control and dispute resolution, and criminal justice and penal policies. The descriptive annotations are brief but do indicate, when available, the broad parameters and findings of research studies. Four appendixes list 1) countries in cross-national data sets, 2) United Nations Interregional Crime and Justice Research Institute publications and staff papers, 3) addresses for United Nations regional institutes for crime prevention, and 4) miscellaneous research aids. Author and subject indexes are provided.

291. Nordquist, Joan, comp. **Violence Against Women: A Bibliography.** Santa Cruz, Calif.: Reference and Research Services, 1992. 68p. (Contemporary Social Issues: A Bibliographic Series, No. 26). $15.00. ISBN 0-937855-50-2.

Focusing on social and feminist perspectives, this bibliography identifies approximately 500 books, book chapters, journal articles, government documents, and pamphlets on the topic of violence against women. References are arranged alphabetically by author within six broad subject sections: violence against women—general, intimate femicide, battered women, rape, sexual harassment, and resources. Many of these sections include subtopics. For example, "Battered Women" includes sections on date violence, race issues, women against women violence, the effect of domestic violence on children, and battered women who kill. The last section, "Resources," has sections for statistics sources, bibliographies, directories, and organizations. This bibliography's strength is its mining of references from alternative sources (e.g., *The Left Index* and *Chicano Database*) in addition to more mainstream indexes and databases.

Indexes, Abstracts, and Databases

292. **Criminal Justice Abstracts.** Vol. 1- , No. 1- . Monsey, N.Y.: Willow Tree Press, 1968- . quarterly, with annual index. $150.00/yr. ISSN 0146-9177.

Each issue abstracts approximately 400 books, book chapters, journal articles, and reports. Coverage is worldwide, including some foreign language sources (though the abstracts are in English). The entries are grouped together in six broad categories: crime, the offender, and the victim; juvenile justice and delinquency; police; courts and the legal process; adult corrections; and crime and control strategies. Since the subject categories are broad, the detailed subject/geographic index is essential for more focused searching of the abstracts. These descriptive abstracts are detailed and run from one to four paragraphs. An author index is also included, as well as a "Quarterly Highlights" listing of interesting subtopics (e.g., violence in schools) and the corresponding entry numbers. This source is also available online through the *WESTLAW* database service and on CD-ROM from SilverPlatter Information Inc.

293. **Criminal Justice Periodical Index.** Vol. 1- . Ann Arbor, Mich.: University Microfilms International, 1975- . 3 issues/yr., with annual cumulations. $285.00/yr. ISSN 0146-5818.

This indexes "over 100 U.S., British and Canadian journals" (p. v) in the areas of criminal justice, criminology, police studies, criminal law, family law, police administration, drug abuse, and more. It is comprised of two major sections: 1) an author index, which includes entries for co-authors; and 2) a subject index, which includes proper names for organizations and police departments, as well as *see* and *see also* references. Complete citations are available for entries in both sections; citations are accompanied by indications of whether article copies or microforms are available from University Microfilms International (UMI). Information on ordering articles is included in the index, as is a user's guide and lists of periodicals indexed (by title and by publisher). This source is also available on the DIALOG database service (*Criminal Justice Periodical Index*, file #177).

294. **NCJRS (National Criminal Justice Reference Service).** Rockville, Md.: National Criminal Justice Reference Service, 1972- . monthly updates. DIALOG file #21.

Included in this DIALOG database are references from the National Institutes of Justice/NCJRS document collection. Books, journal articles, dissertations, audiovisual materials, reports, empirical studies, and other types of sources are covered. All aspects of criminal justice and law enforcement are addressed, including criminology, corrections, evaluation and policy, human resource development, probation and parole, substance abuse, victims services, and more.

Handbooks and Yearbooks

295. **Crime in the United States.** Washington, D.C.: Department of Justice, Federal Bureau of Investigation; distr., Washington, D.C.: GPO, 1930- . annual. ISSN 0082-7592.

Otherwise known as the *Uniform Crime Reports*, this is one of the best government sources for crime statistics. The introductory section briefly explains the reporting program and its methods and procedures. Subsequent sections contain statistics on offenses reported, offenses cleared, persons arrested, homicide patterns, and law enforcement personnel. Data are broken down by age, sex, race, ethnic origin, and a large number of other variables. The tables include plenty of explanatory footnotes. In addition, Appendixes are included dealing with methodology, definitions of offenses, reporting area definitions, state reporting programs, the nation's two crime measures (the National Crime Victimization Survey and the Uniform Crime Reports), a national uniform crime reporting program directory, and a uniform crime reporting publications list.

296. **Criminal Victimization in the United States.** Washington, D.C.: U.S. Department of Justice, Office of Justice Programs, Bureau of Justice Statistics, 1973- . annual. ISSN 0095-5833.

Included here are statistics on crimes reported by their victims on the National Crime Victimization Survey. The data focus particularly on the "personal crimes of rape, robbery, assault, and larceny and the household crimes of burglary, larceny, and motor vehicle theft" (1992 ed., p. iii). A total of 120 tables of data is provided and divided into five major categories: characteristics of personal crime victims; characteristics of household crime victims; victim-offender relationships and offender characteristics; crime characteristics; and reporting crimes to the police. Each of these categories has tables classifying the data by a number of relevant variables (e.g., race, ethnicity, sex, income, locality, etc.). The appendixes include a copy of the survey, as well as a description of the data collection methodology and procedures. An introductory summary of findings is also included, as well as a glossary of basic terms.

297. Morgan, Kathleen O'Leary, Scott Morgan, and Neal Quinto, eds. **Crime State Rankings: Crime in the 50 United States.** Lawrence, Kans.: Morgan Quinto Corporation, 1994- . annual. index. $43.95. ISSN 1077-4408.

Over 400 easy-to-use tables of statistics are drawn from mostly government publications, such as *Crime in the United States* and *Capital Punishment*, as well as sources like the Bureau of Justice Statistics, the American Correctional Association, and the Bureau of the Census. Both published and unpublished data are included. The tables are arranged under a number of major categories: arrests, juvenile arrests, corrections, drugs and alcohol, finance, law enforcement, offenses, and urban/rural crime. Tables of retrospective data are also included. The appendixes list urban, rural, and resident state populations. A list of sources is provided, as is a subject index. Though many of these data are available elsewhere, they are conveniently assembled here in a readable format, with all source documents cited.

298. **National Criminal Justice Thesaurus: Descriptors for Indexing Law Enforcement and Criminal Justice Information.** Washington, D.C.: Department of Justice, National Institute of Justice, 1994. 403p.

This can be used as a guide to indexing terms in criminal justice and criminology literature, particularly the National Criminal Justice Reference Service database (see entry #294). The descriptors (subject headings) are organized into four major sections: substantive (subject) descriptors, organizational descriptors, geographic descriptors, and a permuted (key-word-out-of-context) index. The first three sections list the preferred terms for searching subjects, organizations, and geographic locations. Broader, narrower, and related terms are listed as well. Some terms are accompanied by a scope note (SN) or definition; others have *use* references that direct the user to the preferred subject heading. The permuted index lists alphabetically every key word from every descriptor, followed by the full descriptor in which the word appears. Overall, this thesaurus can help one's search of criminal justice and criminology indexes, abstracts, and databases by identifying potentially fruitful search terms.

299. **Sourcebook of Criminal Justice Statistics.** Washington, D.C.: Department of Justice, Office of Justice Programs, Bureau of Justice Statistics; distr., Washington, D.C.: Government Printing Office, 1973- . annual. index. LC 74-601963. ISSN 0360-3431.

A gold mine of government and nongovernment data on crime, this handbook contains hundreds of tables of data arranged under six sections: characteristics of the criminal justice system, public attitudes toward crime and criminal justice-related topics, nature and distribution of known offenses, characteristics and distribution of persons arrested, judicial processing of defendants, and persons under correctional supervision. These categories are comprised of 50 to 200 tables of data on various subtopics. In addition, appendixes defining terms and discussing survey methodologies and sampling procedures are available. The value of the work is increased by its inclusion, in many tables, of data extending back to the early 1980s, allowing one to chart trends. A subject index complements the access provided by the detailed list of contents. Along with *Crime in the United States*, this should be one of the first places one looks in trying to locate criminal justice statistics.

Dictionaries and Encyclopedias

300. DeSola, Ralph. **Crime Dictionary.** Revised and expanded edition. New York: Facts on File, 1988. 222p. LC 87-20133. ISBN 0-8160-1872-3.

Everyday terms, colloquialisms, abbreviations, and proper names are included in this dictionary, with many terms relating to other countries. The definitions are short, ranging from a phrase to a couple of sentences. Theoretical aspects of crime are not covered. However, for acronyms and slang words, this may be the best place to look. A lack of objectivity does creep through on a few terms. In comparing definitions of the CIA and the Communist International Organization, only the latter is charged with aiding the subversion of unfriendly governments. Overall, however, this is a broad and useful dictionary. Supplemental listings of foreign terms and place-name nicknames are provided. A bibliography of selected sources is also appended.

301. Maguire, Mike, Rod Morgan, and Robert Reiner, eds. **The Oxford Handbook of Criminology.** Oxford: Clarendon Press, 1994. 1,259p. index. $125.00 ISBN 0-19-876242-9.

This handbook has "authoritative overviews of the major issues" (p. 3) comprising the theory and research in criminology. Though the focus is primarily British, this includes much information emanating from and relevant to the United States. The theoretical issues and research findings are important regardless of one's geographic location. In fact, even the discussions of British policies and programs can be instructive for an American audience. The handbook's 25 chapters are arranged into four sections: theoretical and historical perspectives, crime and causation, crime control and criminal justice, and social dimensions of crime and justice. "Crime and causation" addresses violent crime, white-collar crime, the political economy of crime, and the development of criminal careers, among other topics. "Social Dimensions" includes gender, race, mental disorder, youth, and victims of crime. "Crime control" covers such issues as prevention, policing, trials, sentencing, probation, and imprisonment. Each essay is written by an expert in that particular area and includes suggestions for further reading and a list of references. A subject index is provided. This is a superb, one-volume overview for criminology students.

302. Rush, George E. **The Dictionary of Criminal Justice.** 3d ed. Guilford, Conn.: Dushkin, 1994. 432p. $14.95. ISBN 1-56134-297-1.

This much expanded third edition is intended for students, researchers, and practitioners, and includes definitions of thousands of terms drawn from a variety of criminal justice-related disciplines. Concepts, organizations, legislation, and individuals are all included, with definitions running from a sentence to half a page in length. Organization entries are accompanied by addresses. The second part of the dictionary includes paragraph-long summaries of Supreme Court cases affecting criminal justice. These are arranged under an extensive list of legal categories, including various constitutional amendments, amendment issues, Fourth Amendment issues, Fifth Amendment issues, Sixth Amendment issues, Eighth Amendment issues, due process, equal protection, rights of the incarcerated, juvenile court proceedings, and use of illegally obtained evidence. Many of these categories, in turn, have more specific subtopics. Overall, the large number of terms included, the interdisciplinary focus, and the inclusion of court cases make this a useful resource.

Directories

303. Hutchinson, Joyce, comp. **Directory of Criminal Justice Information Sources.** 9th ed. Washington, D.C.: U.S. Department of Justice, Office of Justice Programs, National Institute of Justice, 1994. 165p. index.

The 158 organizations that comprise this directory were included because they provide information, service, and assistance related to criminal justice. A "major function" of the organization, it can be conducted at the local, regional, or national level. The organization entries are arranged alphabetically by parent organization/sponsoring agency name, and most include an address, phone number, the year established, the head of the organization, a contact person, a description of objectives and services offered, the collection size (if applicable), and publications. The appendixes include listings of members of the Criminal Justice Information Exchange, state criminal justice system representatives, and Federal information centers. Entries are also accessible through the information center/library, subject, and geographic indexes.

World Wide Web/Internet Sites

304. **American Society of Criminology (ASC).**
Available: http://sun.soci.niu.edu/~asc/
(Accessed October 8, 1996).

As the Web homepage for the ASC, this site includes information on the organization, its annual conference, and its various divisions (critical, international, and women). A link to the Critical Criminology division's homepage is provided; a link to a page for the organization's journal is currently under development.

305. **Critical Criminology.**
Available: http://www.soci.niu.edu:80/~critcrim/
(Accessed October 8, 1996).

This is a division of the American Society of Criminology (ASC). It provides numerous links to other sites of interest, such as sources of Federal government information, the National Criminal Justice Reference Service, the Department of Justice, the U.S. Criminal Codes, the National Archive of Criminal Justice Data, and the FBI's Uniform Crime Reports. Information is also available about past Critical Criminology award winners, job openings, the ASC annual conference, Master's and Ph.D. programs, resources on prisoners or prisons or punishment, and miscellaneous information (e.g., the Unabomber manifesto and gun control).

306. **The Official Homepage of the Western Society of Criminology.**
Available: http://www.sonoma.edu/cja/wsc/wscmain.html
(Accessed: December 16, 1996).

The Western Society of Criminology is a 23-year-old regional organization. Its Web site includes information about the organization and its membership procedures, annual conference, officers, and newsletter. Additional information on scholarship applications, award recipients, and a student paper competition is provided. Links to related Web sites are also included.

GERONTOLOGY AND AGING

Guides

307. Zito, Dorothea R., and George V. Zito. **A Guide to Research in Gerontology: Strategies and Resources.** New York: Greenwood, 1988. 130p. index. $42.95. LC 88-17773. ISBN 0-313-25904-6.

Relevant gerontological literature can be found not only in specialized gerontology sources, but also in sources for many of the related sciences, social sciences, and humanities. This guide helps to improve one's literature searching by 1) teaching the user about useful research strategies in the field of gerontology, and 2) identifying and describing many of the most fundamental print and electronic tools for research. Students, librarians, researchers, and practitioners should find this guide useful.

The first few chapters are devoted to explaining the types of information sources available and the best research strategies for exploring them. Subsequent chapters deal with specific types of sources, and not only explain what those sources generally do, but also annotate specific titles. These latter chapters cover handbooks, directories, and encyclopedias; indexes and abstracts; agencies and other specialized sources; computerized information retrieval systems; and community resources. Appended are lists of recommended readings, selected indexes and abstracts, gerontology and geriatric journals, and computerized databases. An index is also included. Overall, the instruction on research strategies is excellent. Though a few of the recommended titles have changed, the list of sources is still useful.

Bibliographies

308. Aday, Ron H., comp. **Crime and the Elderly: An Annotated Bibliography.** New York: Greenwood, 1988. 118p. index. (Bibliographies and Indexes in Gerontology, Number 8). $45.00. LC 88-30051. ISBN 0-313-25470-2.

Focusing on the elderly as both victims and offenders, this bibliography includes 361 entries for books, book chapters, articles, dissertations, unpublished papers, and reports published since 1970. These references are organized into three parts. Part one, "Crimes Against the Elderly," includes chapters on criminal justice issues, the elderly as victims, fear of crime, elder abuse and neglect, and crime prevention programs. Part two focuses on the elderly as criminals, with chapters on old age and crime, elderly crime patterns, causes of criminal behavior, aging prisoners, and rehabilitative programs. Entries in all of the above chapters are arranged by author and receive paragraph-long, descriptive annotations. Part three includes lists of crime prevention programs for the elderly, state agencies on aging, state correction agencies, and groups and organizations. Author and subject indexes are provided.

309. Blank, Thomas O., ed. **Topics in Gerontology: Selected Annotated Bibliographies.** Westport, Conn.: Greenwood, 1993. 212p. index. (Bibliographies and Indexes in Gerontology, No. 22). $65.00. LC 93-9311. ISBN 0-313-28337-0.

The purpose of this bibliography is "to give students and professionals a set of essays and annotated bibliographies that individually provide in-depth explorations of specific areas of gerontology and together comprise an introduction to the richness and expanse of aging-related research and theory" (p. vii). The 11 chapters are compiled by experts in their areas and include such topics as the history of gerontology, intergenerational relationships and caregiving, death and dying, Alzheimer's disease, health care decision-making among the elderly, and drug use. Each chapter begins with a brief overview of the topic, followed by the annotated bibliography. Entries are comprised of books, book chapters, journal articles, and conference proceedings, with an emphasis on recent titles. The abstracts are lengthy and quite detailed, particularly for research articles. Author and subject indexes are also provided.

310. Coyle, Jean M., comp. **Families and Aging: A Selected, Annotated Bibliography.** New York: Greenwood, 1991. 208p. index. (Bibliographies and Indexes in Gerontology, No. 14). $49.95. LC 91-29593. ISBN 0-313-27211-5.

As pointed out by Erdman Palmore in the "Series Foreword," family members are the most important group in determining the health and welfare of the aged. This bibliography provides references to and abstracts of 778 books, book chapters, journal articles, reports, dissertations, and films dealing with aging and family relationships. Entries were published from 1980 through 1990 and are listed by author under 11 subject categories: middle-aged families, singlehood, older couples, widowhood, grandparents, adult children, intergenerational relationships, family caregiving, racial and ethnic minority groups, living arrangements of older persons, and general. Additional author and subject indexes are available, though the latter makes too little use of subheadings for some major headings (e.g., "caregiving" has almost 200 reference numbers). An introductory chapter providing brief overviews of some key issues and research relating to each of the subsequent chapters is included.

311. Coyle, Jean M. **Women and Aging: A Selected, Annotated Bibliography.** New York: Greenwood, 1989. 135p. index. (Bibliographies and Indexes in Gerontology, No. 9). $45.00. LC 88-28975. ISBN 0-313-26021-4.

The relationship of women and aging, though historically understudied, comprised a growing segment of the research literature in the 1980s. This bibliography includes annotated references to over 600 books, book chapters, encyclopedia entries, articles, dissertations, films, and government documents "published from 1980 through early 1988" (p. xi). The entries include both popular works and theoretical or research-oriented sources. References are arranged into 13 chapters: roles and relationships, economics, employment, retirement, health, sexuality, religion, housing, racial and ethnic groups, policy issues, international concerns, middle age, and general topics not treated elsewhere. Within these chapters, entries are grouped by type of source, then alphabetically by author. The annotations are brief, ranging from a sentence to a short paragraph. Supplementary subject and author indexes are included, as well as an introductory chapter explaining the scope of the book's coverage and the surprising lack of scholarly attention to middle-aged and older women. This is a useful literature review for the 1980s.

312. Davis, Lenwood G., comp. **The Black Aged in the United States: A Selectively Annotated Bibliography.** 2d ed., rev. and updated. New York: Greenwood, 1989. 277p. index. (Bibliographies and Indexes in Afro-American and African Studies, No. 23). $69.50. LC 88-32359. ISBN 0-313-25931-3.

With coverage through 1987, this bibliography includes 633 annotated references to books, articles, pamphlets, dissertations, theses, and government documents. Its references should interest not only gerontologists, but also sociologists of the family and medical sociologists. Six major chapters are included, most of which are on the type of source: Black aged and slavery; major books and pamphlets; general works; dissertations and theses; government publications; and articles. Within the last four chapters topical subheadings appear, under which references are listed by author. These subheadings, which are not listed in the table of contents, address such topics as the Black aged and children, Black urban aged, families, old folks' homes, mental health, Black aged females, minority aged, counseling, housing, and more. The paragraph-long descriptive abstracts are thorough and well written. Supplementary material includes a list of Black old folks' homes from 1860–1988, a selected list of periodicals with articles on the Black aged, and a combined author/subject index. The introduction is an interesting essay on the black aged during slavery, and it includes a discussion of key books.

313. Harris, Diana K. **The Sociology of Aging: An Annotated Bibliography and Sourcebook.** New York: Garland, 1985. 283p. index. (Garland Bibliographies in Sociology, Vol. 5; Garland Reference Library of Social Science, Vol. 206). LC 83-48220. ISBN 0-8240-9046-2.

Covering the years 1960 to 1980, this bibliography includes books, monographs, and articles focusing specifically on the sociology of aging. It is divided into five parts. Part 1 includes general works and works on theory and methods. Part 2 covers culture and society, with subchapters on culture, socialization, life satisfaction, social groups, and deviance. Part 3 covers social inequality, with subsections on class, age, race, and ethnicity. Part 4 treats social institutions, including "family, religion and education, politics and economy, and work, retirement, and leisure" (p. xii). Part 5 addresses particular problems relating to demography, health, institutionalization, death and dying, and living environments. Chapters on periodicals, reference works, and research centers and associations round out this excellent work. An author index is also provided.

314. Nordquist, Joan, comp. **The Elderly in America: A Bibliography.** Santa Cruz, Calif.: Reference and Research Services, 1991. 64p. (Contemporary Social Issues: A Bibliographic Series, No. 23). $15.00. ISBN 0-937855-44-8.

This is a wide-ranging bibliography of books, government documents, and pamphlets published primarily within the five years preceding this book's publication. However, numerous sources date from the early 1980s. The references are arranged alphabetically by author (or title) in 14 subject chapters: the elderly in America, long-term care, health and medical care, elder abuse, crimes against the elderly, substance abuse, elderly women, elderly minorities, housing, employment, ageism and discrimination, law and the elderly, and statistics. A final chapter of resources lists bibliographies, directories, and organizations; phone numbers for the organizations, in addition to addresses, would be helpful. Though it is unannotated and excludes journal articles, the bibliography's breadth of topics and monographic sources makes it an excellent starting point for research on many subjects in social gerontology.

315. Nordquist, Joan, comp. **Women and Aging: A Bibliography.** Santa Cruz, Calif.: Reference and Research Services, 1994. 76p. (Contemporary Social Issues: A Bibliographic Series, No. 35). $15.00. ISBN 0-937855-68-5.

Approximately 600 books, book chapters, dissertations, journal articles, pamphlets, and government documents on women and aging are cited here by author under 16 topical chapters. These chapters address such important subtopics as psychology, economics, employment, violence against women, substance abuse, women of color, ageism, caregivers, and health and medical care, among others. "Women of Color" includes specific subsections for African Americans, Latinos, Asian Americans, and Native Americans. Within chapters, separate listings for books/documents and articles are included. The final chapter lists various other resources, including statistics sources, directories, bibliographies, periodicals, electronic resources, and organizations. A broad range of major and alternative bibliographic sources were scanned in compiling this bibliography, making it a good guide to both mainstream and alternative critical literature.

316. Parhan, Iris A., ed. **Gerontological Social Work: An Annotated Bibliography.** Westport, Conn.: Greenwood, 1993. 207p. index. (Bibliographies and Indexes in Gerontology, No. 19). $55.00. LC 92-21543. ISBN 0-313-28538-1.

Though ostensibly for social work professionals, this bibliography has much to offer sociologists. It includes over 400 references and abstracts to books, book chapters, journal articles, and reports. These are arranged by author under four major chapters: general works, clinical practice issues, educational issues, and geriatric health services in social work. Many of the entries, especially those in the clinical practice and general chapters, focus on family relations, social networks, and social support, topics that should interest sociologists. The final chapter lists resource information and materials, including journals, audiovisuals, organizations, and media resource guides. Author and subject indexes are provided.

317. Schweitzer, Marjorie M., general ed. **Anthropology of Aging: A Partially Annotated Bibliography.** New York: Greenwood, 1991. 338p. index. (Bibliographies and Indexes in Gerontology, No. 13). $69.50. LC 91-9707. ISBN 0-313-26119-9.

While the focus here is on anthropological literature, this bibliography provides broad coverage of cross-cultural and sociological literature that should be valuable to gerontologists. Though no exact number is specified, approximately 3,000 references are included here to books, book chapters, journal articles, and reports. These are arranged by author under a classification scheme of 13 chapters and numerous subchapters. The major chapters are: general, theoretical, and comparative works; demography, biology, and longevity; medical aspects of aging; nonindustrialized societies; national cultures; modernization; ethnic and rural segments of the United States; social structure; community organization and age-homogeneous residences; urban aged, social networks, and support systems; women; death and dying; and methods. Brief annotations accompany a small percentage of the references. A final chapter provides a list of bibliographies. An author index is also included, although a subject or keyword-in-title index would help in tracking down more specific themes.

Indexes, Abstracts, and Databases

318. **Abstracts in Social Gerontology.** Vol. 33- , No. 1- . Newbury Park, Calif.: Sage, 1990- . quarterly. $186.00/yr.(institutions). ISSN 1047-4862.

This title is published in conjunction with the National Council on the Aging (NCOA) and continues the earlier *Current Literature on Aging*. Each issue includes references to and abstracts of approximately 250 books, journal articles, government documents, pamphlets, reports, and other materials. Entries are arranged by author under an extensive list of some 20 subject categories and many more subtopics. For example, the category "Institutional and Noninstitutional Care" includes subtopics for home care, adult day care, hospitals, and institutionalization/long-term care. In addition to this subject arrangement, every entry is labeled with more specific subject headings that are used in the subject index. The abstracts are lengthy, descriptive, and quite helpful in determining the focus and value of the source. At the end of each issue, a supplementary list of "Related Citations" is included. These unannotated references are arranged by author under an additional list of subject categories; they are not indexed. Each issue includes author and subject indexes, which are cumulated in the final issue of each volume. This is an excellent current awareness source for a broad range of literature in the field.

319. **AgeLine.** Washington, D.C.: American Association of Retired Persons, 1978- . bimonthly updates. DIALOG file #163.

Drawing upon the AARP's National Gerontology Resource Center collection, this DIALOG database covers social, economic, health care, and policy aspects of aging. The database is comprised mostly of journal citations and abstracts, though it also includes references to books, book chapters, and reports. It is an important resource for social gerontologists.

Handbooks and Yearbooks

320. **Annual Review of Gerontology and Geriatrics.** Vol. 1- . New York: Springer, 1980- . annual. $54.00. ISSN 0198-8794.

Issues are comprised of chapter-length articles contributed by various experts on those subjects. Typically, each volume focuses on a particular theme, different aspects of which are explored by the contributors. Recent and forthcoming theme issues address such topics as nutrition or managed care and assuring quality. Articles can focus on medical, management, and social/psychological aspects of the volume's theme.

321. Binstock, Robert H., and Linda K. George, eds. **Handbook of Aging and the Social Sciences.** 4th ed. San Diego, Calif.: Academic Press, 1996. 531p. index. (Handbooks of Aging). $39.95. LC 95-18727. ISBN 0-12-099192-6.

Intended for students, researchers, practitioners, and scholars new to the field, this handbook provides overviews of 25 major social science topics in the study of aging. The 25 topical chapters are arranged under four broad categories: the state of the field, aging and social structure, social factors and social institutions, and aging and social intervention. The signed chapters focus on such topics as social structure, demography, race and ethnicity, stratification, social supports, families, work, economic status, and health care, among others. Each essay includes a list of references, and accompanying author and subject indexes are available. This edition is not simply an update of the earlier editions; 11 new chapters have been added. Eleven other chapters have been rewritten by new authors who brought "their own perspectives to bear upon the subject matter" (p. xvi). The three remaining chapters were revised. Twenty-five of the 40 authors and co-authors are first-time contributors. Some topics from the earlier edition were not included because they were considered still state-of-the-art overviews. Consequently, this edition complements, rather than supersedes, the earlier editions.

322. **Data Collections from the National Archive of Computerized Data on Aging.** Ann Arbor, Mich.: Inter-university Consortium for Political and Social Research, 1996. 344p. free(ICPSR members).

The National Archive of Computerized Data on Aging (NACDA) is a project of the Inter-university Consortium for Political and Social Research (ICPSR) and is funded by the National Institute on Aging. Its purpose is to promote research on aging, in part through the acquisition, preservation, and dissemination of research datasets. This book is the annual guide to NACDA's dataset collection. It provides fairly in-depth descriptions of these datasets arranged under six chapter headings: demographic characteristics of older adults; social characteristics; economic characteristics; psychological characteristics, mental health, and well-being; physical health and functioning; and health care needs, utilization, and financing for older adults. The dataset descriptions include the title, principal investigator, ICPSR study number, summary description, study design information (e.g., sampling), technical information (e.g., data format and file structure), and file specifications (e.g., number of cases, record length, cases per record). All datasets are available through ICPSR. Supplementary indexes for titles, keywords, and principal investigators are available, as well as an appended list of data sources in the United States and other countries.

323. Padgett, Deborah K., ed. **Handbook on Ethnicity, Aging, and Mental Health.** Westport, Conn.: Greenwood, 1995. 347p. index. $95.00. LC 94-11220. ISBN 0-313-28204-8.

A great deal of gerontological research is unavoidably interdisciplinary, a fact reflected in this handbook. Its focus is the use of mental health services by the ethnic elderly, with the intended audience being mental health service providers, administrators, and researchers from the social and behavioral sciences. In exploring this subject, the theories, research, and insights of sociologists, psychologists, social workers, nurses, gerontologists, psychiatrists, and other professionals are drawn upon in profiling African Americans, Hispanics, Asian Americans, and Native Americans. The 16 chapters, which present both empirical research and important theoretical constructs, are arranged into four parts. Part one covers "Approaches to Understanding Aging, Ethnicity, and Mental Health" and focuses primarily on demographic data and theoretical issues. Part two, "Mental Health Status and Needs of the Ethnic Elderly," focuses on the book's four target populations. The chapters in part three, "Help-Seeking and Use of Mental Health Services by the Ethnic Elderly," again focus on the four target ethnic groups and the extent of and obstacles to help-seeking and service use. Finally, part four contains chapters devoted to caregiving and delivery issues. Throughout the book, prominent attention is given not only to demographic data and research findings, but also to social class, race, culture, ethnic differences, and discrimination. Chapters addressing issues of social support and social networks, specifically in the effect of caregiving upon the caregiver, are included. A bibliography and subject index are included.

324. Palmore, Erdman B., ed. **Developments and Research on Aging: An International Handbook.** Westport, Conn.: Greenwood, 1993. 429p. index. $85.00. LC 92-25737. ISBN 0-313-27785-0.

Gerontological research is growing in other countries and is increasingly becoming an "international science." This handbook "attempts to collect and summarize information on the programs and research in gerontology in most of the countries where substantial work is in progress" (p. xvii). This amounts to 25 chapters on countries from all regions of the world, including the United States, the United Kingdom, France, Germany, Italy, Japan, and Mexico, among others. Some smaller countries (e.g., Costa Rica, Denmark, Israel, and Taiwan) are included, as well as nine countries that were not covered in the first edition of this book (*International Handbook on Aging*, 1980). The country essays present not only some demographic data, but also an overview of research efforts, policy issues, and the provision of social and health services. Some of the essays provide a historical review of gerontological research in that particular country. An appended international directory of gerontological/geriatric associations, a selected bibliography, and a combined name/title/subject index are included. As the editor admits, this is not a "representative sample" of countries. Also, some countries covered in the earlier edition are not updated here. Still, the volume should indeed be valuable to students, researchers, administrators, and planners in the field of gerontology.

325. Schick, Frank L., and Renee Schick, eds. **Statistical Handbook on Aging Americans.** 2d ed. Phoenix, Ariz.: Oryx Press, 1994. 335p. index. (Statistical Handbook Series, No. 5). $54.50. LC 93-36711. ISBN 0-89774-721-6.

Drawing primarily upon the 1990 Census and other current surveys, this handbook presents 378 charts, graphs, and tables of data on the elderly. These data are classified under six major topics: demographics, social characteristics, health status, employment, economic conditions, and expenditures for the elderly. A total of 24 subtopics within these chapters is included; each provides numerous tables of data. For example, under the subject, "Social Characteristics," the subtopic "Education" has 13 statistical tables and charts. Though historical statistics are included in many of the tables, data had to be more recent than 1985 and published before June 1993. In most cases, the editors have faithfully reproduced the data found in the original source, which is usually cited. Supplementary information includes a directory of information resources, a list of Census telephone contacts for data users, a glossary of terms, and a list of the statistical sources consulted (arranged by table number). A subject index is also included. This source is more current and more detailed than Vierck's *Fact Book on Aging* (see entry #327).

326. Van Tassel, David D., and Jimmy Elaine Wilkinson Meyer, eds. **U.S. Aging Policy Interest Groups: Institutional Profiles.** New York: Greenwood, 1992. 258p. index. $65.00. LC 91-29198. ISBN 0-313-26543-7.

For those interested in public policy and applied aspects of gerontological research, this handbook describes 83 influential organizations. The descriptions include information on a number of areas: type and purpose, origin and development, organization and funding, policy concerns and tactics, electoral activity, publications, and sources for further information. Significant divisions or units within larger organizations can be profiled as well, though the information is found under the parent organization's entry. Cross-references direct the user from former organizational names to the current one, and from subunit names to the parent organization. Excluded from the handbook are government organizations and groups devoted mainly to research or service. Appended are lists of "Selected

Additional Organizations" and "Organizational Members of Coalitions on Aging, 1991." There is also a selected bibliography and a subject/name index.

327. Vierck, Elizabeth. **Fact Book on Aging.** Santa Barbara, Calif.: ABC-CLIO, 1990. 199p. index. LC 90-34667. ISBN 0-87436-284-9.

There are over 1,500 statistical facts on aging reported here. The author has compiled these data from a variety of mostly government sources and reported them as "statistical one-liners." Thus, a typical entry lists "Remarriage rates for older men as compared to older women: 7 times greater" (p. 47). Both current statistics and projections are included. These facts are arranged into 20 topical chapters, covering such areas as demographic data, life expectancy, geographic distribution, housing, crime, health, attitudes of and toward seniors, long-term care, government spending, and more. Most chapters include three to five subtopics, with as many statistical facts listed under each of those. The statistical source for each fact is cited in "Notes" at the end of each chapter. This may be the most valuable feature of the book, because many of the sources are ongoing publications that could be consulted later for more current data. The detailed subject index allows one to track data across chapters. This is useful because related statistics do not necessarily appear together. A supplementary list of landmark legislation, a list of national professional gerontology associations and membership numbers, and a bibliography are included.

Dictionaries and Encyclopedias

328. **The Encyclopedia of Aging.** 2d ed. George L. Maddox, ed.-in-chief. New York: Springer, 1995. 1,216p. index. $159.00. LC 95-24029. ISBN 0-8261-4841-7.

This reflects the interdisciplinary nature of gerontology by including entries from the social and behavioral sciences; the biological sciences; and social policy, planning, and practice. It has over 600 entries on key terms, theories, physical conditions, organizations, research instruments, and landmark studies. Compared to the first edition, "70% of the original material was updated or revised," and "20% . . . is entirely new" (p. xv). The intended audience is the "educated lay person," which in this case means either advanced students or researchers delving into new areas of gerontological research. The essays, written by experts on their subjects, range in length from a few paragraphs to a couple of pages. They include references to key theories, theorists, and research, as well as *see also* references to related concepts defined elsewhere in the encyclopedia. Full citations to the works cited can be found in the extensive list of references at the end of the volume. A subject index, which includes titles and proper names, is included, as well as a contributor index. This work achieves its goal of providing an "authoritative, comprehensive introduction to gerontology and geriatrics" (p.xiii).

329. Roy, F. Hampton, and Charles Russell. **The Encyclopedia of Aging and the Elderly.** New York: Facts on File, 1992. 308p. index. $45.00. LC 91-23435. ISBN 0-8160-1869-3.

Covering both medical and social/psychological aspects of aging, this encyclopedia is intended to fill "the gap in America's understanding" (p. ix) of aging and its possibilities. Included here are not only key concepts, but also acronyms and proper names for diseases, drugs, and organizations. The definitions, which are well written and reasonably nontechnical, range from a paragraph to a page and include references to further reading and related terms. *See* references, from unused to preferred terms, are included. The appendixes include statistical tables and graphs, a list of national organizations, and a bibliography. A subject/name index is also included. The clear writing should make this suitable for students and interested lay persons.

Directories

330. **National Directory for Eldercare Information and Referral: Directory of State and Area Agencies on Aging.** Washington, D.C.: National Association of Area Agencies on Aging, 1993/94- . LC 94-38911.

State and area agencies providing social services to older Americans are listed in this directory, which continues the earlier *Directory of State and Area Agencies on Aging.* The volume is organized alphabetically by state. The information for each state includes such details as agency addresses, phone numbers, and contact names. Volumes have also included a map designating each state's planning and service areas that are served by the different area agencies. Listings for American Samoa, Guam, Puerto Rico, the Virgin Islands, and the Trust Territory of the Pacific and Northern Mariana Islands have also been included.

331. **National Directory of Educational Programs in Gerontology and Geriatrics.** 6th ed. Washington, D.C.: Association for Gerontology in Higher Education, 1994. 353p. index. $85.00. ISSN 0148-4508.

This directory lists higher educational institutions that offer formal credit (both undergraduate and graduate) and post-doctoral training in gerontology, geriatrics, and aging. The entries are arranged alphabetically by state, then by institution. For each institution, one or more listings for each organizational unit that offers programs may be available. A description of each unit's activities is provided, along with an address, phone, fax number, E-mail address, number of teaching faculty, credit courses offered, and special resources available. This information is followed by a description of each individual program offered, including the director's name, the level at which the program is offered (e.g., bachelor's), the credential earned (e.g., degree, certificate, or minor), the subject focus, and recent student enrollments and completions. Institutional members of the Association for Gerontology in Higher Education (AGHE) are noted. A second, smaller section of the directory lists 41 additional AGHE member schools that provide other offerings, though no formal programs. Finally, a list of AGHE organizational affiliate members is included, such as the American Association of Retired Persons (AARP) and the National Council on the Aging. Indexes for primary contact persons, discipline/area of study, and educational level of the program are provided. This is clearly a valuable resource for those identifying appropriate programs for further study in gerontology.

World Wide Web/Internet Sites

332. **Directory of WEB and Gopher Aging Sites.**
Available: http://www.aoa.dhhs.gov/aoa/webres/craig.htm
(Accessed: November 21, 1996).

This directory has links to Web sites for government and aging network organizations, academic and research institutions, foundations, professional organizations, and international sites. Specific links to topics on long-term care are provided, including family caregiver options, programs and policy, and Alzheimer's disease. Additional links relate to topics and resources, like elder abuse, primary health care, E-mail discussion groups, and libraries and databases.

333. **Gerontological Society of America.**
Available: http://www.geron.org
(Accessed: November 16, 1996).

Included here is an overview of the society, its annual conference, its publications, its membership procedures, and its professional opportunities. A section on the National Academy on Aging is available, as well as numerous links to other World Wide Web sites, such as the Social Security Administration, the Alzheimer's Association, the National Institutes of Health, the National Institute on Aging, and the World Congress on Gerontology. See entry #234 for a description of the organization.

334. **GeroWeb.**
Available: http://www/iog.wayne.edu/GeroWebd/GeroWeb.html
(Accessed: November 20, 1996).

Developed by the Graduate Student Organization and GeroInformatics Workgroup at Wayne State University's Institute of Gerontology, this provides both browsing and searching of Web sites on aging.

335. **Internet and E-Mail Resources on Aging.**
Available: http://www.aoa.dhhs.gov/aoa/pages/jpostlst.html
(Accessed: November 20, 1996).

Revised in May and November each year, this is an up-to-date guide to discussion lists, World Wide Web sites, electronic journals, and more. The browsing list of over 24 categories includes such topics as caregiving; associations, conferences; aging; research; intergenerational relationships; psychology, psychiatry; and demographic centers, datasets, and statistical information. Each category provides links to anywhere from two to one hundred sites.

336. **The National Archive of Computerized Data on Aging (NACDA).**
Available: http://www.icpsr.umich.edu/nacda
(Accessed: December 7, 1996).

This site has information about NACDA, allows for searching of NACDA's data holdings, and has information on NACDA publications, services, and programs. Links to other sites of relevance to gerontology and geriatrics, and descriptions of cooperative initiatives and datasets on aging in Europe are also included. NACDA is a project of the Inter-university Consortium of Political and Social Research (ICPSR) and is funded by the National Institute on Aging.

INDUSTRIAL SOCIOLOGY/ SOCIOLOGY OF WORK

Bibliographies

337. Ferber, Marianne A. **Women and Work, Paid and Unpaid: A Selected, Annotated Bibliography.** New York: Garland, 1987. 408p. index. (Garland Reference Library of Social Science, Vol. 315). $44.00. LC 87-8652. ISBN 0-8240-8690-2.

Though focusing primarily on economics literature, this bibliography nonetheless includes a significant amount of research from other social sciences, including sociology. Over 1,000 annotated citations to books, journal articles, and book chapters are included, with most having been published since the 1960s. These are arranged by author under nine subject chapters: general works, the family, labor force participation, occupational distribution, earnings and the female-male gap, discrimination, unemployment, women in individual occupations, and women throughout the world. The citations indicate, by code number, whether the reference focuses on theory, methodology, empirical evidence, or policy. Some entries are accompanied by *see* references to related entries. Throughout, one finds numerous entries from the major sociology journals. Also, some research from other countries is included for comparative purposes. Additional searching of the entries is provided by author and subject indexes.

338. Ghorayshi, Parvin. **The Sociology of Work: A Critical Annotated Bibliography.** New York: Garland, 1990. 214p. index. (Garland Library of Sociology, Vol. 17; Garland Reference Library of Social Science, Vol. 591). $39.00. LC 90-2840. ISBN 0-8240-3438-4.

This is a selective bibliography intended to "highlight the present themes, debates, problems and issues in the sociology of work and industry" (p. xviii). Most of the 405 entries were published in the 1980s and are multidisciplinary, international, and theoretically diverse. Books, articles, and reports are included and arranged alphabetically by author in six subject chapters: the world of work; division of labor; new technology at work; hazards of work; the trade union, industrial conflict and strike; and industrial democracy. Numerous subtopics are covered in each of these chapters. For example, "Division of Labor" includes entries on labor market segmentation, immigrant workers, race, elderly and young workers, gender, and the social construction of skill, among others. "Hazards of Work" includes plant closure, deindustrialization, personal and social costs of unemployment, occupational hazards, and union responses. "The World of Work" covers such subjects as the ideology of work, the global economy, work relations, and labor market trends. A subject index provides more detailed access to the entries. The annotations, though brief, are adequately descriptive and also include some evaluative comments. Some annotations include cross-references, by author and entry number, to related entries. An author index is also provided.

339. Nordquist, Joan, comp. **Comparable Worth.** Santa Cruz, Calif.: Reference and Research Services, 1986. 62p. (Contemporary Social Issues: A Bibliographic Series). $15.00. ISBN 0-937855-03-0.

On average, women in the workforce earn significantly less than men. Pay differentials persist even when one controls for factors, such as occupation and experience. This fact has helped establish the issue of comparable worth, or equal pay for equal work, as a major economic and social issue. Sociologists interested in the causes and consequences of these circumstances should find many useful sources in this bibliography. It includes hundreds of entries for books, pamphlets, documents, and articles on comparable worth and related topics. References are listed by author within seven subject sections: introduction–occupational segregation, earnings differentials; general; the literature of business, specific industries, occupations and trade unions; law and legislation; states, cities; federal documents; and international aspects. Within these sections, references are listed separately for 1) books, pamphlets, and documents; or 2) articles. Periodical article entries date mainly from the 1980s, though some other entries extend back to the mid-1970s. A final section lists relevant bibliographies, organizations, and periodicals.

340. Wilson, Joseph, comp. and ed., with the assistance of Thomas Weissinger. **Black Labor in America, 1865-1983: A Selected Annotated Bibliography.** New York: Greenwood, 1986. 118p. index. (Bibliographies and Indexes in Afro-American and African Studies, No. 11). $42.95. LC 86-349. ISBN 0-313-25267-X.

With a specific focus on African American workers, this bibliography briefly annotates 583 books, studies, pamphlets, government documents, and dissertations. Articles are included only if they were also published as pamphlets. Entries are arranged alphabetically by author, with accompanying one- or two-sentence annotations in most cases. Sociologists may be interested in this bibliography's historical coverage, as well as its focus on race and, to some extent, its intersection with class. Citations for dissertations do not include full references to *Dissertation Abstracts International*, where a full abstract could be found. Also, while the bibliography is selective, the introduction is unclear about the specific criteria used in selection. Finally, the subject index is not suitably detailed. This, combined with the brief abstracts, makes specific subject access more difficult. However, the topic of the bibliography is important and many of the sources would be difficult to identify otherwise. A title index is also provided.

World Wide Web/Internet Sites

341. **Organizations, Occupations, and Work.**
Available: http://www.princeton.edu/~orgoccwk/
(Accessed: December 31, 1996).

This is the Web page of one of the American Sociological Association's interest group sections. Included here is membership information, a list of committees, a list of sessions sponsored at the annual ASA conference, information about the newsletter, calls for papers, job announcements, and more. Links to other Web sites of interest are also provided.

MARRIAGE AND THE FAMILY

Guides

342. Card, Josefina J., et al, comps. **The American Family: A Compendium of Data and Sources.** New York: Garland, 1994. 1v.(various paging). index. (Garland Reference Library of Social Science, Vol. 925). $76.00. LC 93-24328. ISBN 0-8153-1492-2.

Large-scale data collection for research projects can be a costly and time-consuming undertaking. However, on many subjects, existing, high-quality datasets may be available that will allow students, faculty, and researchers to conduct a secondary data analysis on their chosen research focus. This book is an invaluable guide to identifying some of those existing, major datasets in the area of family research. It provides thorough descriptions of 29 datasets addressing "family-related issues such as child care, children and youth, education, health, economic and social issues, labor force participation, violence, family therapy, and marriage and divorce" (p. x). For each dataset, detailed information is provided on the study's purpose, methods (e.g., sampling, response rates), questionnaire, variables, topics covered, limitations, file structure, documentation, cost, availability, and bibliography. All of the studies are available in various machine-readable formats (e.g. CD-ROM, cartridge, and diskette) from suppliers, such as the Sociometrics Corporation or the Inter-university Consortium for Political and Social Research (ICPSR). By comparison, the descriptions are far more thorough than one finds in ICPSR's *Guide to Resources and Services* (see entry #4), though the latter covers many more studies on a wider range of topics. Author/organization and subject indexes are provided.

343. Zill, Nicholas, and Margaret Daly, eds. **Researching the Family: A Guide to Survey and Statistical Data on U.S. Families.** Washington, D.C.: Child Trends, Inc., 1993. 460p. ISBN 0-932359-03-5.

This is a guide to 60 major datasets relating to the family, covering "an assortment of substantive issues, including health, education, employment and unemployment, poverty, crime, family formation and dissolution, child development, and substance abuse" (p. xiv). For each dataset, information is provided on the purpose, sponsorship, design, periodicity, content, limitations, availability, and publications using the data. Checklists are also included indicating specific variables covered for family-level characteristics, characteristics of adult family members, and characteristics of child family members. Many of these datasets are also available from the Inter-university Consortium for Political and Social Research (see entry #215).

Bibliographies

344. **Black American Families, 1965-1984: A Classified, Selectively Annotated Bibliography.** Walter R. Allen, Editor-in-Chief. New York: Greenwood, 1986. 480p. index. (Bibliographies and Indexes in Afro-American and African Studies, No. 16). $59.95. LC 86-14959. ISBN 0-313-25613-6.

This is an invaluable guide to sociological and related research on the African American family. Though somewhat dated, the bibliography nonetheless covers an important period in the historical development of the research base. Included are 1,153 references to books, book chapters, journal articles, dissertations, government documents, and university publications. More popular works are generally excluded. The citations are listed alphabetically by author in the main, bibliography section of the book. Most references also include two subject headings that are used to track articles in the classified (subject) index. This index lists article titles and entry numbers under an extensive list of 12 categories and 120 subject headings. The major categories cover marriage and family trends, organizations and services, family relationships and dynamics, mate selection, reproduction issues, sexual attitudes and behavior, special problems (e.g., abuse, stress, suicide, and juvenile delinquents), psychology and sociology, family counseling and education, minority groups, and aids for theory and research. A keyword (in title) index is also included that cites complete titles and entry numbers from the bibliography section. Yet another index traces co-authors and co-editors. A list of the periodicals scanned is provided, as is an extensive introduction explaining the scope, organization, and use of the bibliography.

345. Dixon, Penelope. **Mothers and Mothering: An Annotated Feminist Bibliography.** New York: Garland, 1991. 219p. index. (Women's History and Culture, Vol. 3; Garland Reference Library of Social Science, Vol. 646). LC 90-24981. ISBN 0-8240-5949-2.

The subject of mothers and mothering relates to numerous sociological topics, including marriage and the family, gender socialization, and the social division of labor, to name a few. This bibliography is a selective guide to books and articles on this topic. Sources cited were published since 1970, and popular, historical, fictional, cross-cultural, and psychologically oriented works are excluded, as are theses and dissertations. The entries are arranged alphabetically by author in 11 topical chapters: mothering today; mothers and daughters; mothers and sons; single mothers; working mothers; lesbian and Black mothers, daughters and sons; mothering and the family; the children; feminism; psychoanalysis; and abortion, surrogacy, and the new reproductive technologies. Each chapter begins with an essay overview of the topic and some of the key works and authors in that area. All entries have well-written, paragraph-long annotations. Sources cited more than once are cross-referenced to the annotated entry. An author index is provided.

346. Engeldinger, Eugene A. **Spouse Abuse: An Annotated Bibliography of Violence Between Mates.** Metuchen, N.J.: Scarecrow, 1986. 317p. index. $29.50. LC 85-14546. ISBN 0-8108-1838-8.

Though not particularly current, this bibliography does serve an important function in literature reviews on spouse abuse. It includes paragraph-long annotations for 1,783 books, chapters, articles, reports, government documents, theses, and dissertations. Both scholarly and popular works are included for the time period covering the 1970s through 1983, a major period of growth in the "discovery" of and attention to the problem. The entries are arranged alphabetically by author. An extensive subject index to aid searching is provided, though some of the headings (e.g., marital rape and victims characteristics) could use subheadings to be truly helpful. A name index is also included.

347. Gondolf, Edward W. **Research on Men Who Batter: An Overview, Bibliography and Resource Guide.** Bradenton, Fla.: Human Services Institute, 1988. 93p. index. $11.95. LC 87-34229. ISBN 0-943519-05-5.

Intended for "social workers, therapists, and researchers" (p. v) working with or studying batterers, this bibliography cites approximately 1,000 books, chapters, and journal articles from the late 1970s and 1980s. The entries are arranged by author under five major categories: the dynamics of men who batter; the roots of wife battering; men who batter; intervention with the batterer; and program resources. These categories are further subdivided by some 40 subtopics. For example, "Dynamics of Wife Battering" includes theory, power and status, incidence and impact, and premarital abuse, among others. The chapter "Roots of Wife Battering" has subtopics for patriarchy; masculinity and sex-roles; and anger, aggression, and violence. "Men Who Batter" includes self-esteem, personality traits, and alcohol abuse. "Intervention" covers such topics as men's programs, couples counseling, and police intervention. The "Program Resources" chapter lists self-help books, films, program manuals, resource centers, periodicals, and reference books. A useful introductory chapter providing an overview of the research on men who batter is included. An author index is appended.

348. Gouke, Mary Noel, and Arline McClarty Rollins. **One-Parent Children, the Growing Minority: A Research Guide.** New York: Garland, 1990. 494p. index. (Reference Books on Family Issues, Vol. 14; Garland Reference Library of Social Science, Vol. 344). $59.00. LC 84-48876. ISBN 0-8240-8576-0.

Single-parent families have been growing, as have the numbers of children living in such families. This changing family structure has serious implications for a range of social issues and problems, including child development, the feminization of poverty, educational achievement, and the incidence of childhood poverty, among others. This bibliography abstracts over 1,100 books, book chapters, journal articles, ERIC documents, and conference papers on various aspects of one-parent children; it also cites, but does not abstract, dissertations. (*Dissertation Abstracts* references are provided.) The bibliography is divided into four parts: general aspects of one-parent children, children in different types of one-parent families, children who lack or have lost a parent, and single-parent children and the schools. The "different types" of families include reconstituted, fatherless, motherless, single-parent adoptive, and alternative lifestyle families; subtopics for "parental loss" cover illegitimacy, illness, employment, imprisonment, military service, divorce/desertion/separation, and death. The descriptive abstracts are long and very well written; if an entry is a research study, key methodological information is provided, as is a summary of the findings. Supplementary geographic, author, and subject indexes are included. This is an excellent bibliography with clear relevance for the sociology of the family, educational sociology, and social psychology.

349. Nordquist, Joan, comp. **Domestic Violence: Spouse Abuse, Marital Rape.** Santa Cruz, Calif.: Reference and Research Services, 1986. 64p. $15.00. (Contemporary Social Issues: A Bibliographic Series, No. 4). ISBN 0-937855-07-3. ISSN 0887-3569.

Nordquist has identified books, book chapters, articles, pamphlets, handbooks, and guides on some of the issues that comprise domestic violence. Coverage extends back approximately five years from the bibliography's 1986 publication date, though some earlier works of "historical interest" are included as well. The bibliography is arranged into three sections. Section one, "Domestic Violence/Spouse Abuse," includes categories for general works, therapy/counseling, the batterer, the children, husband abuse, the police, law and legislation, the states, the federal government, and international references. Section two addresses "Marital Rape" and includes categories on general works, law and legislation, and international references. Within chapters, references are usually subarranged by categories for books, articles, and handbooks/pamphlets; they are then listed alphabetically by author. Section three contains separate lists of bibliographies, resource lists/directories, organizations, and periodicals. As with other Nordquist bibliographies, this source's strength is its identification of useful references across a range of sources and disciplines.

350. Sadler, Judith DeBoard. **Families in Transition: An Annotated Bibliography.** Hamden, Conn.: Archon Books/Shoestring Press, 1988. 251p. index. LC 87-37347. ISBN 0-208-02180-9.

The structure of the American family includes not only the nuclear family, but also single-parent families, commuter families, stepfamilies, and a variety of other forms of the family. This annotated bibliography is a guide to information on changing family structures and their related problems. It provides one-paragraph, descriptive annotations on almost 1,000 books, articles, handbooks, media materials, research studies, popular works, and other sources. Over 90 percent of these materials were published since 1975; 65 percent were published in the 1980s, including some as recently as 1987.

The entries are arranged into 16 chapters; within each chapter, entries are sorted into subsections for books or articles, and then arranged alphabetically by author. Chapter titles include "Single-Parent Families," "Stepfamilies," "Divorce," "Adoptive and Foster Care Families," "Divorce and Remarriage," "Custody and Child Support," "Parental Kidnapping," "Children of Divorce," "Working Parents & Latchkey Children," "Fathers," "Teen Pregnancy and Parenthood," "Homosexual Relationships," and "Works for Children & Youth." A chapter listing media is included, as well as two general chapters covering such topics as surrogate parents, commuter families, and living-together arrangements, among others. A final chapter lists bibliographic citations for recently identified works. Separate subject, author, book title, and article title indexes are provided, as well as an appended list of family-related associations and organizations.

This is a commendable bibliography, both for its broad coverage of topics and for its inclusion of material for nonprofessional and professional audiences. However, it excludes relevant indexes, abstracts, and databases (e.g., *Family Studies Database* and *Sage Family Studies Abstracts*) that would be useful for those wanting to do further research.

Indexes, Abstracts, and Databases

351. **Family Index.** John Touliatos, ed. Fort Worth, Tex.: Human Sciences, 1996- . annual. $149.95/yr. ISSN 1089-6147.

Over 850 source journals are indexed in this new, annual guide to family literature. Included here are references to 4,106 articles from 1995; these are accessible both by subject and author. Coverage is international and multidisciplinary, including journals in such areas sociology, social work, gerontology, family therapy, family medicine, child welfare, child development, education, counseling, law, medicine, history, and feminist studies.

These fields are distilled into eight broad categories for the contents: foundations of family studies; institutions, policy, and families; diverse families; martial, family, and other relationships; sexuality, reproduction, and families; individual development and behavior in families; family problems; and education, therapy, and services for families. Each of these categories, in turn, has a number of subtopics.

352. **Family Studies Database.** [CD-ROM]. Baltimore, Md.: National Information Services Corp., 1995- . updated quarterly.

This CD-ROM database is the electronic equivalent of and supersedes the *Inventory of Marriage and Family Literature* and covers from 1970 to the present. The latter volumes comprised a multivolume, continuing index to marriage and family journal and book literature. While they were published from 1974–1995, their coverage actually spanned the entire twentieth century. Each volume included author, subject, and keyword-in-title indexes. Over 300 source journals were scanned for relevant articles.

353. **Sage Family Studies Abstracts.** Vol. 1- , No. 1- . Thousand Oak, Calif.: Sage, 1979- . quarterly, with annual cumulative index. $355.00/yr.(institutions). ISSN 0164-0283.

Approximately 250 books, chapters, and articles are descriptively abstracted in each issue. The entries are arranged alphabetically by author within a large number of subject categories and subcategories. These include such subjects as sexual attitudes, gender roles, early socialization, child care, late socialization, family relations, life cycles, family services, divorce, economics, minority relations, theory, and many more. All citations include subject headings, which are used in the subject index; book citations include prices. Each index issue also provides subject and author indexes, which are annually cumulated. A source list of over 100 journals consulted is listed in the last issue of the volume.

Handbooks and Yearbooks

354. Chadwick, Bruce A., and Tim B. Heaton., eds. **Statistical Handbook on the American Family.** Phoenix, Ariz.: Oryx Press, 1992. 295p. index. $59.50. LC 91-44175. ISBN 0-89774-687-2.

Both government and nongovernment data comprise this handbook's more than 400 tables, charts, and graphs on the family. Government sources include ongoing publications, such as the *Current Population Reports* and the *Statistical Abstract of the United States*, though data from the 1990 Census was not yet available. Nongovernment sources include books and journal articles (including *The Gallup Report*), as well as research studies, such as the *General Social Survey* and the *National Survey of Families and Households*. Retrospective data are included whenever possible. The data are arranged into nine subject chapters: marriage; quality of marriage and family life; divorce; children; sexual attitudes and behavior and contraceptive use; living arrangements and kinship ties; working women, wives, and mothers; family violence; and elderly families. Each of these chapters has numerous subtopics with many tables of data. The data source for each table is fully cited in the supplementary "List of Sources." Every chapter begins with a brief overview of each subtopic. A fairly detailed subject index complements the list of contents and the more thorough "List of Tables and Charts."

355. Hawes, Joseph M., and Elizabeth I. Nybakken, eds. **American Families: A Research Guide and Historical Handbook.** New York: Greenwood, 1991. 435p. index. $79.50. LC 90-25221. ISBN 0-313-26233-0.

This is intended as an introductory guide to the history of the American family. According to the editors, research in this field is flourishing and they see this work as bringing some organization and structure to the more recent scholarship. The handbook is a collection of overview essays, arranged both historically and topically. Historical chapters cover the preindustrial family (1600–1815), the new model middle-class family

(1815–1930), families during the Depression (1930–1940), World War II and the Baby Boom (1940–1955), and postwar families (1955–present). Topic chapters focus on women and families, African American families, Native American families, and immigrant working-class families. Two introductory chapters on the study of the family and changing approaches to that study are also included. Throughout, the essays are fascinating and well written, and they reinforce the idea that good social analysis must also be historical. Each essay includes a "notes" section of works cited as well as an author listing of references. A selected bibliography is appended, as is a thorough subject/name index.

356. McCue, Margi Laird. **Domestic Violence: A Reference Handbook.** Santa Barbara, Calif.: ABC-CLIO, 1995. 273p. index. (Contemporary World Issues). $39.50. LC 95-44080. ISBN 0-87436-762-X.

This provides a broad and fairly in-depth overview of domestic violence, including its causes, extent, personal consequences, available services, and possible solutions. The handbook includes a wide variety of facts, references, and analyses, arranged into seven chapters. The first chapter provides a description of the types of domestic violence, their causes and history, and various groups' responses. The second chapter is an annotated chronology of key historical events, while chapter three includes biographies of 21 important figures, both living and dead. Chapter four presents facts, statistics, and legal issues, organized around 13 often-asked questions. Each question is accompanied by a well written, concise discussion of the issues involved and the known facts. All data sources are cited and fully referenced at the end of the chapter. Chapter five includes directories of national and state organizations and coalitions; the national organizations are annotated. The last two chapters are annotated bibliographies of books, articles, curricula, program materials, manuals, periodicals, films, audiocassettes, and videos relating to domestic violence. A combined subject/name/title index provides additional access to the material.

357. Schmittroth, Linda, ed. **Statistical Record of Children.** Detroit, Mich.: Gale Research, 1994. 983p. index. $105.00. ISBN 0-8103-9196-1.

Sociologists of the family, medical sociologists, educational sociologists, and others should find useful data in this statistical compilation. It includes 929 tables, from both government and nongovernment sources, arranged into 10 chapters: population; vital statistics; education; health, nutrition, and medical care; child care; income and expenditures; crimes, misdemeanors, and violence; domestic life; sports and recreation; and international comparisons. Many of the tables include retrospective data, in some cases extending back to the 1960s. Each table indicates its data source, including the specific volume, year, and page references where appropriate. The sources are listed alphabetically in the supplementary "List of Sources Consulted." A keyword index that includes place names is also included.

358. Sussman, Marvin B., and Suzanne K. Steinmetz, eds. **Handbook of Marriage and the Family.** New York: Plenum, 1987. 915p. index. $110.00. LC 86-25135. ISBN 0-306-41967-X.

The 30 chapters that comprise this handbook address such topics as theory, methodology, history, demography, ethnicity, stratification, work, religion, nontraditional family forms, socialization, gender roles, sexuality, divorce, family stress, violence, law, and family therapy, among others. Experts from a variety of social science disciplines authored these chapters, which review the historical development of each topic, its major issues and subtopics, its key theories and theorists, and significant research. Because the chapters are thorough and historical, they would be an excellent starting point for students beginning to do research on subtopics within marriage and the family. For more recent references on these topics, one could consult current bibliographies (cited elsewhere in this section), *Sage Family Studies Abstracts*, *Sociological Abstracts*, or the *Family Studies Database*, to name a few sources. Because so many topics are discussed across chapters, the extensive subject index should be useful.

359. Touliatos, John, Barry F. Perlmutter, and Murray A. Straus, eds. **Handbook of Family Measurement Techniques.** Newbury Park, Calif.: Sage, 1990. 797p. index. $85.00. LC 89-10542. ISBN 0-8039-3121-2.

Intended for clinicians and researchers, this book describes 976 research instruments available for various aspects of family research. The descriptions are arranged by author under a classification scheme of five major categories and 16 subcategories. The major categories are dimensions of marital and family interaction, intimacy and family values, parenthood, roles and power, and adjustments. "Adjustments" includes family functioning, stress, divorce, separation, and remarriage. Each major category is introduced by an essay that attempts to integrate "conceptual evaluation with progress in measurement" (p. 9). Over half of the instruments have been cited since 1975 and are given more detailed descriptions in the first part of the book. For each instrument, information is available including the author(s), title, availability, variables measured, type of instrument, instrument description, sample items (if permission was granted), comments (e.g., validity, reliability, and Cronbach's alpha), and references that describe the instrument. The older research instruments that have not been recently cited are given abbreviated abstracts in the last, smaller section of the book. Instrument author, title, and classification indexes are provided, as well as an introductory essay on the evolution of family research principles and techniques.

Dictionaries and Encyclopedias

360. DiCanio, Margaret. **The Encyclopedia of Marriage, Divorce and the Family.** New York: Facts on File, 1989. 607p. index. LC 89-11838. ISBN 0-8160-1695-X.

All aspects of family life are addressed in this multidisciplinary encyclopedia, including social roles and relationships, economic circumstances, reproduction, the physical and emotional health of family members, demographic aspects, family dysfunctions, legal issues, types of families, and more. The entries range from a few paragraphs to three or four pages in length. They often cite both relevant statistical information and key references, which are fully cited in the supplementary bibliography. DiCanio also includes a number of appended consumer guides and directories: family counseling and mental health services; choosing therapists/mental health agencies; divorce procedures; choosing divorce attorneys; antenuptial agreements; living-together agreements; resources (organizations); state child-care licensing agencies; and state child-support enforcement offices. A combined name/title/subject index is also included. This is concise, well written, and wide-ranging in the topics covered; it should make an excellent resource for students.

361. **Encyclopedia of Marriage and the Family.** David Levinson, ed.-in-chief. New York: Simon and Schuster Macmillan, 1995. 2v. $175.00. LC 95-18682. ISBN 0-020897235-X.

The study of marriage and the family is necessarily interdisciplinary, drawing heavily from such fields as sociology, psychology, and anthropology. The 160 articles comprising this two-volume set represent state-of-the-art overviews of primarily social and behavioral science aspects of marriage and the family. The signed essays cover such topics as child abuse, conflict, measures of family characteristics, single parents, divorce, dysfunctional families, gender roles, family systems theory, homeless families, poverty, social networks, and teenage parenting, among others. In addition, some topics are covered from a medical or health sciences perspective, including conception, birth control, and abortion. Entries typically range from two to seven pages and include both a bibliography of cited sources and *see also* references to related topics. Throughout, the essays are very well written and should be equally usable for undergraduates, graduate students, and faculty. A thorough index is included on subjects, some cited authors, organization names, acronyms, legislation, court cases, and some titles of important books.

World Wide Web/Internet Sites

362. **Family Development Page.**
Available: http://www.uakron.edu/hefe/fam1.html
(Accessed: October 23, 1996).

Available here are links to a range of Web sites related to the sociology of the family, touching on such topics as marriage, family economics, death/widowhood/bereavement, family violence, sexuality, women's issues, and the media.

MEDICAL SOCIOLOGY

Bibliographies

363. Levine, Paul L., John G. Bruhn, and Norma H. Turner. **The Psychosocial Aspects of AIDS: An Annotated Bibliography.** New York: Garland, 1990. 540p. index. (Garland Reference Library of Social Science, Vol. 547). LC 90-32919. ISBN 0-8240-5835-6.

AIDS researchers and interested medical sociologists will find this a useful guide to the 1980s research and writing on the social and psychological aspects of AIDS. Approximately 1,200 annotated references to books, articles, dissertations and reports are included. Arrangement of the entries is by author within six major chapters, each with numerous subsections. The chapters address "The Acquired Immune Deficiency Syndrome," "Epidemiological Aspects of the HIV infection and AIDS," "AIDS and Society," "Education and Prevention," "Services for Persons Affected by AIDS," and "Coping with AIDS." Among the many subtopics covered are issues of public policy, social support and networks, epidemiology, race and gender, attitudes and beliefs, and ethics. A glossary of key terms is provided, as well as author and detailed subject indexes.

364. Rice, Mitchell F., and Woodrow Jones, Jr., comps. **Black American Health: An Annotated Bibliography.** New York: Greenwood, 1987. 140p. index. (Bibliographies and Indexes in Afro-American and African Studies, No. 17). $49.95. ISBN 0-313-24887-7.

Medical sociologists interested in the intersection of race, class, and health may find this helpful, though not current. Included are references and abstracts to books, book chapters, monographs, journal articles, and conference papers. These are arranged alphabetically by author under seven chapter headings: cardiovascular system; mental health;

health care problems; assessment studies; cancer; political/social issues; and sickle cell anemia. Sociological concerns are reflected throughout and are not limited to the chapter on political and social issues. A brief introduction on some indicators of the health of African Americans is presented. An author index is included, and a list of "Black Health Organizations" is appended.

365. Selin, Helaine. **Science Across Cultures: An Annotated Bibliography of Books on Non-Western Science, Technology, and Medicine.** New York: Garland, 1992. 431p. index. (Garland Reference Library of the Humanities, Vol. 1597). LC 92-26370. ISBN 0-8153-0839-6.

Among the subjects covered in this bibliography are comparative aspects of medicine and health care. A total of 836 annotated references to books and monographs is included, arranged alphabetically by author under 10 mostly geographic chapters: multicultural; Africa; the Americas; Asia; China; Japan; India; Islamic Science; the Middle East; and the Pacific. Entries deal with social and cultural aspects of not only medical and health care, but also science and technology. Author, title, and subject indexes are provided for additional access.

366. Thomas, Richard R. **The Sociology of Mental Illness: An Annotated Bibliography.** New York: Garland, 1989. 129p. index. (Garland Library of Sociology, Vol. 15; Garland Reference Library of Social Science, Vol. 578). LC 88-37538. ISBN 0-8240-6672-3.

Covering literature from the 1970s and 1980s, this bibliography includes references to 367 books, book chapters, and articles exploring the issues, research, and controversies in this subfield of medical sociology. References are arranged by author within 11 chapters that cover major aspects of the field: definitions and classification of mental illness; historical perspectives; causes; incidence and prevalence; correlates of mental illness; diagnosis and treatment; the mental patient career; implications of stress, social support and life events; mental health occupations and professions; attitudes toward and perceptions of mental illness; and critiques and controversies. All references have paragraph-long descriptive annotations with occasional evaluative comments. References that relate to more than one chapter are cited more than once; a cross-reference locates the entry with the abstract. One of this bibliography's strengths, which is evident in the entries and in the introduction, is the full airing of the debates over the existence, definition, extent, nature, and explanation of mental illness. It provides an excellent overview of the field for the average researcher. An author index is provided.

Indexes, Abstracts, and Databases

367. **AIDSLINE.** Bethesda, Md.: National Library of Medicine, 1980- . monthly updates. DIALOG file #157.

All aspects of AIDS are covered by the literature in this database, including clinical studies, treatment, epidemiology, and policy issues. A number of these subjects are of interest to medical sociologists. Over 4,000 journals from 70 countries are scanned for citations; most references are in English. Approximately 50 percent of the citations include abstracts. *AIDSLINE* is also available on CD-ROM (from SilverPlatter; Aries Systems Corp.), and may also be found in online library catalogs (e.g., from Ovid Technologies).

368. **CINAHL.** [CD-ROM]. Peabody, Mass.: EBSCO Publishing, 1983- . monthly updates.

CINAHL is the CD-ROM version of the printed *Cumulative Index to Nursing and Allied Health Literature.* It indexes and abstracts articles in approximately 500 serial publications in nursing. However, because it deals with the provision of health care, much of interest may be here for medical sociologists and sociologists studying health care professions. An online database version of this is available from DataStar (DataStar label: NAHL). Another CD-ROM version of the database is available from Ovid Technologies.

369. **Medline.** Rockville, Md.: National Library of Medicine, 1966- . weekly updates. DIALOG files #154 (1985-) and #155 (1966-).

The *Medline* database is equivalent to three print sources: *Index Medicus, Index to Dental Literature, and International Nursing Index.* For medical sociologists, it is an excellent source for citations dealing with health care accessibility; health care policies; the treatment and epidemiology of various conditions (e.g., AIDS); aspects of the work of health care professionals; treatment related to race, ethnicity, and gender; and much more. Abstracts accompany about 50 percent of the citations added since 1974, and about 60 percent of the citations added after 1984. Foreign language articles are included and constitute about 25 percent of the of the database. Numerous versions of the *Medline* database are also available on CD-ROM from such publishers as SilverPlatter and EBSCO. Increasingly, this database is also accessible on many online library catalogs and networks.

Handbooks and Yearbooks

370. Dorgan, Charity Anne, ed. **Statistical Record of Health & Medicine.** New York: Gale Research, 1995. 1,218p. index. $99.00. ISBN 0-8103-9745-5.

Medical sociology students and researchers should find this not only an excellent compilation of data, but also an important guide to source documents for future reference. In all, it includes 961 tables of data from both government and nongovernment sources. A number of the tables include historical data or projections. The tables are arranged under 12 subject categories: summary indicators; health status of Americans; health care establishment; lifestyles and health; health in the workplace; health expenditures and funding; health care programs; health care industries; medical professions; medical establishment; politics, opinion, and law; and international comparisons. Each of these chapters includes additional subtopics for further grouping of the tables. Data sources are cited with the tables and again in the accompanying bibliography of sources. A substantial keyword index is included covering subjects, diseases, medical specialties, names, geographic locations, companies, hospitals, schools, and more. This is scheduled to be a biennial publication.

371. Roemer, Milton I. **National Health Systems of the World.** New York: Oxford University Press, 1993. 2v. index. $140.00/set. ISBN 0-19-505320-6(v. 1); 0-19-507845-4(v. 2).

Medical sociologists, particularly those doing comparative studies of health care systems, should find this handbook useful. It is comprised of two complementary volumes. Volume one, *The Countries*, provides overviews of countries at different levels of development and with different types of health care systems. Countries are classified as industrialized, transitional, or very poor, categories that comprise the major sections of volume one. Within these categories, countries are further classified as to whether their health care systems are entrepreneurial, welfare-oriented, comprehensive, or socialist. The country essays are located within these categories, though not all countries are included. For most health care systems covered, information is available on the system's social background, organizational structure, resources, economic support, management, and delivery of services. The introductory four chapters discuss some of these evaluative and analytical categories. The concluding chapters discuss health systems in oil-rich developing countries, as well as broad social trends and issues related to health systems.

Volume two, *The Issues*, contains essays addressing major components of and issues in health care systems and service delivery. The 18 chapters are arranged under five major parts: resources; programs; economic support and management; health services delivery; and world perspectives. "Resources" has chapters addressing health care personnel, facilities, and knowledge. "Programs" includes governmental health agencies, social security, voluntary health agencies, and private sector health care. "Economic Support and Management" addresses those issues, as well as health system regulation and legislation. "Health Services Delivery" discusses primary health care, hospital services, and programs for certain populations, disorders, and special health services. "World Perspective" includes international health activities and world trends. A subject/name index is included in both volumes.

World Wide Web/Internet Sites

372. **Duke Medical Sociology.**
Available: http://www.soc.duke.edu/~mmusick/oth_site.html
(Accessed: December 31, 1996).

This provides links to government and medical research sites, epidemiology and public health research sites, research institutions, the Triangle Health and Social Issues Group, the Duke University Center for Aging and Human Development, and other Sociology departments and sites.

373. **Section on Medical Sociology.**
Available: http://www.asanet.org/medical.htm
(Accessed: December 31, 1996).

Medical sociology is one of the American Sociological Association's interest groups, and this is its Web site. One can find here a list of officers, section announcements, highlights from the section newsletter and, in the future, home pages of section members.

POPULATION AND DEMOGRAPHY

Bibliographies

374. Gerhan, David R., comp. **Bibliography of American Demographic History: The Literature from 1984-1994.** Westport, Conn.: Greenwood, 1995. 339p. index. (Bibliographies and Indexes in American History, Number 30). $79.50. LC 94-42117. ISBN 0-313-26677-8.

A follow-up to Gerhan and Wells' *A Retrospective Bibliography of American Demographic History from Colonial Times to 1983* (see entry #375), this bibliography adds another 9,802 references to the literature on this growing field. Books, scholarly journal articles, local and state historical journal articles, and essays/book chapters are included; dissertations, biographical/autobiographical works, critiques/responses, and unrevised new editions are excluded. The arrangement of the works into subject chapters and subtopics is identical to the earlier volume by Gerhan and Wells, with the addition of some "general" categories in some chapters. The major chapter topics are 1) theory, methods, and general background; 2) marriage and fertility; 3) health and death; 4) migration, pluralism, and local patterns; 5) family and demographic history; and 6) population and economics, politics, and society. Each chapter and subsection begins with an overview of that particular topic, followed by the references listed alphabetically by author. Additional access to the entries is provided by author, place, ethnicity/national origin, and topic indexes. The topic index has been newly added since the previous volume and could use subheadings under some of the larger subject headings.

375. Gerhan, David R., and Robert V. Wells, comps. **A Retrospective Bibliography of American Demographic History from Colonial Times to 1983.** New York: Greenwood, 1989. 474p. index. (Bibliographies and Indexes in American History, Number 10). $105.00. ISBN 0-313-23130-3.

Demographic history "includes not only the basic patterns of population, but also the study of such things as family patterns and the social, economic, and political consequences of demographic trends" (p. xi). Consequently, many of this bibliography's 3,840 references should interest sociologists. Books, articles, studies, and government documents are included if they are research works and are historically oriented. Diaries and memoirs are excluded, as are twentieth-century journal articles without sufficient historical focus. Publication dates span the twentieth century, with some items published in the nineteenth century. References are arranged by author into six chapters: introduction and general background; marriage and fertility; health and death; values and attitudes; migration, pluralism, and local patterns; family and demographic history; and population, economics, politics, and society. Many more subtopics, for both subjects and historical periods, are available within each of these chapters. Each chapter and section is introduced by a brief essay describing the focus of the entries. Author, place, and subject indexes are provided. Though it makes insufficient use of subheadings, the subject index does indicate this work's extensive coverage of various racial, ethnic, and religious groups.

376. Nordquist, Joan, comp. **Recent Immigration from Latin America: Social, Economic and Political Aspects: A Bibliography.** Santa Cruz, Calif.: Reference and Research Services, 1995. 68p. (Contemporary Social Issues: A Bibliographic Series, No. 37). $15.00. ISBN 0-937855-72-3.

Over 700 books, book chapters, pamphlets, government documents, dissertations, and journal articles are cited on the causes and consequences of immigration from Latin America. Both legal and illegal immigration are addressed, with the entries focusing primarily on social, economic, and immigration policy issues. The references are arranged by author under 10 chapters. Chapter one includes general sources on the issue, with subtopics on economic and social conditions, employment, health, education, and women. Chapter two focuses on undocumented immigrants, with the same subtopics as chapter one. Chapter three specifically addresses the economic impact of legal and illegal immigration. Chapters four through eight cite references to Mexican immigrants, Central American immigrants, other Latin American Immigrants, Cuban immigrants, and Puerto Rican immigrants, respectively. Chapter nine is on immigration policy, while the final chapter lists relevant bibliographies. Most books cited are less than five years old, while journal articles are less than three years old. An impressive variety of indexes, abstracts, and databases were scanned to create this politically and ideologically diverse list of references.

377. Obudho, R. A., and Jeannine B. Scott, comps. **Afro-American Demography and Urban Issues: A Bibliography.** Westport, Conn.: Greenwood, 1985. 433p. index. (Bibliographies and Indexes in Afro-American and African Studies, No. 8). $65.00. LC 85-17752. ISBN 0-313-24656-4.

Though now a bit dated, this includes references to 5,235 books, book chapters, journal articles, papers, theses, public documents, and dissertations, with some entries dating from the eighteenth century. This historical coverage compensates, somewhat, for the lack of more recent citations. The entries are arranged alphabetically by author within eight chapters: bibliographies; demography and population; urbanization and disurbanization; housing and residential patterns; ghettoization, slum and squatter settlements; suburbanization and reurbanization; geography and rural studies; and urban and regional planning policies. Lists of 1) major research collections on Afro-American demography and urban studies; and 2) periodicals consulted are provided. An author/main entry index is included, though a keyword-in-title or subject index would have been desirable.

Indexes, Abstracts, and Databases

378. **CENDATA.** Washington, D.C.: U.S. Bureau of the Census, 1980- . daily updates. DIALOG file CENDATA.

This DIALOG file is both current and cumulative, encompassing all of the various CENDATA files (files #578-580). It is a menu-driven database that selectively includes both current and historical data. There are U.S., state, and local data, as well as data on 200 other countries. Two of the 18 subject categories cover population data (number 16) and 1990 Census data (number 18). Tract level data are available in DIALOG file #580, which is a command-driven, not menu-driven file.

379. **POPLINE.** [CD-ROM]. Norwood, Mass.: SilverPlatter Information, Inc., 1970- . semiannual updates.

This is a CD-ROM version of the *POPLINE* database, which was begun in 1970 and now includes over 200,000 references and abstracts for books, articles and reports on population, demography, family planning, fertility, AIDS, health care, public policy, and related issues. Some of the references are historical, dating back to the nineteenth century. It is updated semiannually and adds approximately 10,000 references each year. *POPLINE* is produced at Johns Hopkins University by the Population Information Program. *POPLINE* is also searchable online through *MEDLARS* (from the National Library of Medicine).

380. **Population Demographics.** New York: Market Statistics, 1990- . annual updates. DIALOG file #581.

Though probably intended as a marketing database, this nonetheless provides ready access to 1990 Census data on population, households, income, education, and occupation. Data in these categories are easily broken down by numerous other variables, such as age, race, gender, metropolitan area, county, state, etc. Current year estimates and five-year projections are also included.

381. **Population Index.** Vol. 1- , No. 1- . Princeton, N.J.: Office of Population Research, Woodrow Wilson School of Public and International Affairs, Princeton University, 1935- . quarterly, with annual cumulative indexes. $90.00/yr. ISSN 0032-4701.

Each issue contains approximately 900 annotated citations "designed to cover the world's demographic and population literature, including books and other monographs, serial publications, journal articles, working papers, doctoral dissertations, and machine-readable data files" (p. 175). Items from Princeton University's Office of Population Research, as well as other major research centers, are included. Items are arranged alphabetically by author under an extensive list of topics and subtopics. Each citation receives a number code that refers to the index volume and citation number; these codes are used in the author and geographical indexes. The bibliography is international in scope, including source documents in other languages. Citations and abstracts, however, are in English, though the untranslated title is included as well. Each entry also includes an address for correspondence and the location of at least one holding library for that item. The author and geographical indexes in each issue are annually cumulated. This source is also now on the World Wide Web for searching the years 1986–1996. Available: http://opr.princeton.edu/popindex/ (Accessed October 3, 1996).

Handbooks and Yearbooks

382. Barrett, Richard E. **Using the 1990 U.S. Census for Research.** Thousand Oaks, Calif.: Sage, 1994. 86p. (Guides to Major Social Science Data Bases, 3). $24.00. LC 94-17655. ISBN 0-8039-5389-5.

Census data are relevant to any number of sociological research topics. These data are also valuable because they have been collected since 1790, and because they are readily available in microfiche, print, or electronic formats (CD-ROM and computer tape) at many public and academic libraries. This guide will enable one to make best use of the data found in the 1990 Census. Its chapters describe not only the history and current contents of the 1990 Census, but also its design, procedures and problems, and data analysis. Each of these topics is broken down into various subtopics. However, taken as a whole, this description of the content and methodology of the Census should be invaluable to researchers doing secondary analysis of the data. Institutional members of the Inter-university Consortium for Political and Social Research (ICPSR), as well as U.S. government depository libraries, will likely have the 1990 Census and many of its earlier versions.

383. Bos, Eduardo, et al. **World Population Projections: Estimates and Projections with Related Demographic Statistics.** Baltimore, Md.: Johns Hopkins University Press, 1994. 521p. $34.95. ISBN 0-8108-4947-0.

Published on behalf of the World Bank, this contains detailed population projections broken down by categories for the world, geographic regions, income groups, countries, economies, and territories. An introductory chapter discusses trends, data sources, and projection methodology relating to fertility, mortality, migration, and age structure. Detailed projections are then presented for the world, geographic regions, fertility transition status groups, and income groups; these are broken down further by subtopics. Following this are projections for countries, economies, and territories; these are alphabetically arranged. For each geographic entity, data projections are included for age groups, birth rates, death rates, migration rates, growth rates, and fertility rates. Throughout this section, the projections are presented in 25-year periods from 1990 through 2150.

384. Domschke, Eliane, and Doreen S. Goyer. **The Handbook of National Population Censuses: Africa and Asia.** New York: Greenwood, 1986. 1,032p. $215.00. LC 85-31712. ISBN 0-313-25361-7.

See entry #387.

385. Frey, William H., and Alden Speare, Jr. **Regional and Metropolitan Growth in the United States.** New York: Russell Sage Foundation, 1988. 586p. index. (The Population of the United States in the 1980s). $70.00. LC 88-6727. ISBN 0-87154-293-5.

Drawing extensively upon the Census and other government and nongovernment data, this handbook focuses on explaining the redistribution of the American population across regions and metropolitan areas. The 11 chapters address such issues as the components, determinants, and consequences of metropolitan growth and decline; the growth of the African American population in metropolitan areas; city-suburb redistributions within large metropolitan areas; race and status dimensions of these redistributions; and household, family, workplace, and residence dimensions of city-suburb redistributions. The essays are extensively footnoted and accompanied by tables, charts, and graphs drawn from the 1950–1980 Censuses and the *Current Population Reports*, among other sources. Though well written, the analyses are sophisticated and, therefore, most suitable for advanced students and faculty. While this does not include the 1990 Census, the historical analysis is valuable. Name and subject indexes are provided.

386. Goyer, Doreen S., and Eliane Domschke. **The Handbook of National Population Censuses: Latin America and the Caribbean, North America, and Oceania.** Westport, Conn.: Greenwood, 1983. 711p. $135.00. LC 82-9390. ISBN 0-313-21352-6.

387. Goyer, Doreen S., and Gera E. Graaijer. **The Handbook of National Population Censuses: Europe.** New York: Greenwood, 1992. 544p. $99.50. LC 91-39111. ISBN 0-313-28426-1.

All three volumes of *The Handbook of National Population Censuses* are organized identically and provide a comprehensive, historical overview of censuses conducted worldwide. For each country, a multipage description of the various censuses that have been done is included, as well as the types of questions asked. For more recent censuses, additional categories of information for special elements or features, the quality of the census, and the publication plan are provided. In some cases, an accompanying national topic chart is included that lists, for each census, the topics surveyed. At the end of each volume, an international topics chart is provided that lists, for each country, census topics covered within five-year periods from 1945 through 1984. An appended cross-reference list of variant country names and capital cities is available.

388. Keyfitz, Nathan, and Wilhelm Flieger. **World Population Growth and Aging: Demographic Trends in the Late Twentieth Century.** Chicago, Ill.: University of Chicago Press, 1990. 608p. index. $78.00. LC 90-11015. ISBN 0-226-43237-8.

This presents both regional and country data from the 1950s through 1985, with projections to 2020. The data tables are organized into three main sections: summary tables, tabulations based on United Nations data and estimates, and detailed country tabulations. Summary tables include region and country data on population, age structure, vital rates, mortality, and fertility, with some further breakdown of these categories. The United Nations data include tables and graphs for each region and country, with specific categories for observed and projected population data, population ratios, mortality measures, fertility measures, and aging measures. These tables typically span from 1950 to 2020, with projections beginning in 1990. The detailed country tabulations have extensive population data taken at five- to ten-year intervals, though this varies from country to country. A lengthy introductory chapter explains the methodology involved in the collection and estimation of the data. The appendixes include, among other things, lists of data sources and cooperating national statistics agencies. a region/country/territory index is also included.

389. **Sourcebook of County Demographics.** 8th ed. Arlington, Va.: CACI Marketing Systems, 1995. 277p. ISBN 0-918417-57-0.

Though intended primarily for market researchers, this nonetheless has useful data for students of population and demography. It may be particularly suitable as a current data source for courses doing statistical analysis on select population and demographic variables. The data are arranged alphabetically by state, then by county. For each county one finds data on population, population composition, households, income, and purchase potential. The population section includes projections to the year 2000, annual change from 1990–1995, and percentage by race. Population composition covers percentage Hispanic origin, age distribution, median age, and the ratio of males to females. Household data include the number of households (with projections), the annual percentage change from 1990 through 1995, the number of families, and median household income. Income data include per capital income, household income base, household income distribution, and average disposable income by age of householder. The purchase potential indexes indicate potential demand for various categories of products. Summary data are included for metropolitan statistical areas (MSA), as well as Nielsen (DMA) and Arbitron (ADI) market areas. Country maps are included, as are appendixes for state, MSA, ADI, and DMA codes and definitions.

Dictionaries and Encyclopedias

390. Petersen, William, and Renee Petersen. **Dictionary of Demography: Terms, Concepts, and Institutions.** New York: Greenwood, 1986. 2v. index. $195.00. LC 83-12571. ISBN 0-313-24134-1(set).

To be most beneficial to readers of the literature, this dictionary has included terms not only from demography, but also from its related disciplines. As a result, individuals will not be forced to consult other dictionaries. Included among the 1,484 entries are basic terms, acronyms, countries, demographic institutions, important publication titles (e.g., *Current Population Survey*), and research studies. Definitions range in length from a few sentences to a number of pages, with some definitions including references to sources. In all definitions, asterisks indicate words that are defined elsewhere in the dictionary; daggers indicate biographies found in another title, the *Dictionary of Demography: Biographies*. The supplementary material includes a comprehensive subject/name index, as well as a classified international list of institutes, organizations, associations, and agencies.

391. Pressat, Roland. **The Dictionary of Demography.** Christopher Wilson, ed. Oxford: Blackwell, 1985. 243p. index. LC 84-28407. ISBN 0-631-12746-1.

The core of this dictionary is an adaptation and translation of the French edition of Pressat's *Demographic Dictionary*. Additional entries to this edition are provided by over two dozen demographic scholars from England, the United States, Europe, and Australia. The signed entries are well written, though the concepts are sometimes too complex for beginners. Definitions include references to other terms defined in the dictionary; these cross-referenced terms are in capital letters. Another useful feature is the inclusion of references and suggested readings at the end of many definitions. A subject index, an unusual feature for a dictionary, is also included; it helps locate uses of a term in other definitions.

World Wide Web/Internet Sites

392. **Population Index.**
Available: http://opr/princeton/edu/popindex/
(Accessed October 29, 1996).

Among other things, this site offers electronic searching from the last 10 years of the *Population Index* by subject, author, geographical region, and publication date. Full-text searching of the database is also offered, on an experimental basis, for the years 1994–1996. Also included is information on subscribing and submitting materials to *Population Index*.

393. **Progressive Population Network.**
Available: http://csf.colorado.edu/mail/ppn/
(Accessed October 3, 1996).

The Progressive Population Network (PPN) encourages alternative approaches to the study of population, particularly sociological, anthropological, Marxist, neo-Marxist, feminist, and environmentalist perspectives. Special emphasis in this discussion list is made on class, racial/ethnic, and gender divisions.

Address to subscribe to list: listproc@csf.colorado.edu
Message: SUB PPN Yourfirstname Yourlastname

394. **U.S. Census Bureau Home Page.**
Available: http://www.census.gov/
(Accessed: December 16, 1996).

Regular users of the Census will find this a relevant Web site to monitor. It includes news, data access tools (software), a list of subjects on which information is available, a list of 1,000 documents that are available online in PDF (portable document format), a search engine that allows searching available online documents by some basic variables, other available Census products, and more. Links to other official statistics are also available.

RACE AND ETHNIC RELATIONS

General Sources

Bibliographies

395. Fairchild, Halford H., et al, comps. and eds. **Discrimination and Prejudice: An Annotated Bibliography.** 2d ed. San Diego, Calif.: Westerfield Enterprises, 1992. 312p. index. $89.95. LC 92-11244. ISBN 0-942259-03-3.

Major social science indexes, abstracts, and databases were scanned to find approximately 4,300 references to books, articles, dissertations, and government documents on prejudice and discrimination. The bibliography has five parts: four on major racial/ethnic groups (African Americans, American Indians, Asian Americans, and Hispanic Americans); and one for multiethnic references. For each group, references are arranged by author under subtopics. With some variation from group to group, these subtopics include: attitudes and bias; criminal justice; civil rights; education; employment; political participation; economic rights; housing; immigration; health and public services; and women. Most references receive brief, descriptive abstracts. A separate subject index for each part of the bibliography is included. However, the subject categories are too broad to be particularly useful; often dozens, if not hundreds, of entry numbers are cited under one term. More subheadings are needed for this index to be truly useful. Though not comprehensive, this bibliography is appropriately broad in the literature it cites on discrimination and prejudice.

396. Weinberg, Meyer, comp. **Racism in the United States: A Comprehensive Classified Bibliography.** New York: Greenwood, 1990. 682p. index. (Bibliographies and Indexes in Ethnic Studies, Number 2). $89.50. LC 89-78118. ISBN 0-313-27390-1.

As Weinberg argues in the introduction, personal prejudice and institutional racism have a tenacious hold on U.S. society. Racism has deep historical roots, as well as recent and varied manifestations. This bibliography identifies over 10,000 books, journal and newspaper articles, reports, hearings, theses, dissertations, and other sources on a wide variety of topics relating to the history and current dimensions of racism. The references, which are unannotated, are arranged by author under 87 subject headings. These headings address such compelling topics as affirmative action, antiracism, blacks and Jews, class structure, slavery, economics of racism, family, I.Q. and race, institutional racism, migration, racist groups, stereotypes, violence against minorities, wealth and income, antisemitism, and sexism, among others. Virtually all of the headings should include entries of interest to sociologists. Where titles do not adequately indicate the content and focus of an article, an annotation of a few words has been added. Cross-references at the end of each section to other relevant sections in the bibliography are included. While the entries in each section are clearly selective and not comprehensive, they nonetheless identify enough important sources to be a valuable starting point. An author index is provided.

397. Weinberg, Meyer, comp. **World Racism and Related Inhumanities: A Country-by-Country Bibliography.** New York: Greenwood, 1992. 1,048p. index. (Bibliographies and Indexes in World History, Number 26). $125.00. LC 92-4094. ISBN 0-313-28109-2.

Weinberg has cited over 12,000 books, articles, and dissertations published worldwide on racism and related subjects. The entries are arranged first by country, then by author. Sources in languages other than English are included. Over 135 countries are covered, with some additional chapters for references on various regions of the world (e.g., Latin America and the Middle East). In addition to racism, the "related inhumanities" covered include slavery, class domination, sexism, national oppression, imperialism, colonialism, and antisemitism. A few of the larger chapters, such as Canada or China, categorize the entries further by subtopic or group. While the entries in any one chapter are just a subset of what could be included, they nonetheless provide a useful guide to discussions of racism and other forms of oppression in that particular country. Furthermore, racism is addressed in a variety of institutional contexts, including the economy, politics, and education, among others. Additional access to the entries is provided by author and subject indexes. The latter includes a breakdown of countries within each subject heading.

Indexes, Abstracts, and Databases

398. **Ethnic Newswatch.** [CD-ROM]. Stamford, Conn.: Softline Information, Inc., 1992- . bimonthly. ISSN 1068-1272.

This is a CD-ROM database providing full-text of articles from ethnic and minority magazines and newspapers in the United States. A total of 163 publications are covered and the articles are searchable by a number of variables, such as publication name, keyword, author, article type, ethnic group, geographical location, and publication date. Virtually any subject of interest to sociologists is covered, including drug use, crime, religion, health care, inequality, AIDS, social change, and more.

399. **Sage Race Relations Abstracts.** Vol. 1- . London: Sage, 1975- . quarterly. $256.00/yr. ISSN 0307-9201.

Published on behalf of the Institute of Race Relations (London), each issue includes abstracts of approximately 200 books and articles. Coverage is multidisciplinary and international, with most citations coming from England, the United States, and Canada. Entries are arranged alphabetically by author under broad subject categories, such as bibliographies, area studies, community relations, culture and identity, demographic studies, education, family and adoption, housing, immigrant communities, and more. Some abstracts are accompanied by *see also* references to other abstracts. Cumulative author and subject indexes are provided in the last issue of each volume. Issues may also include an introductory article or bibliographic essay.

Handbooks and Yearbooks

400. Buenker, John D., and Lorman A. Ratner, eds. **Multiculturalism in the United States: A Comparative Guide to Acculturation and Ethnicity.** New York: Greenwood, 1992. 271p. index. $55.00. LC 91-35116. ISBN 0-313-25374-9.

A common focus of all of the essays in this handbook is the acculturation of various groups to American society. Included are chapters on African Americans, American Indians (Native Americans), German Americans, Irish Americans, Scandinavian Americans, Polish Americans, Jewish Americans, Italian Americans, Chinese Americans, and Mexican Americans. While not all ethnic groups are represented, the editors believe that the sample is varied and representative enough to allow for useful comparisons and generalizations. The essays touch on such issues or variables as the pace and degree of acculturation, group strategies, social mobility, identity formation, marriage patterns, social class, occupation, religion, and more. These chapters provide useful overviews for students and are accompanied by bibliographical essays discussing important literature. A subject/name index is included.

401. Sigler, Jay A. **International Handbook on Race and Race Relations.** New York: Greenwood, 1987. 483p. index. $125.00. LC 86-33651. ISBN 0-313024770-6.

Though the category of "race" is debatable among social scientists, race relations is nonetheless an important subject of study worldwide. This handbook provides overview essays on the state of race relations in 20 countries, with the descriptions contributing to a comparative analysis of the issues and problems. The countries represent a geographic and political variety and include: Australia, Brazil, Canada, Fiji, France, India, Japan, Malaysia, Netherlands, New Zealand, Singapore, South Africa, Sudan, Switzerland, Thailand, Trinidad, Union of Soviet Socialist Republics, United Kingdom, and West Germany. Clearly, events have overtaken the analysis in some of these countries (e.g., USSR, West Germany, and South Africa), somewhat dating the essays. However, the historical information for each country will be valuable. Furthermore, some seemingly homogeneous countries (i.e., Japan, West Germany, France, United Kingdom, Netherlands, and Switzerland) were included because of emerging issues regarding racial minorities. An appendix lists percentages for racial and ethnic divisions within the countries treated in the volume. A subject index that includes names is also included.

Dictionaries and Encyclopedias

402. Auerbach, Susan, ed. **Encyclopedia of Multiculturalism.** New York: Marshall Cavendish, 1994. 6v. index. $449.95. LC 93-23405. ISBN 1-85435-670-4(set).

These six volumes include 1,438 entries "on people, places, concepts, events, laws, and organizations that have shaped multiculturalism in the United States" (p. vi). The signed entries range from a short paragraph on basic terms to 5,000 words for major topics. Both contemporary and historical subjects are covered, as are some aspects of popular culture (e.g., sports and media). Many sociological topics are addressed, either separately or in the context of particular ethnic groups. These include social movements, discrimination, intergroup relations, education, family life, gender and sexism, and race and racism, to name but a few. The essays are straightforwardly written and include both suggested readings and references to terms defined elsewhere in the encyclopedia.

Volume six also has a U.S. multiculturalism time line, a directory of resource organizations, a filmography of multicultural films, a general bibliography, a listing of subject entries by population and by major subject area, and a subject index. This encyclopedia would be most appropriate for students and general readers.

403. Levinson, David. **Ethnic Relations: A Cross-Cultural Encyclopedia.** Santa Barbara, Calif.: ABC-CLIO, 1994. 293p. index. (Encyclopedias of the Human Experiences). $49.50. LC 94-40253. ISBN 0-87436-735-2.

Aimed primarily at undergraduate students, this encyclopedia contains essays describing approximately 90 terms on racial and ethnic relations. A number of terms deal with specific racial or ethnic groups, such as the Kurds, Bosnians/Croats/Serbs, Gypsies, and Sikhs. However, many of the remaining terms deal with important theories and concepts in the study of racial and ethnic relations. These include colonialism, ethnocentrism, cultural relativism, pluralism, race and racism, indigenous rights, and hate crimes, among others. The well-written essays range from one to nine pages and are accompanied by bibliographic references. A supplementary directory of organizations concerned with ethnic relations, such as OXFAM, Human Rights Watch, and Amnesty International, is provided. For each organization, an address and description of its purpose is included. The encyclopedia also includes a bibliography and subject index.

World Wide Web/Internet Sites

404. **Sociology of Ethnicity: Ethnic Relations, Migration and Racism.**
Available: http://www.pcsw.uva.nl/sociosite/TOPICS/Ethnic.html
(Accessed: February 11, 1997).

A subsection of the *SocioSite* Web site, this provides links to a variety of Web sites dealing with race, ethnicity, racism, and more. Coverage is international, and electronic journals and discussion lists are included. A link to the *Yahoo* category for ethnic and racial minorities is also provided.

African Americans

Bibliographies

405. **Black Adolescence: Current Issues and Annotated Bibliography.** The Consortium for Research on Black Adolescence. Boston, Mass.: G. K. Hall, 1990. 157p. $40.00. LC 89-26995. ISBN 0-8161-9080-1.

Adolescents constitute a growing and significant percentage of the African American population. They are also disproportionately beset by a range of social, economic, behavioral, and institutional problems that can have serious consequences for their development. In the interest of helping policymakers, activists, and other professionals promote that development, the Consortium for Research on Black Adolescence developed this annotated bibliography. Its entries are arranged into 11 chapters that span a variety of sociological specialties: psychosocial development, psychological health. physical health, drug abuse, suicide, academic performance, education and occupational choice, employment, family-adolescent relationships, sexuality and contraception, and teen parenting. Each chapter begins with a brief essay discussing key themes and issues in the literature. Accompanying this essay is a small number of annotated references, as well as an unannotated list of other relevant sources.

406. Hall, Christine C. Iijima, Brenda J. Evans, and Stephanie Selice, eds. **Black Females in the United States: A Bibliography from 1967 to 1987.** Washington, D.C.: American Psychological Association, 1989. 189p. index. (Bibliographies in Psychology, No. 3). $25.00. LC 89-112. ISBN 1-55798-048-9.

While the primary focus of this bibliography is empirical psychological research, many references should interest sociologists. In all, 664 annotated and 1,839 unannotated journal article references that were drawn from the *Psychological Abstracts/PsycLIT/PsycINFO* database are included. These are arranged by author under 13 major categories for psychological research, including psychometrics, human experimental psychology, personality, treatment and prevention, physiological psychology, applied psychology, physical and psychological disorders, developmental psychology, educational psychology, social psychology, communication systems, professional personnel and professional issues, and social processes and social issues. Many of these categories include research examining the intersection of race and gender in such areas as family relations, identity and self concept, stress and coping, aging, and social problems (e.g., poverty, drug abuse, and teen pregnancy). Entries under educational psychology, for example, address the causes and consequences of differential school achievement, an important topic in the sociology of education. Author and subject indexes are included, as well as an appendix showing the computer search strategy used to retrieve the references. This would be valuable in updating a subject search in the future.

407. Hay, Fred J. **African-American Community Studies from North America: A Classified, Annotated Bibliography.** New York: Garland, 1991. 234p. index. (Garland Reference Library of Social Science, Vol. 420; Applied Social Science Bibliographies, Vol. 5). $45.00. LC 91-8158. ISBN 0-8240-6643-X.

For sociologists interested in community studies, particularly of African American communities, this identifies and describes the monographic literature from 1890 through the 1980s. The citations are arranged first by decade, then by community size, geographic region, state, community name, and finally author. Each entry includes a complete reference and a paragraph-long annotation. An accompanying keyword "ID" field indicates the decade when the study was completed, the community ecology (e.g. urban inner city), the geographic area, community name and state (or province if in Canada), the discipline of the primary investigator, and the investigator's race. In addition, codes are available for the Oke-She-Moke-She-Pop Classification Numbers and Document Numbers, which are fully explained at the end of the book. Additional access to the studies is provided by three indexes: author and personal name, state and community, and geographic region/feature (e.g., Midwest, Great Lakes).

408. Nordquist, Joan, comp. **The African-American Woman, Social and Economic Conditions: A Bibliography.** Santa Cruz, Calif.: Reference and Research Services, 1993. 76p. (Contemporary Social Issues: A Bibliographic Series, No. 32). $15.00. ISBN 0-937855-62-6.

Included here are over 1,000 unannotated references arranged by author under 20 subject categories. Topics covered include education, employment, violence against African American women, substance abuse, male/female relationships, families, teenage pregnancy, feminism, and more. Within each subject section, references are listed under format for either articles (journal and book chapters) or books, pamphlets, documents, and dissertations. The entries were drawn from searches of not only standard print and electronic bibliographic sources (e.g., *ERIC*, *PAIS*, *Books in Print*, and *PsychLIT*), but also small, alternative, radical, feminist, and African American presses and indexes (e.g.,

Alternative Press Index, *Ethnic Newswatch*, *Index to Black Periodicals*, and *The Left Index*). The inclusion of "alternative" literature helps to broaden the political, theoretical, and ideological perspectives covered in the bibliography. Also included are listings of directories and bibliographies on the topic. Most of the references were published within five years of the publication date.

409. Nordquist, Joan, comp. **African Americans, Social and Economic Conditions: A Bibliography.** Santa Cruz, Calif.: Reference and Research Services, 1992. 72p. (Contemporary Social Issues: A Bibliographic Series, No. 27). $15.00. ISBN 0-937855-52-9.

The almost 1,000 unannotated references that constitute this bibliography are arranged into five sections: race relations; social conditions; economic conditions; specific populations; and resources. "Social Conditions" is subdivided by topics such as education, health, AIDS, substance abuse, crime, and housing. Similarly, "economic conditions" includes employment and affirmative action. "Specific Populations" is subdivided by topic: male; female; male/female relations; family; children; youth; teenage pregnancy; and the aged. Within these various subtopics, entries are listed by author under categories for articles or for books/pamphlets/documents. The chapter on "resources" includes statistics sources, bibliographies, directories, and a list of organizations. Throughout, references are current, with books having been published within five years and articles within three years of the bibliography's publication date. Furthermore, as seen in the list of bibliographic sources, this bibliography includes literature from alternative sources (e.g., *The Left Index*, *Alternative Press Index*, and *Ethnic Newswatch*) and small presses. Overall, it provides easy access to a quality body of literature on the topic.

410. Stevenson, Rosemary M. **Index to Afro-American Reference Resources.** New York: Greenwood, 1988. 315p. index. (Bibliographies and Indexes in Afro-American and African Studies, No. 20). $47.95. LC 87-28028. ISBN 0-313-24580-0.

A large number of reference books on African Americans is available, including encyclopedias, bibliographies, indexes, handbooks, almanacs, biographical sources, and more. Collectively, these contain information on a variety of important topics that span the social sciences, humanities, and natural sciences. However, when researching a specific subject, the difficulty is knowing in which reference book to look. This index and bibliography solves that problem. It identifies, by subject, entries found in any of dozens of reference books on African Americans. The arrangement of this book is alphabetical by subject, with many headings also indicating the type of source (e.g., Slavery–Religion–Bibliography). Under these headings appear the titles of relevant entries and brief references to the works in which they are found. A list of cited works at the beginning of the volume provides complete bibliographic details on these sources. Author and title indexes supplement the subject arrangement of the bibliography.

Indexes, Abstracts, and Databases

411. **Index to Black Periodicals.** New York: G. K. Hall, 1988- . annual. price on request. ISSN 0899-6253.

This continues the *Index to Periodical Articles By and About Blacks*, which in turn continued some earlier titles. Approximately 40 journals focusing on African Americans are indexed, with the exact volumes and issues cited in the "List of Periodicals Indexed." Both popular (e.g., *Jet* and *Ebony*) and scholarly (e.g., *Race and Class* and *Journal of Negro Education*) journals are included. The citations themselves are arranged alphabetically in one list by either author or subject. Book, film, music, record, and theater reviews are included among the entries and are indexed by author, reviewer, and subject. The subjects covered span all of the social sciences and humanities, with many references on sociological topics, such as class and race identity, aging, health care, the production of educational inequality, families, gender, and more. Users should be aware that there is a lag of over a year between the journal articles identified and the release of this index (e.g., the 1994 index was published in 1996).

Handbooks and Yearbooks

412. Estell, Kenneth, ed. **The African-American Almanac.** 6th ed. Detroit: Gale, 1994. 1,467p. index. $160.00. ISBN 0-8103-5409-8.

Formerly *The Negro Almanac*, this award-winning book provides an excellent one-volume overview of important people, events, and historical developments in the African American experience. A total of 27 chapters is included covering a wide range of topics in history, the arts, social and economic conditions, politics, and popular culture. Of particular interest to sociologists may be the chapters on population, religion, education, the family, employment and income, the law, Black nationalism, and civil rights. The chapters make liberal use of illustrations, charts, and statistical tables. Many chapters also include historical overviews of their topic, as well as biographies of key individuals. An extensive chronology is provided, as are copies of or excerpts from significant historical documents. An appended list of African American award winners is provided, as well as a bibliography, picture and text credits, and a subject index.

413. Hornor, Louise L., ed. **Black Americans: A Statistical Sourcebook.** 1996 edition. Palo Alto, Calif.: Information Publications, 1996. 321p. $50.00. ISBN 0-929960-20-3.

The data compiled in this sourcebook are drawn from many common U. S. government document statistics sources, such as the *Statistical Abstract of the United States*, the *Digest of Education Statistics*, the *Handbook of Labor Statistics*, *Health United States*, *Employment and Earnings*, and the *Current Population Reports*. They are organized into eight subject chapters: demographics and characteristics of the population; vital statistics and health; education; government, elections, and public opinion; crime, law enforcement, and corrections; labor force, employment, and unemployment; earnings, income, poverty, and wealth; and special topics (e.g., social security and Black-owned firms). The tables of data are reasonably current, with some retrospective data included as well. Source documents are clearly cited, and descriptive notes, units of measure, and SuDoc (Superintendent of Documents) numbers are included. While many of the sources are easy to use, this work has nonetheless mined them for significant statistics and presented them in a straightforward and accessible manner. A handy glossary and subject index are also included.

414. Smith, Jessie Carney, and Carrell Peterson Horton, comps. and eds. **Historical Statistics of Black America.** New York: Gale, 1995. 2v. index. $125.00. LC 94-29718. ISBN 0-8103-8542-2(set).

The historical statistics presented here cover the eighteenth century through 1975, with the data being drawn from both government and nongovernment sources. Tables are arranged under 19 subject chapters, including sociological areas, such as crime/law enforcement/criminal justice, education, family, labor and employment, health, housing, income/spending/wealth, population, religion, and vital statistics, among others. For each of the 2,320 tables, the source document is fully cited; many of these documents could be mined more systematically on areas of special interest. While the historical coverage is this work's strength, it should be noted that the tables vary noticeably in the time periods covered. Some tables include data for just a year or two; other tables present data that span decades, making historical trends more apparent. Appended is a list of the reference sources consulted, as well as subject and year indexes.

415. **Statistical Record of Black America.** Detroit: Gale, 1990- . biennial. $109.00. ISSN 1051-8002.

Statistical information on African Americans is spread across a wide range of government and nongovernment sources. This handbook compiles data from many of those sources and reproduces them in over 1,000 tables. These tables are arranged under 19 subject categories: the arts; attitudes, values, and behavior; business and economics; crime, law enforcement, legal justice; education; family; health and medical care; housing; income, spending, and wealth; labor and employment; military affairs; miscellany; politics and elections; population; the professions; religion; social services; sports and leisure; and vital statistics. Most of these chapters include from four to over a dozen subtopics for the further categorization of the data. Many of the tables include historical data, and all fully cite the source document. The reference sources that were consulted are listed at the end of the volume. A subject index is also available.

416. Washington, Valora, and Velma LaPoint. **Black Children and American Institutions: An Ecological Review and Resource Guide.** New York: Garland, 1988. 432p. index. (Garland Reference Library of Social Science, Vol. 382; Source Books on Education, Vol. 16). $77.00. LC 88-16490. ISBN 0-8240-8517-5.

To what extent do major U.S. social institutions promote or impair the development of African American children? This is a central question that underlies this resource guide, with the major focus being on families, the economy, schools, health care institutions, the criminal justice system, and social welfare institutions. The initial six chapters provide overviews of many of these key issues and institutions and their effect on the development of African American children. These chapters are: Black children, American institutions, and human ecology; the status of Black children: developmental features and trends; Black children in educational systems; family support, public assistance, and child welfare services; the criminal justice system; and physical and mental health. Each of these chapters includes numerous subtopics. Overall, the essays focus on the issues, facts, and historical contexts of African American children's interaction with these institutions. The remaining chapters provide a directory of advocacy organizations and programs, a list of policy recommendations, and a selectively annotated bibliography (arranged by author) that comprises half of the book. An author/name index and a fairly brief subject index are included.

Dictionaries and Encyclopedias

417. Williams, Michael W., ed. **The African American Encyclopedia.** New York: Marshall Cavendish, 1993. 6v. index. $449.95. LC 93-141. ISBN 1-85435-545-7(set).

Included here are over 2,000 entries on African American history, politics, social and cultural life, business and economic life, performing arts and artists, and more. The entries, which range in length from a few paragraphs to approximately 5,000 words, include biographies, concepts, historical events, institutions and organizations, court cases, and social issues, among others. The longer entries are signed and include a bibliography of suggested readings. Sociology students may find useful overview essays on a variety of topics, including family life, health, Black nationalism, civil rights and race relations, religion, and virtually any other subtopic in the discipline. To aid access to the encyclopedia's many biographical entries, a supplementary list of people by profession is provided. A bibliography arranged by broad topical area (e.g., Black nationalism, performing arts, health, etc.) is included, as well as a subject index. Other appended materials include directories of relevant research centers and libraries; the 100 most profitable Black-owned businesses; a list of historically African American colleges and universities; and lists of African American-owned newspapers, periodicals, radio stations, and television stations. The writing is excellent throughout, making this a good starting point for those researchers new to some of these topics.

Asian Americans

Bibliographies

418. Nordquist, Joan, comp. **Asian Americans: Social, Economic and Political Aspects: A Bibliography.** Santa Cruz, Calif.: Reference and Research Services, 1996. 80p. (Contemporary Social Issues: A Bibliographic Series, No. 42). $15.00. ISBN 0-937855-82-0.

Over 800 books, pamphlets, theses, dissertations, and government documents are cited in 27 subject chapters of two general types: those focusing on sociological topics relating to Asian Americans in general; and those focusing on specific Asian American groups. The topical chapters cover such subjects as employment, education, health, substance abuse, immigration, crime, family, discrimination, the elderly, and women, among others. The chapters on groups cover Chinese Americans, Japanese Americans, Korean Americans, Indochinese Americans, Cambodian Americans, Vietnamese Americans, Hmong Americans, Laotian Americans, Filipino Americans, and Asian Indian Americans. In all chapters, the unannotated references are listed alphabetically by author. Some chapters include accompanying indexes of the entries by topic and nationality. One of the bibliography's strengths is its inclusion of many theses and dissertations. Also, as with other volumes in this series, it cites radical and alternative publications that broaden the ideological scope of the entries.

Handbooks and Yearbooks

419. **The Asian American Almanac: A Reference Work on Asians in the United States.** Susan Gall, managing ed. Detroit: Gale, 1995. 834p. index. $95.00. LC 95-8520. ISBN 0-8103-9193-7.

The distinct histories and common experiences of Asian Americans are examined through the social, political, economic, cultural, and historical circumstances that have shaped their lives. This almanac is organized into 42 chapters, 14 of which focus on distinct groups that comprise the Asian American community: Asian Indian Americans; Cambodian Americans; Chinese Americans; Filipino Americans; Hmong Americans; Indonesian Americans; Japanese Americans; Korean Americans; Laotian Americans; Nepali Americans; Pacific Islanders; Pakistani Americans; Thai Americans; and Vietnamese Americans. For each group, a lengthy essay is included discussing such issues as its history, immigration and acculturation, religion, language, education, work experiences, family life, and more. The remaining chapters of the book address topics that cut across all of the Asian American groups. These include population growth, immigration, civil rights, voting rights, the military, family, language, education, work, literature, and more. Most of these chapters are broken down by subtopics, which are often for specific groups. Other chapters include significant documents, a chronology, historic landmarks, and speeches. The text is complemented by 350 illustrations. A bibliography of recommended readings is also available, arranged by group. A keyword index provides detailed access to the entire almanac.

420. Gall, Susan B., and Timothy L. Gall, eds. **Statistical Record of Asian Americans.** Detroit: Gale, 1993. 796p. index. $105.00. ISBN 0-8103-8918-5.

The 850 data tables and graphs comprising this handbook are arranged under 14 major subject categories: attitudes and opinions; business and economics; crime, law enforcement, and civil rights; domestic life; education; employment and occupations; health; housing; immigration; income, spending, and wealth; the military; population and vital statistics; public life; and religion. These chapters are subdivided by up to 13 subtopics for the more precise location of relevant tables. The data were drawn from government and nongovernment sources. Wherever possible, the Asian/Pacific Islander category was subdivided further by nationality group. The data cover primarily the 1980s through 1991, with some tables including retrospective data to the mid-1970s. Each table fully cites its data source; many of these are ongoing publications that could be revisited for more current or additional data. The supplementary information includes a bibliography, arranged by specific group, definitions of terms used in the tables, and a subject index. Because of its broad subject coverage and diverse data sources, this is an excellent starting point for gathering sociologically relevant statistical information on Asian Americans.

421. **Reference Library of Asian America.** Susan Gall, managing ed. Detroit: Gale, 1995. 3v. ISBN 0-7876-0841-6.

Asian Americans are a diverse segment of the population, comprised of some 20 ethnic and nationality groups. These three volumes assemble a great deal of textual information on Asian Americans and supplement it with statistical data, illustrations, biographies, and more. Of the 41 chapters included here, the first 15 describe various Asian American groups, including Asian Pacific Americans, Asian Indian Americans, Cambodian Americans, Chinese Americans, Filipino Americans, Hmong Americans, Indonesian Americans, Japanese Americans, Korean Americans, Laotian Americans, Nepali Americans, Pacific Islanders, Pakistani Americans, Thai Americans, and Vietnamese Americans. These chapters are accompanied, in volume one, by a chronology of key events and excerpts of important historical documents (e.g., the Immigration Act of 1924). The chapters in the remaining volumes focus on various topics and institutions, including the family, religion, education, population, civil rights, literature, the military, women, languages, entrepreneurship, and more. Some additional chapters describe important organizations, prominent Asian Americans, historic landmarks, and more than a dozen significant speeches. A supplementary bibliography, arranged by group, is included, as is a detailed subject index that includes names, book titles, and organizations.

Dictionaries and Encyclopedias

422. Ng, Franklin, ed. **The Asian American Encyclopedia.** New York: Marshall Cavendish, 1995. 6v. index. $449.95. LC 94-33003. ISBN 1-85435-677-1.

Both the common experiences and the unique characteristics of the Asian American community are described in this multivolume set. Over 2,000 entries discuss important events, places, people, organizations, court cases, and concepts related to the Asian American experience. The entries range in length from a paragraph to 4,000 words. This textual information is complemented by portraits, maps, charts, graphs, and tables; in all, over 1,100 illustrations are included. The entries for groups focus primarily on Chinese Americans, Filipino Americans, Japanese Americans, Asian Indian Americans, Korean Americans, and Vietnamese Americans, with less coverage of groups such as the Hmong Americans and Pacific Islander Americans. The signed entries are clearly written and, for the longer essays, accompanied by suggested readings. Volume six includes a timeline, as well as directories of organizations; museums; research centers and libraries; Asian American studies programs; films and videos; and newspapers, newsletters, magazines, and journals. A bibliography arranged by both populations groups and by subjects is available; a subject list of entries is arranged similarly. Finally, the general index includes subjects, people, places, events, and other proper names or titles appearing in the entries. Entries related to women, discrimination, immigration, social movements, community studies, and the family are particularly relevant for sociology students.

Hispanic Americans, Latinos/ Latinas, Chicanos/ Chicanas, Mexican Americans

Bibliographies

423. Nordquist, Joan, comp. **Latinos in the United States, Social, Economic and Political Aspects: A Bibliography.** Santa Cruz, Calif.: Reference and Research Services, 1994. 92p. (Contemporary Social Issues: A Bibliographic Series, No. 34). $15.00. ISBN 0-937855-66-9.

The "Latinos" in this title includes Latinos/Hispanics, Mexican Americans/Chicanos, Puerto Ricans, and Cuban Americans. For these groups, 1,130 references are cited for books, documents, dissertations, theses, and periodical articles. Most items date from the last five years, though some important works produced within 10 years are included.

Entries are arranged by author under 16 subject categories and, further, by specific group and format (i.e., either books or articles). The subject categories include such areas as gangs, education, family, health, substance abuse, women, employment, AIDS, and social conditions, among others. The citations are drawn from a diverse list of indexes, abstracts, and databases, lending some theoretical and ideological variety to the sources cited. Lists of statistics sources, directories, and other bibliographies are included. In all, this is a valuable bibliography that touches on any number of sociologically interesting topics.

Indexes, Abstracts, and Databases

424. Castillo-Speed, Lillian, comp. and ed. **The Chicana Studies Index: Twenty Years of Gender Research 1971-1991.** Berkeley, Calif.: Chicano Studies Library Publications Unit, University of California at Berkeley, 1992. 427p. index. (Chicano Studies Library Publication Series, No. 18). $90.00. LC 92-10870. ISBN 0-918520-21-5.

This is an index to 1,150 unannotated references for books, book chapters, journal articles, dissertations, and reports "on all aspects of the Chicana experience" (p. i). The citations are arranged alphabetically by author under an extensive list of subject headings/ descriptors. Much of interest is here for sociologists, with subject headings on academic achievement, aging (ancianos), attitudes, cultural characteristics, mental health, family, identity, feminism, sex roles, stereotypes, working women, acculturation, employment, social classes, and more. Extensive use of cross-references from unused to preferred headings, many of which are in Spanish, is available. The sources themselves can be in English or Spanish; Spanish titles are not necessarily translated into English. Title and author indexes are also provided.

425. **Chicano Database on CD-ROM.** [CD-ROM]. Berkeley, Calif.: Chicano Studies Library Publications, University of California, 1990- . semiannual updates. ISSN 1056-2516.

Included in this CD-ROM version of the *Chicano Database* are parts of the *Chicano Periodical Index* (1967-1988), *The Chicano Index* (1989-present), *The Chicano Anthology Index*, and the *Arte Chicano: An Annotated Bibliography of Chicano Art* (1965-1981). Overall, this provides access to references dealing with the Chicano experience. Searching uses terms from the Chicano thesaurus, which is part of the database.

426. **Hispanic American Periodicals Index.** Los Angeles: UCLA Latin American Center, University of California Los Angeles, 1970/74- . annual. $385.00/yr. ISSN 0270-8558.

This provides author, subject, and book review indexing to articles from approximately 250 journals dealing with Latin America, Hispanics in the United States, and the United States-Mexico border region. The subject headings are primarily in English, except for proper names and untranslatable concepts. However, two introductory sections translate the main subject headings into Spanish and Portuguese. Article citations are presented in their original language. The journals covered span the social sciences and humanities, and important sociological concepts are indexed. These include the family, sex roles, population, cultural identity, social change, social classes, old age, religion, educational sociology, mobility, and many more. This index is also available on CD-ROM from the National Information Services Corporation.

Handbooks and Yearbooks

427. **Handbook of Hispanic Cultures in the United States.** Nicolas Kanellos and Claudio Esteva-Fabregat, general eds. Houston: Arte Publico Press; Madrid: Instituto de Cooperacion Iberoamericana, 1993-1994. 4v. index. $240.00. LC 93-13348.

These four volumes focus on four major aspects of Hispanic communities in the United States: history, anthropology, sociology, and literature and art. Each volume consists of lengthy essays, written by experts, that provide overviews of a variety of topics in that subject area. The "Sociology" volume contains broad essays on the topics of immigration, the labor market, politics, education, families, women and feminism, religion, identity, newspapers, and mass communication. Within these topics, sections are often devoted to specific populations, such as Mexican Americans, Cuban Americans, and Puerto Ricans. Throughout, the emphasis is on structural or institutional explanations for the "Hispanic experience" (p. 14). Every essay is accompanied by a bibliography of works cited. Tables of data are included in some essays, with their source documents noted. Each volume includes its own subject index. Overall, the essays are detailed and well written, and should be appropriate for students, faculty, and other interested researchers.

428. **Hispanic Americans: A Statistical Sourcebook.** Palo Alto, Calif.: Information Publications, 1991- . annual. $50.00. ISSN 1056-7992.

Like its companion volume, *Black Americans: A Statistical Sourcebook*, this volume draws its statistics on Hispanic Americans from U.S. government documents. Specifically, it has consulted such works as *Employment and Earnings*, *Current Population Reports*, *Health United States*, *Statistical Abstract of the United States*, *Digest of Education Statistics*, the *Handbook of Labor Statistics*, and *The Hispanic Population in the United States*, among others. The tables of data are arranged into chapters covering such topics as demographics; social characteristics; household and family characteristics; education; government and elections; labor force, employment, and unemployment; earnings, income, poverty, and wealth; crime and corrections; and special topics (e.g., AIDS and housing). While most tables use only "Hispanic" as a category, some include categories for Mexican, Puerto Rican, Cuban, Central/South American, and other Hispanic. Source documents for all tables are cited, and explanatory notes and units of measure are included as well. A supplementary glossary defines many key terms encountered in the tables and their data categories.

429. **Hispanic Databook of U.S. Cities and Counties.** Milpitas, Calif.: Toucan Valley Publications, 1994. 555p. $56.00. ISBN 1-884925-00-6.

As statistical sourcebooks go, this one's strength is its geographical breakdown of the data. Its source is the *Census of Population and Housing, 1990: Summary Tape Files 3B and 3C*, from which it lists data for states, cities with populations over 10,000, counties, and zip codes (for cities with populations over 100,000). The hierarchical arrangement is alphabetical by state, then counties, then cities within counties, then zip codes within large cities. While this organizational scheme can be useful, the range of data presented is limited. Data categories include total population, percent Hispanic, percent speaking Spanish, percent speaking only Spanish, per capita income, percent high school graduates, and the percent reporting that they are Mexican, Puerto Rican, Cuban, Dominican, Central American, South American, or other. A supplementary city finder list that locates cities by their page number is included. An introductory table ranks the states by their percentage of population that is of Hispanic origin.

430. Kanellos, Nicolas. **The Hispanic Almanac: From Columbus to Corporate America.** Detroit: Visible Ink Press, 1994. 644p. index. $16.95. ISBN 0-7876-0030-X.

This is an abridged edition of *The Hispanic-American Almanac* (see entry #431).

431. Kanellos, Nicolas. **The Hispanic-American Almanac: A Reference Work on Hispanics in the United States.** Detroit: Gale, 1993. 780p. index. LC 92-075003. ISBN 0-8103-7944-9.

Intended for students and general readers, this provides an excellent introduction to Hispanic Americans' history, culture, and social conditions. A total of 25 chapters is included, written by experts, focusing on history, the arts, language, literature, media, population growth, law and politics, education, religion, labor and employment, women, the family, and more. The essays are complemented by over 400 illustrations and, in some cases, historical documents. Many of the chapters, not just those that are historical, provide a historical overview of the development of their topics. Chapters include references for further reading. A glossary, a general bibliography, and a keyword index are also included. Sociology students will find these essays useful introductions to key areas like the family, education, women, religion, and work. This book has been repackaged in *The Hispanic Almanac* (see entry #430). A second edition (1996) is now available.

432. Schick, Frank L., and Renee Schick, comps. and eds. **Statistical Handbook on U.S. Hispanics.** Phoenix: Oryx Press, 1991. 255p. index. $49.50. LC 90-48167. ISBN 0-89774-554-X.

This is a collection of over 300 tables, charts, graphs, and diagrams of statistical data on Hispanic Americans. Data were drawn from government (primarily *Census*) and nongovernment sources, with the restriction that "information based entirely on pre-1985 data is not included" (p. xv). While reasonably current, many of the tables also include retrospective data extending back a number of decades. The tables are organized under eight subjects: demographics, immigration and naturalization, social characteristics, education, health, politics, labor force, and economic conditions. Each of these, in turn, has from two to five subtopics, with multiple tables or charts presenting relevant statistics. The source documents for each table are fully cited in the back of the volume. A subject index and a glossary of key terms are also included. This book's strengths are the variety of topics covered, the nice layout of the data, and the inclusion of some retrospective statistics. However, it does not include data from or since the 1990 *Census*, as do some of the more current statistical sourcebooks.

433. **Statistical Record of Hispanic Americans.** Detroit: Gale, 1993- . biennial. $105.00. ISSN 1082-0507.

Approximately 900 tables of statistical data profiling Hispanic Americans are included in this source. The tables are arranged into major chapters for demographics, the family, education, culture, health and health care, social and economic conditions, business and industry, government and politics, and law enforcement. These chapters have a few subtopics as well. The "family" includes characteristics, child care, divorce, income, and marriage; "social and economic conditions" includes poverty, homelessness, support networks, employment, income, housing, and public assistance. These data are assembled from both government and, to a lesser extent, nongovernment sources. Many of the tables include retrospective data to the 1970s. Most tables specify only Hispanic as a category, though some also include Mexican, Puerto Rican, Cuban, Central or South American, or Other Hispanic. The data sources are noted both with the table and in an appended source list. An extensive keyword index that includes subjects, names, geographic entities, and organizations is also included.

Native Americans

Guides

434. Klein, Barry T. **Reference Encyclopedia of the American Indian.** 7th ed. West Nyack, N.Y.: Todd Publications, 1995. 883p. index. $125.00. ISBN 0-915344-45-9.

Included here are thousands of reference and information sources for those researching Native Americans in the United States and Canada. The materials are divided into four sections. Section one, the largest, contains directories or lists on such topics as federally recognized tribes, reservations, government agencies, regional or state organizations, college courses and programs, financial aid, health services, libraries and research centers, communications, audiovisual aids, and periodicals, among others. Complete addresses and phone numbers are provided where appropriate. Section two focuses exclusively on Canada and has listings of reserves and bands, national and regional associations, museums, libraries, periodicals, colleges, and communications. Section three is a bibliography of 4,500 books that is arranged alphabetically by title. Each entry includes a complete bibliographic citation; most include prices, and some include brief descriptions. These titles are listed again in a subject section that includes topics and tribes. An alphabetical directory of publishers completes this section. Section four is a collection of 2,500 biographies, accompanied by a name index.

Bibliographies

435. Bataille, Gretchen M., and Kathleen M. Sands. **American Indian Women: A Guide to Research.** New York: Garland, 1991. 423p. index. (Women's History and Culture, Vol. 4; Garland Reference Library of Social Science, Vol. 515). LC 91-2961. ISBN 0-8240-4799-0.

According to Bataille and Sands, Native American women have historically been understudied, particularly in terms of scholarly research. Traditionally, the focus has been on men, with women stereotypically portrayed as either "princesses" or "squaws." This bibliography is intended to remedy the above biases and oversights. It has 1,573 multidisciplinary entries for books, book chapters, articles, government documents, and reports, some dating back to the turn of the century. The focus is on North American Indian women, including women in Canada; excluded are works on Indians of Mexico or Central and South America, popular fiction, travel journals, dissertations, conference papers, and book reviews. The arrangement of the entries is alphabetical by author within eight subject chapters: bibliographies and reference works; ethnography, cultural history, and social roles; politics and law; health, education, and employment; visual and performing arts; literature and criticism; autobiography, biography, and interviews; and film and video. All entries include annotations ranging from a sentence to a paragraph. Though these are mostly descriptive, some critical or evaluative comments are sometimes included to indicate an item that is not suitable for research purposes. Plenty is available here for any number of sociological specialties. The index covers subjects, names, tribes, and periods.

436. Hoxie, Frederick E., and Harvey Markowitz. **Native Americans: An Annotated Bibliography.** Pasadena, Calif.: Salem Press, 1991. 325p. index. LC 91-16427. ISBN 0-89356-670-5.

Focusing on books and selective articles published in the last 25 years, this bibliography identifies approximately 1,000 sources on the history, culture, and social life of Native Americans. The citations are arranged by author within four broad sections, with numerous subsections of sociological interest. The first section covers general studies and reference works, with general studies comprised of works spanning more than one culture area or time period. The second section focuses on historical works, with subsections on the Colonial period, the United States from 1776–1990, and Canada from 1776–1990. The third section covers the eight different culture areas identified by the Smithsonian Institution (e.g., Northeast, Plains, and Great Basin). For each, typical subtopics include folklore, religious beliefs, family and society, material culture, and tribal life, among others. Section four covers social issues related to contemporary life, including family, religion, health and alcoholism, education, images and self-identity, urban Indians, and more. All entries are descriptively annotated. An author index is included.

Handbooks and Yearbooks

437. Reddy, Marlita A., ed. **Statistical Record of Native North Americans.** 2d ed. Detroit: Gale, 1995. 1,272p. index. $105.00. ISBN 0-8103-6421-2.

A total of 1,007 tables of historical and current data on Native Americans is included in this statistical compilation. The data are drawn from both government and nongovernment sources and are arranged into 12 chapters, including such important sociological areas as demographics, the family, education, culture and tradition, health and health care, social and economic conditions, and law and law enforcement. These chapters do group the tables by a modest number of subtopics. A separate "History" chapter that includes data and estimates extending back decades and even centuries is included. However, historical data for more recent decades are also found in other chapters. Data for specific tribes, as well as for other racial or ethnic groups, are included throughout this source. The final chapter includes Canadian data, with subtopics corresponding to the other major chapter topics. Source documents are cited with each table and in a supplementary listing. An extensive keyword index includes subjects, names, tribes, organizations, and places.

RESEARCH METHODS AND STATISTICS

Guides

438. Weitzman, Eben A., and Matthew B. Miles. **Computer Programs for Qualitative Data Analysis: A Software Sourcebook.** Thousand Oaks, Calif.: Sage, 1995. 369p. index. $65.00. LC 94-40467. ISBN 0-8039-5536-7.

According to the authors, the last 10 years have seen a stunning growth in the availability of PC-based software for the analysis of qualitative data. This volume is designed to review the features and functionality of the currently available programs, and to discuss some of the issues involved in selecting the most appropriate program for one's research needs and data. The book is divided into three parts. Part one addresses the basic required questions in choosing software. It also provides an overview of the various software types and functions. Part two contains software reviews for more than two dozen programs, arranged according to five categories: text retrievers; textbase managers; code-and-retrieve programs; code-based theory-builders; and conceptual network-builders. For each program, information on a variety of characteristics is available: price and availability, hardware requirements, overview, database structure, data entry, working on the data, output, searching, user friendliness, and more. Sample screens are also reproduced to indicate the features and look of the software interface. A sixth chapter provides a matrix for comparing the programs. Part three includes the authors' reflections, researcher needs, and expectations for development. An appended directory of program developers and distributors is included, as well as a glossary, annotated references, other references, and a name/subject index that includes programs.

Bibliographies

439. Bausell, R. Barker. **Advanced Research Methodology: An Annotated Guide to Sources.** Metuchen, N.J.: Scarecrow, 1991. 903p. index. $84.50. LC 91-16135. ISBN 0-8108-2355-1.

Intended for "serious, practical researchers" (p. vii) in all of the social and behavioral sciences, this work identifies and annotates 2,660 books and articles on the research process. The entries are divided into three major parts and 78 topical categories addressing various issues, methods, and techniques in conducting research. Part one covers research methods and procedures and includes 24 chapters on literature reviewing, research design (e.g., experimental design, sampling, assigning subjects to groups, and response rate), types of research (e.g., survey, secondary analysis, qualitative), and related issues (e.g., fraud, informed consent, ethics, grantsmanship). Part two, on psychometrics, has 24 chapters relating to theory, reliability theory, validity, instrument selection, and instrument use. Part three focuses on statistical analysis. Its 30 chapters address the broad topics of univariate procedures, causal modeling, multivariate procedures, and specific data analysis. Within every chapter, books and articles are listed separately and arranged alphabetically by author. All entries are accompanied by paragraph-long, well-written descriptive annotations. Author and subject indexes provide additional access.

440. Huttner, Harry J. M., and Pieter van den Eeden. **The Multilevel Design: A Guide with an Annotated Bibliography, 1980-1993.** Westport, Conn.: Greenwood, 1995. 276p. index. (Bibliographies and Indexes in Sociology, No. 23). $69.50. LC 94-36760. ISBN 0-313-27310-3.

For researchers interested in multilevel research design, this volume includes both an overview of that method and a substantial annotated bibliography of 589 books and articles. The first six chapters address various aspects of the design: principles, multilevel theories and their explanations of contextual effects, the multilevel design, interpretation of an analytical group characteristic, multilevel design in evaluation research, and further developments of multilevel research. References in the bibliography are arranged by author under eight subject categories. The first two categories cover theoretical and methodological issues. Five chapters address applications in the areas of educational research, voting behavior, deviant behavior and healthcare, organizations, and spatial contexts. A final chapter covers miscellaneous items that had an insufficient number of entries to form distinct chapters. The paragraph-long abstracts are all in English, though some of the sources are in other languages (primarily Dutch and German). Author, title, and subject indexes are provided.

441. **ICPSR Summer Program in Quantitative Methods: 1995 Bibliography.** Ann Arbor, Mich.: Inter-university Consortium for Political and Social Research, 1996. 314p. free(members).

Each Summer, the Inter-university Consortium for Political and Social Research (ICPSR) offers courses and workshops in quantitative research methods and techniques. This book includes the outlines for these courses, as well as bibliographies of required and supplementary readings. Therefore, it should be useful for those interested in reading about particular techniques, as well as for those wanting to register for a course. These courses, offered by experts from U.S. and Canadian universities, are intended to provide state-of-the-art information on approximately 40 topics. These include regression analysis, LISREL, Logit and Log-Linear models, nonlinear systems, social network analysis, time series analysis, and nonparametric regression, among others. Classes focusing on quantitative research in particular subject areas, such as criminal justice, health, mental health, historical analysis, and Latin America, are also available. The 1996 edition of this bibliography, and very likely future editions, will only be available on the ICPSR Website (http://www.icpsr.umich.edu).

Dictionaries and Encyclopedias

442. Vogt, W. Paul. **Dictionary of Statistics and Methodology: A Nontechnical Guide for the Social Sciences.** Newbury Park, Calif.: Sage, 1993. 253p. $46.00. LC 93-728. ISBN 0-8039-5276-7.

The terminology used in social science statistical and methodological discussions can be intimidating. Knowing that, this author has assembled fairly readable definitions of key statistical and methodological terms. The focus here, as the author points out, is on explaining concepts, not equations. Jargon is kept to a minimum in the definitions themselves, though it is not entirely avoidable. When definitions use words defined elsewhere in the dictionary, those words are marked with an asterisk. Another nice feature of the dictionary is its use of examples. These greatly clarify definitions that, though well written, may not have been fully understood. This is an excellent and helpful dictionary from a well-known and respected publisher of monographs and book series on social science research methods and statistics.

World Wide Web/Internet Sites

443. **Software and Datasets for Sociology and Demography.**
Available: http://www.stat.washington.edu/raftery/Research/Soc/soc_software.html
(Accessed: February 11, 1997).

Included here are five software programs for conducting certain kinds of statistical analysis. These are available for free for educational use; they may also be shared for this purpose. Also available are two datasets: Irish educational transition data; and social mobility data.

RURAL SOCIOLOGY

Bibliographies

444. Berndt, Judy. **Rural Sociology: A Bibliography of Bibliographies.** Metuchen, N.J.: Scarecrow, 1986. 176p. index. $20.00. LC 85-26070. ISBN 0-8108-1860-4.

Though now a bit dated, this source lists "and annotates all English language bibliographies in rural sociology published separately since 1970" (p. vii). The entries are arranged into 15 subject sections covering the aged, crime, development, education, general, health, housing, irrigation, labor/industry, land tenure and use, migration, nomadism, peasantry, transportation, women, and youth. The citations are drawn from books, book chapters, articles, ERIC documents, and other sources. Most entries are annotated, with some of these annotations taken from the author's introduction or the abstracting source (e.g., ERIC). Additional access to the citations is provided by name, title, and geographical indexes.

445. Larson, Olaf F., Edward O. Moe, and Julie N. Zimmerman, eds. **Sociology in Government: A Bibliography of the Work of the Division of Farm Population and Rural Life, U.S. Department of Agriculture, 1919-1953.** Boulder, Colo.: Westview Press, 1992. 301p. index. LC 92-2514. ISBN 0-8133-8529-6.

As pointed out in the introduction, the Department of Agriculture's Division of Farm Population and Rural Life was a significant source of sociological research from 1919–1953. The rural sociologists engaged in research on families, health, population and demography, social groups, social organizations, and communities. This bibliography is a guide to that body of literature, both published and unpublished. Entries are arranged chronologically within categories for the type of source. These include bibliographies and reference lists, books, Congressional testimony and reports, research publications (the largest category), restricted use reports and manuscripts, unpublished addresses, and periodic publications issued by the division. Though unannotated, the citations do include a series of keywords indicating the subject, groups, and geographic entity studied. These are fully indexed in the substantive area (i.e., subject), ethnic-cultural group, and geographic indexes. This is an important historical guide to pioneering research in rural sociology and methodological techniques. A 1997 edition, with a slightly different title, is forthcoming from the same publisher.

Indexes, Abstracts, and Databases

446. **World Agricultural Economics and Rural Sociology Abstracts.** Vol. 1- , No. 1- . Oxford, England: Commonwealth Bureau of Agricultural Economics; distr., New York: UNIPUB, 1959- . monthly. $725.00/yr. ISSN 0043-8219.

While the bulk of this source's entries are on agricultural economics, a section in each issue is provided on rural sociology. This includes articles, books, book chapters, and reports on such topics as demography, stratification, rural communities, conflict and political movements, rural families, and more. Few rural sociology entries are included per issue, but they are international in coverage. Copies of cited documents can be obtained through a photocopy service. Besides the topical arrangement of the abstracts, access is provided by author and subject/geographical indexes, which annually cumulate.

World Wide Web/Internet Sites

447. **Urban and Rural Sociology.**
Available: http://www.pcsw.uva.nl/sociosite/TOPICS/City.html#RURAL
(Accessed: February 11, 1997).

The subsection here on rural sociology provides links to the Center for Rural Studies at the University of Vermont, the Rural History Center, and *Rural Society*, a "quarterly journal of rural social issues" (Web page).

SOCIAL CHANGE, MOVEMENTS, AND COLLECTIVE BEHAVIOR

Bibliographies

448. Wallace, Steven P., and John B. Williamson, with Rita Gaston Lung. **The Senior Movement: References and Resources.** New York: G.K. Hall, 1992. 204p. index. (Reference Publications on American Social Movements). $45.00. LC 91-40851. ISBN 0-8161-1841-8.

Sociologists of social movements, as well as gerontologists and policy sociologists, should find this annotated bibliography most beneficial. It cites approximately 857 books and articles dealing with the senior movement as a social movement. References are divided into four chapters. Chapter one includes general works. Chapter two focuses on the movement, with specific subsections on leaders, organizations, advocacy, electoral strategy and behavior, and other political strategies. Chapter three focuses on the issues, with subsections on public policies and government, social security, pensions and poverty, health care, ageism, intergenerational conflict, and the legal system. Chapter four includes reference sources for research and advocacy. An appendix lists addresses and missions of advocacy organizations. An excellent introduction that discusses the senior movement in historical perspective and as a social movement is included. Author and subject indexes are also provided, though the latter needs subheadings under some of the larger topics (e.g., poverty, history, Medicare, and Social Security).

World Wide Web/Internet Sites

449. **Section on Collective Behavior and Social Movements.**
Available: http://www.ssc.wisc.edu/~myers/cbsm/
(Accessed: December 31, 1996).

This is the World Wide Web site for one of the American Sociological Association's interest groups. Among other things, one can learn how to join, find a directory of members and officers, obtain a copy of the by-laws, and see the current contents of the newsletter, *Critical Mass Bulletin*. Also included are teaching resources, links to sociology department Web pages, links to sociology associations worldwide, and announcements of upcoming meetings and special journal issues, among other items.

SOCIAL INDICATORS

Handbooks and Yearbooks

450. **The Economist Book of Vital World Statistics.** New York: Times Books/Random House, 1990. 254p. (Economist Books). $35.00. LC 90-33986. ISBN 0-8129-1877-0.

Focusing on social and economic development, this volume presents data on approximately 200 countries. Though data cover only through the late 1980s, a number of important social measures are treated. These include education, health, family life, demography, poverty and inequality, religion, crime, and employment. A number of tables and graphs is provided for each of these areas, giving one a useful comparative picture of social conditions and development in various countries. An equally large number of tables provide various indicators of economic development. Topics here include economic strength, agriculture, trade, inflation, industry and energy, commodities, transport and communications, government finance, and debt. Overall, this provides quick and readable, albeit somewhat dated, comparative information on social and economic development.

451. Hauchler, Ingomar, and Paul M. Kennedy, eds. **Global Trends: The World Almanac of Development and Peace.** New York: Continuum, 1994. 416p. index. $39.50. ISBN 0-8264-0674-2.

Unlike many other books on social and economic development, this one is more closely focused on the various social consequences of development. Its data and analyses are divided into seven chapters focusing on world development, world order, world society, world peace, world economy, world ecology, and world culture. Each chapter treats specific subtopics. For example, "world society" encompasses living conditions (e.g., poverty and distribution of wealth), social development (e.g., education), political human rights, populations, and migration. Tables and charts are explained and elaborated upon by well-written text. Throughout, the emphasis of the volume is on the growing interdependence of the world and the promises and perils of social indicators in some of these areas of development. Appended are country statistics, world maps of poverty, a bibliography, and a subject index.

452. O'Donnell, Timothy S., et al. **World Quality of Life Indicators.** 2d ed. Santa Barbara, Calif.: ABC-CLIO, 1991. 199p. $40.00. ISBN 0-87436-657-7.

This could be a useful source for beginning sociology students looking for social data on a variety of countries, or for those doing some rudimentary statistical analysis. Included here are comparative statistics on 171 countries arranged alphabetically by their "familiar" names. The entries include such data categories as population, vital statistics, health care, ethnic composition, religion, the economy, and education. Within these categories, a number of subcategories of data can be available. For example, "vital statistics" includes average life expectancy, male and female life expectancy, age distribution, median age, maternal mortality, and infant mortality. While no analysis of the meaning of these data is provided, the same categories are included for all countries.

453. **Social Indicators of Development 1996.** Baltimore: Johns Hopkins University Press, 1995. 397p. $26.95. ISBN 0-8018-5274-9. ISSN 1012-8026.

Sponsored by the World Bank, this 1996 edition focuses on poverty, its indicators and characteristics, and efforts toward its elimination. Covering almost 200 countries, data tables on each country include three different time periods and contain poverty-related measures as well as "underlying economic variables" (p. vii). Specifically, indicators fall under categories for poverty, short-term income, social indicators (e.g., life expectancy, expenditures on social services, and infant mortality), human resources, natural resources, income (household), expenditure (food, housing, etc.), and investment in human capital (health and education). Each of these categories has numerous, specific subcategories of data. Some supplementary tables provide comparative data on the social and economic conditions of over 100 of the countries, covering such categories as the illiteracy rate, malnutrition, primary school enrollment rate, GNP per capita, infant mortality, and share of agriculture in GDP. This is the last print edition of this source, though it will be available in the future on diskette, with time-series data covering 25 years.

Dictionaries and Encyclopedias

454. Welsh, Brian W. W., and Pavel Butorin, eds. **Dictionary of Development: Third World Economy, Environment, Society.** New York: Garland, 1990. 2v. (Garland Reference Library of Social Science, Vol. 487). $150.00. LC 90-3051. ISBN 0-8240-1447-2.

The focus here is on social and economic development in the developing world or Third World. Included are descriptions and definitions of concepts and worldwide organizations relating to development. Entries can range from a paragraph to a page in length and are often accompanied by bibliographic references. Many of the social aspects of development may interest sociologists, in particular, the entries on demography, aging, homelessness, health, poverty, ethnicity, family planning, women, population growth, child labor, social welfare, and many more. This source's large amount of information on other countries more easily facilitates a comparative focus. Additionally, the extensive number of entries on organizations, with addresses, aids further research. The dictionary also uses numerous *see* references to direct the user from unused names or acronyms to preferred ones. An introductory section ("Developing Country Indicators") lists basic data on countries, arranged by region and name. Appended is an extensive list of relevant periodicals, with addresses, under 16 broad subject categories.

SOCIAL PROBLEMS

Alcoholism and Drug Abuse

Bibliographies

455. Barnes, Grace M., and Diane K. Augustino, comps. **Alcohol and the Family: A Comprehensive Bibliography.** New York: Greenwood, 1987. 461p. index. (Bibliographies and Indexes in Sociology, No. 9). $69.50. LC 86-27112. ISBN 0-313-24782-X.

The possible causes of alcoholism are many, but high on the list should be the organization and functioning of the family. Specifically, this includes such processes as childhood socialization, parental role modeling, marital interactions, family violence, and more. The relation of these and other family variables to alcoholism are the focus of this bibliography. Almost 6,500 references to books, articles, papers, chapters, and dissertations are included. Most are in English, though some foreign language sources, with titles translated into English, are cited as well. References are arranged alphabetically by author or, lacking an author, by title. An introductory chapter outlines some of the types of family-related research that has been conducted on the causes of alcoholism. A subject index that is useful for more specific terms is included. However, many of the broader terms make no use of subheadings and can include hundreds of reference numbers. In other respects, this is a useful retrospective bibliography covering the twentieth century up to the mid-1980s.

456. Lobb, Michael L., and Thomas D. Watts. **Native American Youth and Alcohol: An Annotated Bibliography.** New York: Greenwood, 1989. 165p. index. (Bibliographies and Indexes in Sociology, No. 16). $55.00. LC 88-32345. ISBN 0-313-25618-7.

Intended for researchers, human service professionals, and tribal leaders, this bibliography focuses on the various causes and consequences of alcohol abuse among Native American youth, aged 15 to 24. While the approximately 400 references draw from a range of social science disciplines, there is a distinct sociological focus to the topics covered and sources cited. Books, chapters, articles, reports, conference papers, dissertations, and government documents are listed by author under 11 subject chapters: accidental death, biomedical factors, crime, etiology, gender, policy and prevention, reservations, sociological factors, suicide, treatment, and urban versus rural. The descriptive abstracts range in length from a few sentences to a paragraph. An introduction and review of the literature that provides a detailed overview of the key topics in the bibliography is available. Author and subject indexes are included.

457. Miletich, John J., comp. **Treatment of Cocaine Abuse: An Annotated Bibliography.** Westport, Conn.: Greenwood, 1992. 234p. index. (Bibliographies and Indexes in Medical Studies, No. 9). $55.00. LC 91-35403. ISBN 0-313-27839-3.

The well-publicized abuse of cocaine and crack in the United States raises a host of public policy and public health questions, not the least of which concern the physiological correlates, effects, and treatment of cocaine abuse. This bibliography annotates over 600 books, book chapters, articles, dissertations, government documents, and other items on these and related aspects of cocaine abuse. Its scholarly and popular entries, which span the late nineteenth and twentieth centuries, are intended to be of use to sociologists, psychologists, nurses, lawyers, chemists, librarians, and interested laypersons.

Entries are arranged into four large chapters: "Definitions, Identification, Diagnosis"; "Treatment"; "Specific Occupations"; and "Women and Children." Within these sections, arrangement is alphabetical by author or, lacking this, by title. The annotations are descriptive and range in length from a sentence to a paragraph; they also often indicate the number of tables, figures, and footnotes or references in articles. The book also includes a list of acronyms, as well as appendixes for various names for cocaine, relevant videocassettes, and a cocaine time line. Author and subject indexes are also provided. The title is a bit misleading in that much more than treatment issues are addressed. This bibliography should be of most use to medical sociologists, policy sociologists, and sociologists of work.

458. Nordquist, Joan, comp. **Substance Abuse I: Drug Abuse: A Bibliography.** Santa Cruz, Calif.: Reference and Research Services, 1989. 68p. $15.00. ISBN 0-937855-31-6.

Policy sociologists, medical sociologists, and criminologists, among others, may find useful material in this interdisciplinary bibliography. Over 500 books, book chapters, journal articles, government documents, and pamphlets are cited within eight subject chapters. These chapters address general works, specific populations (women, minorities, youth, elderly), crime, the workplace, AIDS, treatment, legal aspects, and the war on drugs (including policy and prevention). Within these chapters, references are divided into sections for books or articles, then arranged alphabetically by author. References generally date from the 1980s, with articles dating primarily from the late 1980s. A final chapter lists reference resources, including other bibliographies, directories and guides, statistics sources, and organizations.

459. Page, Penny Booth. **Alcohol Use and Alcoholism: A Guide to the Literature.** New York: Garland, 1986. 164p. index. (Garland Reference Library of Social Science, Vol. 350). LC 83-49073. ISBN 0-8240-9020-9.

Though not intended for researchers, this bibliography should be useful for students researching alcohol use/abuse and its consequences. It is targeted at not only general readers, but also counselors, social service workers, and health professionals, among others. Included are 405 annotated references to books, pamphlets, and government documents; audiovisual materials and journal articles are excluded. Most entries were published between the mid-1970s and 1985. References are arranged alphabetically by author within 16 subject chapters, covering such topics as the history of alcohol use/abuse, alcoholism, treatment, children of alcoholics, alcohol use among women, alcohol use among youth, problems in industry, education and prevention, legal and social issues, and more. The descriptive annotations, which range from a few sentences to a paragraph, often indicate the target audience for the source. Most chapters include cross-references to related sources found elsewhere in the bibliography. Appendixes for alcohol-related periodicals and resource organizations are provided. Author and title indexes are included.

460. Page, Penny Booth. **Children of Alcoholics: A Sourcebook.** New York: Garland, 1991. 249p. index. (Garland Reference Library of Social Science, Vol. 461). $40.00. LC 91-19611. ISBN 0-8240-3045-1.

The last 25 years have seen a growing interest in the effects on young and adult children of growing up in an alcoholic family. Both children of alcoholics and those who work with, study or treat them should find useful items in this annotated bibliography. It includes 347 references to books, monographs, and articles published from 1969 through early 1990, though the articles are concentrated since 1985. The bibliography is organized into two major parts: children of alcoholics; and adult children of alcoholics. "Children of Alcoholics" includes subtopics for general reference works, research, family issues, treatment, recovery, and fiction. Part two, on adult children of alcoholics, has subtopics for research, family issues, treatment, recovery, and fiction. Within each of these sections, references are arranged by author under categories for books and articles. The paragraph-long descriptive abstracts are well-written and detailed. Cross-references to related entries are located at the end of chapters. Appended are directories of resource organizations, audiovisual review sources and producers/distributors, and relevant periodicals. Author, title, and subject indexes are included, as is a publisher listing. While only a fraction of the items here are research-oriented, the anecdotal and autobiographical sources do provide compelling descriptions of the problem.

461. Rebach, Howard M., et al. **Substance Abuse Among Ethnic Minorities in America: A Critical Annotated Bibliography.** New York: Garland, 1992. 469p. index. (Garland Library of Sociology, Vol. 20; Garland Reference Library of Social Science, Vol. 737). $76.00. LC 91-45032. ISBN 0-8153-0066-2.

Intended primarily for social and behavioral science researchers, this bibliography cites and thoroughly annotates 168 articles on substance abuse among ethnic minorities.

While most of the sources cited are empirical research articles, some literature reviews and case histories are also included. To be included, articles had to have appeared in refereed journals and to have been published from 1980 onward. Furthermore, racial or ethnic minorities had to be a major focus of the article, not just an incidental variable. The primary racial and ethnic groups in focus are African Americans, American Indians/Alaska Natives, Hispanics, and Asians and Pacific Islanders. Entries are arranged alphabetically by the primary author. Each reference receives a detailed, three- to four-page annotation that describes the type, purpose, background, methodology, and results of the study. A general discussion of the research and its critical evaluation provided by the bibliography's compilers are included. An introductory table lists, for each article, the ethnic group, age group, topic, and substance studied. Supplementary material includes lists of periodicals and references, as well as an author index. The thoroughness of the abstracts, along with the brief introduction, makes this an excellent, state-of-the-art literature review.

462. Watts, Thomas D., and Roosevelt Wright, Jr. **Black Alcohol Abuse and Alcoholism: An Annotated Bibliography.** New York: Praeger, 1986. 265p. index. $65.00. LC 85-28245. ISBN 0-275-92083-6.

According to the bibliography's compilers, alcoholism among African Americans has been understudied. This annotated bibliography is an attempt to bring together from a variety of disciplines all of the relevant research on this topic. It includes references and paragraph-long annotations to 553 books, articles, dissertations, reports, and papers dealing with alcoholism in the African American community. The entries are arranged chronologically, spanning 1943 through 1985. Within a particular year, their arrangement is alphabetical by author. Most of the references are concentrated in the late 1970s to 1985, reflecting a growth in interest in and research on the topic. Appended is a list of national alcoholism-related organizations, as well as a state-by-state directory of alcoholism programs. A combined index that includes authors, minority populations, cities, agencies, and tests is provided.

Handbooks and Yearbooks

463. Woods, Geraldine. **Drug Abuse in Society: A Reference Handbook.** Santa Barbara, Calif.: ABC-CLIO, 1993. 269p. index. (Contemporary World Issues). $39.50. LC 93-11858. ISBN 0-87436-720-4.

Unemployment, hopelessness and alienation, family dysfunction, and a host of other factors can be involved in the explanation of drug abuse, a problem that cuts across racial, ethnic, gender, and class boundaries. This handbook provides a wide-ranging description of the extent and changing nature of drug abuse and its many consequences.

The book is arranged into seven chapters covering various aspects of and sources on drug abuse. Chapter one presents an essay overview of drug abuse, relating it to such subtopics as health, crime, sports, pregnancy, legalization, homelessness, the workplace, drug testing, the international drug trade, and treatment and prevention. Chapters two, three, and four provide a chronology of drug abuse, biographical sketches of important individuals, and statistics and key documents, respectively. The key documents include the drug policies of major sports, recent presidential policy speeches, and a speech arguing for the legalization and decriminalization of drugs. Chapter five provides a directory of governmental and private drug abuse-related agencies and organizations, while chapters six and seven are annotated bibliographies of print and nonprint sources of information. A glossary of key terms and a combined name/subject/title index are also included.

Dictionaries and Encyclopedias

464. **Encyclopedia of Drugs and Alcohol.** Jerome H. Jaffe, ed.-in-chief. New York: Macmillan, 1995. 4v. index. $290.00. LC 95-2321. ISBN 0-02-897185-X.

Intended as a "comprehensive source" on substance use and abuse, this set includes approximately 500 signed essays discussing topics related to pharmacology and epidemiology, treatment, prevention, policy, and law enforcement. The well-written essays range from one to ten pages long and include bibliographic references and cross-references to other terms; some are also supplemented with tables, charts, diagrams, or graphs. The last volume includes five appendixes: a list of poison control centers for drug overdoses; a U.S. and state government drug resources directory; a directory of drug abuse and alcoholism treatment and prevention programs (by state and city); a Bureau of Justice Statistics overview of how the government combats illegal drugs; and schedules of controlled drugs. A supplementary subject index is provided. Overall, nonspecialists interested in policy, social support, and addiction should find these essays a useful starting point for further research.

465. O'Brien, Robert, et al. **The Encyclopedia of Drug Abuse.** 2d ed. New York: Facts on File, 1992. 500p. index. $45.00. LC 89-71531. ISBN 0-8160-1956-8.

This represents an expanded, revised, and updated edition of the authors' earlier (1984) work. Its entries address a variety of causes and effects of drug abuse, including medical, physical, legal, psychological, and political factors. It is intended both for general readers and professionals, and its entries make minimal use of jargon, except where unavoidable. Drug terms, particular drugs, organizations, and relevant legislative acts are all included, with entries ranging in length from a paragraph to a few pages. Descriptions of particular drugs generally include their activity, dosage, and effects. Many entries use *see* and *see also* references to preferred and related terms, while longer entries also cite a few bibliographic references. The appendixes include glossaries of street language and slang synonyms for drugs, tables and figures of data on drug use and abuse, and a directory of sources of information. A bibliography and a subject/name index are also included. This is a companion volume to *The Encyclopedia of Alcoholism* (see entry #466).

466. O'Brien, Robert, and Morris Chafetz. **The Encyclopedia of Alcoholism.** 2d ed. New York: Facts on File, 1991. 346p. index. $45.00. LC 89-23333. ISBN 0-8160-1955-X.

A companion volume to *The Encyclopedia of Drug Abuse* (see entry #465), this encyclopedia provides descriptions of hundreds of terms relating to alcohol use and abuse. Though alcoholism is treated in the *Encyclopedia of Drug Abuse*, it is not given as much attention as in this work. Included here are slang terms, medical or physiological terms and conditions, organizations, acronyms, legislation, biographies, groups, alcoholic beverages, countries, and more. The descriptions vary from a paragraph to a few pages; some entries include tables and charts, and longer entries have a few bibliographic references. Appended are tables and figures of data, sources of information, and a bibliography. A subject index that includes proper names, titles, and organizations is also included.

Homelessness

Bibliographies

467. Henslin, James M. **Homelessness: An Annotated Bibliography.** New York: Garland, 1993. 2v. index. (Garland Reference Library of Social Science, Vol. 534). $135.00/set. LC 92-41254. ISBN 0-8240-4115-1.

The literature on homelessness is spread across a wide range of disciplines, sources, and historical periods. More than any other bibliography on homelessness, this book attempts to pull together that variety of sources. The first volume is a straightforward annotated bibliography arranged alphabetically by author. Sources include books, book chapters, newspaper articles, reports, and government documents. Furthermore, no historical limit on the date of publication seems to be in place, as a work by Martin Luther, dating from 1528, is included. The descriptive annotations range from a sentence to a paragraph. In the second volume, the author has listed the same references under 41 subject headings, including such topics as advocacy, homeless children, hunger, deinstitutionalization of the mentally ill, runaways, social work issues, soup kitchens, welfare hotels, voting, and suburban homelessness. The annotations are not reprinted in this subject section. Furthermore, because of the subject categories, no subject index is included. However, an author index is provided. While the bibliography's coverage is limited, it is still a massive and very useful resource.

468. Nordquist, Joan, comp. **The Homeless in America: A Bibliography.** Santa Cruz, Calif.: Reference and Research Services, 1988. 64p. (Contemporary Social Issues: A Bibliographic Series, No. 12). $15.00. ISBN 0-937855-23-5.

This bibliography provides a broad and useful, albeit selective, guide to literature on the problem of homelessness, with entries having been published from the late 1970s through 1988. The citations, which are not annotated, are arranged under eight sections: general; specific populations; health issues; services/shelters; federal policy; cities, counties and states; legal issues; and resources. The section on specific populations includes families, children and youth, women, minorities, and the elderly. "Health Issues" are comprised of general works, mental health, and alcohol and drug-related problems. Within every section of the book, separate author listings for books/documents/pamphlets and for articles (journal and book chapter) are included. Neither discussion as to how items are selected for the bibliography nor a cumulative author index is provided. However, the references do reflect a range of political and ideological viewpoints.

469. Van Whitlock, Rod, Bernard Lubin, and Jean R. Sailors, comps. **Homelessness in America, 1893-1992: An Annotated Bibliography.** Westport, Conn.: Greenwood, 1994. 215p. index. (Bibliographies and Indexes in Sociology, No. 22). $59.95. LC 93-11876. ISBN 0-313-27623-4.

This is another of many useful bibliographies on homelessness (see entries in this section by Henslin, Hombs, and Nordquist). It includes 1,703 references to books, book chapters, articles, and dissertations, 717 of which are given brief annotations. Items published back to the turn of this century are included. Subject coverage is broad, reflecting the variety of perspectives needed in addressing the problem. However, the compilers gave preference to empirical studies when deciding which items to abstract. Entries are arranged by author under 11 subject chapters: early research, 1893-1965; mental health; alcohol and drug abuse; single homeless; health; families and children; legal issues; social and historical perspectives; elderly, minorities, veterans; programs, services, and training; and housing. Author and subject indexes are included, though the latter would be more helpful if it made more extensive use of subheadings.

Handbooks and Yearbooks

470. Fantasia, Rick, and Maurice Isserman. **Homelessness: A Sourcebook.** New York: Facts on File, 1994. 356p. index. LC 92-37762. ISBN 0-8160-2571-1.

After an excellent introductory essay on the history of homelessness as a social issue, the bulk of this handbook is comprised of a dictionary. Included are key terms, organizations, persons, court cases, and legislation relating to homelessness. The well-written definitions range from a paragraph to a few pages, with *see* and *see also* references to preferred and related terms. Some important appendixes are also included: groups and resources for the homeless; homeless persons in selected locations (e.g., shelters, on the street, etc.), arranged by state; and the United States Conference of Mayors' *A Status Report on Hunger and Homelessness in America's Cities: 1993*. An extensive bibliography of books, articles, government documents, reports, and bibliographies on homelessness is also included. Additional access is provided by an extensive name/title/subject index.

471. Hombs, Mary Ellen. **American Homelessness: A Reference Handbook.** 2d ed. Santa Barbara, Calif.: ABC-CLIO, 1994. 272p. index. (Contemporary World Issues). $39.50. LC 94-33788. ISBN 0-87436-725-5.

Estimates range as high as 3 million Americans currently homeless, with fully a third of these being families with children. This handbook attempts to identify and partially untangle the variety of causes and institutional responses to homelessness, while also providing sources for additional information. The book's 10 chapters provide an overview of the topic; a chronology of key events; biographical sketches of key figures; facts and statistics; excerpts from key documents and reports; descriptions of federal legislation; overviews of significant litigation; a directory of organizations and agencies; and an annotated bibliography of print and nonprint resources. The introductory overview clarifies many of the key concepts on homelessness and discusses the parameters of the problem. The statistics chapter includes descriptions of various programs, services, and guidelines. Entries for the court cases, organizations, and print/nonprint resources are all annotated. Also, the legislation chapter provides extensive discussion of the Stewart B. McKinney Homeless Assistance Act (PL 100-77), a landmark piece of legislation first passed in 1987. A glossary of key terms and a combined author/subject/title index are included.

Rape, Sexual Assault, and Harassment

Bibliographies

472. Hartel, Lynda Jones, and Helena M. VonVille. **Sexual Harassment: A Selected, Annotated Bibliography.** Westport, Conn.: Greenwood, 1995. 158p. index. (Bibliographies and Indexes in Women's Studies, No. 23). $59.95. LC 95-21267. ISBN 0-313-29055-5.

Sexual harassment is a social problem, not a "women's" problem. Its causes and manifestations are varied, but they certainly include such sociologically relevant areas as sex role socialization, gender inequality in work and other institutions, and more. This annotated bibliography is a guide to these and other aspects of sexual harassment. It includes 534 references to scholarly books, articles, and dissertations; popular treatments are excluded, though selective items on the Anita Hill-Clarence Thomas hearings are available. The references were published between 1984 and the end of 1994 and are arranged by author under 18 topical chapters. These chapters fall under four broad categories: the history, theories, and consequences of harassment; harassment in various workplace settings; harassment in academic, social, and living environments; and legal aspects. Author and subject indexes are provided, as is a chronology of important legislation, court cases, and publications. For coverage of the previous 10 years, see McCaghy's *Sexual Harassment* bibliography (see entry #473).

473. McCaghy, M. Dawn. **Sexual Harassment: A Guide to Resources.** Boston, Mass.: G. K. Hall, 1985. 181p. index. LC 84-25148. ISBN 0-8161-8669-3.

Covering the period from 1974 to 1984, this annotated bibliography includes references to books, book chapters, articles, reports, dissertations, and government documents on various aspects of sexual harassment. Entries are arranged by author within five subject chapters: general works; the academic setting; coping strategies; the legal perspective; and the management response. Some subtopics within each of these chapters are included. "Coping Strategies" include legal, personal, and extralegal tactics. The "Legal Perspective" covers legislative and judicial reviews, individual cases, employer liability, Equal Employment Opportunity commission guidelines, and related legal issues. Both the "General Works" and "Academic Setting" chapters include subsections for surveys and research, which may be particularly interesting to sociologists. The descriptive and evaluative annotations are detailed and range in length from a paragraph to a page. Author/title and subject indexes are included. This work complements Hartel and VonVille's *Sexual Harassment* bibliography (see entry #472), which treats the years 1984 through 1994. Between them, they cover the major time period for written works on this topic.

474. Nordquist, Joan, comp. **Violence Against Women: A Bibliography.** Santa Cruz, Calif.: Reference and Research Services, 1992. 68p. (Contemporary Social Issues: A Bibliographic Series, No. 26). $15.00. ISBN 0-937855-50-2.

Books, book chapters, journal articles, pamphlets, and government documents are included in this unannotated bibliography. Most of the references were published within five years of the bibliography's compilation. The entries are arranged under five major chapters: violence against women, intimate femicide, battered women, rape, and sexual harassment. "Violence Against Women" includes both general entries and entries on the effects of pornography and violence in the media. "Battered Women" has subsections on date violence, race issues, women against women violence, the effect of domestic violence on children, and battered women who kill. The chapter on "Rape" covers date rape, marital rape, and race issues. "Sexual Harassment" has subsections for general references, the workplace, and school. A sixth chapter, "Resources," has sections listing statistical sources, bibliographies, directories, and organizations. The organizations are listed according to the particular problem they address; entries include addresses and phone numbers. For more specific bibliographies on wife abuse, see the chapter on Marriage and the Family.

475. Ward, Sally K., et al., comps. **Acquaintance and Date Rape: An Annotated Bibliography.** Westport, Conn.: Greenwood, 1994. 218p. index. (Bibliographies and Indexes in Women's Studies, No. 21). $55.00. LC 94-21870. ISBN 0-313-29149-7.

A total of 192 annotated references to books, book chapters, and journal articles on date and acquaintance rape is included in this bibliography. Most of the entries were published since 1980, though some key earlier works are included. Emphasis is on scholarly research or reviews of such research; popular works are excluded. The primary arrangement of the entries is by author under 13 subject categories: incidence, social correlates, misperceptions of sexual intent, research on perpetrators, theoretical perspectives, attitudes toward acquaintance rape, attribution of responsibility, legal issues, campus rape, marital rape, gang rape, treatment of victims and perpetrators, and prevention programs. The annotations are typically a paragraph to a page long and usually describe the study's purpose, its research method, and its findings; a sociological focus is prominent throughout the annotations. An introductory chapter provides a brief overview of each chapter and lists, alphabetically by author, references and citation numbers for all entries in the bibliography. Author and subject indexes are provided.

Suicide

Bibliographies

476. McIntosh, John L., comp. **Research on Suicide: A Bibliography.** Westport, Conn.: Greenwood, 1985. 323p. index. (Bibliographies and Indexes in Psychology, No. 2). $75.00. LC 84-15706. ISBN 0-313-23992-4.

Part of the difficulty of researching suicide is the multidisciplinary origins of its literature; thorough literature searching is made difficult. This bibliography brings together 2,300 English-language works published in a variety of fields between the mid-1970s and 1984. It is topically arranged into 10 subject chapters, including theories of suicide; general overviews; demography and epidemiology of suicide; and prevention, intervention, treatment, assessment, and prediction of suicidal behavior. Demography includes sections on such variables as age, sex, race, ethnicity, and marital status; these chapters should interest sociologists. Author and subject indexes are provided, and reference works are cited in the overview chapter.

Violence

Bibliographies

477. Nordquist, Joan, comp. **Violence in American Society: A Bibliography.** Santa Cruz, Calif.: Reference and Research Services, 1994. 68p. (Contemporary Social Issues: A Bibliographic Series, No. 33). $15.00. ISBN 0-937855-64-2.

The focus here is on the extent of violence in America, its types, and its causes. In all, 639 entries in 18 subject chapters are included: violence in general, urban violence, youth violence, gangs, school violence, children and violence, family violence, violence against women, the effect of pornography and media violence on women, hate crimes, hate crimes on college campuses, the mass media, television, movies, music, video games, guns, and sports. References for books and articles are listed separately in each section and are arranged alphabetically by author. "Books" also includes pamphlets and government documents; "articles" includes both journal articles and book chapters. Mostly scholarly sources are cited here, though some popular works are also included. Most items were published in the late 1980s and early 1990s (through 1994). As with other bibliographies in this series, its strength is the variety of bibliographic sources consulted in compiling the list of references.

Handbooks and Yearbooks

478. Dobrin, Adam, et al. **Statistical Handbook of Violence in America.** Phoenix, Ariz.: Oryx Press, 1996. 394p. index. $54.50. LC 95-42437. ISBN 0-89774-945-6.

The extensive data on violence in the United States indicate what violent crimes are committed, who is committing them, who its victims are, where the crimes are committed, what weapons are used, and what the population thinks about crime, among other things. However, these data are scattered across a variety of sources, government and nongovernment, published and nonpublished. This handbook assembles almost 400 tables and figures of data to document the extent and nature of violence in the United States. The tables are arranged into five subject chapters. Chapter one is on fatal violence and includes data on victims, offenders, weapons, rates by cities and regions, homicide patterns, and legal executions. Chapter two includes data on other types of violence, such as rape, robbery, and assault. These tables, too, often include breakdowns by victim characteristics, the victim-offender relationship, weapons used, and the location of the crime, among other factors. Chapter three arranges data on crime for vulnerable groups and situations, including subtopics for youth, elderly, women, minority groups, the workplace, socioeconomic status, institutionalized populations, and high-risk groups (e.g., police). Chapter four, on the impact of violence, has data on psychological trauma, physical injury, economic costs, loss of productivity, and premature mortality. Chapter five includes survey data of U.S. opinion on crime. All tables include references to sources; these are fully described, including data collection methods and target populations, in an appendix. A small glossary defining some key statistical concepts is available, as well as a subject index for more detailed access to the tables.

SOCIALIZATION, GENDER ROLES, AND SOCIAL PSYCHOLOGY

Bibliographies

479. August, Eugene R. **The New Men's Studies: A Selected and Annotated Interdisciplinary Bibliography.** Littleton, Colo.: Libraries Unlimited, 1994. 2d ed. 440p. index. $47.50. LC 94-32454. ISBN 1-56308-084-2.

While agreeing that traditional scholarship has ignored women, thus giving rise to the need for women's studies, August suggests that most ordinary men are also ignored. Men's studies, therefore, fills a natural and complementary role to women's studies in its exploration of gender, according to the editor. This second edition of August's bibliography has over 1,000 annotated entries, including most of those from the first edition. Both popular and more scholarly works are included, though the criteria for including more recent works are more stringent than for the first edition. Entries are arranged into 27 chapters covering such subjects as boys' socialization, divorce and custody, feminism, pornography, AIDS, masculinity, minority males, patriarchy, sexuality, spirituality, homosexuality, sports, and more. Within chapters or subsections, references are arranged alphabetically by author. All entries are given very useful abstracts, which range from being fairly descriptive to somewhat partisan (e.g., compare Robert Blys' *Iron John* to Andrea Dworkin's *Pornography*). At the end of each section, cross-references to other sections of the book or to other specific entries that relate to the topic are available. Both a combined author/title index and a helpful subject index, which was missing in the first edition, are included.

480. Canary, Daniel J., and David R. Seibold. **Attitudes and Behavior: An Annotated Bibliography.** New York: Praeger, 1984. 221p. index. $55.00. LC 84-3389. ISBN 0-03-060293-9.

The relationship between attitudes and behavior is fundamental to the social sciences. This multidisciplinary bibliography attempts to bring together a selective list of research articles in this area. Most of the works were published between 1969 and December 1982. In all, "more than 600 articles converging on meta-theoretical, theoretical, methodological, or applied aspects of attitude-behavior relationships" (p. 6) are included. Arrangement of the entries is alphabetical by author.

The annotations use a coding system intended to make them brief as well as thorough. These codes indicate the type of study, procedure used, moderating factors, and the attitude-behavior relationship. While the annotations do what they are supposed to do, they presume a fair amount of knowledge of existing tests and measures in attitude-behavior research. Consequently, one intended audience, students and investigators new to the field, may not benefit from the annotations as much as advanced students or researchers, for whom this source should be most useful.

Subject access to the entries is modestly provided by a broad subject category index. Authors are listed under any of 15 categories to which their entries relate.

481. Ridinger, Robert B. Marks, comp. **The Homosexual and Society: An Annotated Bibliography.** New York: Greenwood, 1990. 444p. index. (Bibliographies and Indexes in Sociology, No. 18). $65.00. LC 90-31738. ISBN 0-313-25357-9.

In essence, this is a guide to literature on the issue of homophobia in a variety of social and institutional contexts. Included are almost 1,600 annotated references to books and articles, with abstracts ranging in length from a paragraph to a page. The articles are drawn from mainstream journals in the homosexual community (*The Ladder*, *The ADVOCATE*, and *The Mattachine Review*) and from popular periodicals, such as *New Republic*, *The Nation*, or *Newsweek*. Literature from the legal perspective is also included, though sources dealing with AIDSphobia are not. The cutoff date for inclusion was the end of 1987. The references are arranged randomly under seven topical chapters: adoption/foster care; child custody; the military; employment discrimination; censorship; religion; and police attitudes and actions. A detailed index includes subjects, names, and court cases, though some of the subject headings have too many entries and are in need of subheadings.

482. Signorielli, Nancy, comp. and ed. **Role Portrayal and Stereotyping on Television: An Annotated Bibliography of Studies Relating to Women, Minorities, Aging, Sexual Behavior, Health, and Handicaps.** Westport, Conn.: Greenwood, 1985. 214p. index. (Bibliographies and Indexes in Sociology, No. 5). $55.00. LC 85-9823. ISBN 0-313-24855-9.

Television is an important agent of socialization, and this bibliography revolves around its stereotyping of particular social groups. Over 400 articles, books, book chapters, reports, and government documents are included; the cutoff date for inclusion is the end of 1984. While a few of these entries are from popular sources, most are scholarly or research-oriented. The entries are arranged alphabetically by author under five major subject chapters: women and sex roles, racial and ethnic minorities, aging and age-roles, sexual behavior and orientations, and health and handicaps. Since most of the sources cited use content analyses of programs, the annotations include a description of both the sample and the findings. Author and subject indexes are provided.

Handbooks and Yearbooks

483. Adler, Leonore Loeb, ed. **International Handbook on Gender Roles.** Westport, Conn.: Greenwood, 1993. 525p. index. $99.50. LC 92-45080. ISBN 0-313-28336-2.

The comparative study of gender role socialization across countries can be a rich source of insight and research possibilities. This handbook provides concise and well-written overviews of gender roles in 31 countries worldwide. For each country, an initial overview of the extent of equality/inequality between males and females is provided, followed by a comparison of gender roles over the course of the life cycle. The periods covered here include infancy and early childhood, school years, young adulthood, adulthood, and old age. A list of references for works cited accompanies each chapter. Though brief, these 10- to 12-page essays provide real insight into the reproduction of gender roles in the different countries, with plenty of attention given to the role of schools, marriage and the family, and the economy. A supplementary "Selected Bibliography" is included as well as a combined name/title/subject index.

484. Beere, Carole A. **Gender Roles: A Handbook of Tests and Measures.** New York: Greenwood, 1990. 575p. index. $89.50. LC 89-17033. ISBN 0-313-26278-0.

Developing a valid and reliable research instrument for data collection is a laborious process. An alternative would be to identify existing measures for the researcher. This handbook is a guide to instruments that focus on gender roles and related subjects. In all, 211 surveys/questionnaires/scales are fully described in the handbook. These measures are subarranged by seven categories: gender roles, children and gender, stereotypes, marital and parental roles, employee roles, multiple roles, and attitudes toward gender role issues. For each measure, the information provided includes the title, author(s), date first mentioned, variable, type of instrument, description, sample items, previous subjects, appropriate subjects, administration, scoring, development, validity, reliability, notes and comments, availability, sources using the scale, and a bibliography of citations relating to the scale's development. The author thoroughly discusses her criteria for inclusion. Supplementary indexes to scale authors, titles, variables measured, and users are available. Compared to other guides to existing research instruments, this handbook is extremely thorough and well organized. Beere has also authored a companion handbook, *Sex and Gender Issues: A Handbooks of Tests and Measures* (1990), that focuses on related issues.

485. Beere, Carole A. **Sex and Gender Issues: A Handbook of Tests and Measures.** New York: Greenwood, 1990. 605p. index. $99.50. LC 90-32466. ISBN 0-313-27462-2.

This handbook is a companion volume to Beere's *Gender Roles: A Handbook of Tests and Measures* (1990). It provides a guide to and thorough descriptions of almost 200 scales/surveys/questionnaires related to sex and gender issues. These issues, which constitute the chapters, cover heterosocial relations, sexuality, contraception and abortion, pregnancy and childbirth, somatic issues, homosexuality, rape and sexual coercion, family violence, body image and appearance, eating disorders, and other scales. For each measure, Beere provides information on the authors, variable, type of instrument, description, sample items, previous subjects, appropriate subjects, administration, scoring, development, reliability, validity, notes and comments, availability, sources using the scale, and a bibliography of sources relating to the scale's development. For sociologists requiring a research instrument in any of these areas, this detailed and thorough handbook could be invaluable. Supplementary indexes for scale titles, scale authors, variables measures, and scale users are available.

486. Lindzey, Gardner, and Eliot Aronson. **Handbook of Social Psychology.** New York: Random House, 1985. 2v. index. LC 84-18509. ISBN 0-394-35049-9(v. 1); 0-394-35050-2(v. 2).

These two volumes reflect an overview of the state of the art, as of 1985, in research and writing on social psychology. In all, 30 chapters written by various experts on the major research areas in the field are included. Volume 1 focuses on theory and methods. This includes chapters not only on the historical development of social psychology, but also on learning theory, symbolic interaction and role theory, attitude and opinion measurement, and quantitative methods. Volume 2 deals with special fields and applications. Chapter topics include sex roles, socialization in adulthood, attitudes and attitude change, leadership and power, intergroup relations, deviance, and more. This work is a massive undertaking and an excellent, albeit somewhat dated, review of the field. Chapters are accompanied by lengthy bibliographies. Subjcct and name indexes are also included.

487. Robinson, John P., Phillip R. Shaver, and Lawrence S. Wrightsman, eds. **Measures of Personality and Social Psychological Attitudes.** San Diego, Calif.: Academic Press, 1991. 753p. $134.00. LC 90-91. ISBN 0-12-590241-7.

This is a selective guide to 150 attitude and personality scales. The descriptions for these measures are separated into 11 chapters focusing on the more specific subtopics of response bias, subjective well-being, self-esteem, social anxiety/shyness, depression and loneliness, alienation and anomie, interpersonal trust and attitudes toward human nature, locus of control, authoritarianism, sex roles, and values. In each of these chapters, an expert in that subject area has selected "10 or 20 of the most interesting or promising measures in their area" (p. 1). For each instrument or scale, discussion of the variable measured, overall description, samples, reliability, validity, location, comments and, in many cases, sample items is included. The "comments" section is often particularly valuable, as are many of the comments on validity and reliability. Each chapter begins with a useful three- or four-page overview of the subject and ends with a recommended bibliography. The opening chapter provides a well-written and informative discussion of criteria for scale selection and evaluation. Overall, this is a valuable source for identifying existing, high-quality social psychological scales.

Dictionaries and Encyclopedias

488. Manstead, Antony S. R., and Miles Hewstone, eds. **The Blackwell Encyclopedia of Social Psychology.** Oxford: Blackwell, 1995. 694p. index. $100.00. LC 93-51074. ISBN 0-631-18146-6.

Providing a comprehensive collection of signed entries on "all key topics in social psychology" (p. xv), this encyclopedia is intended for students, faculty, and researchers. Four different types of entries are included, with each type varying in length and in the length of its accompanying bibliography. A total of 93 "feature items," with 3,000-word essays and approximately 10 bibliographic references are included. The entries for 101 "major items" are less extensive, with 1,000-word essays and five bibliographic references. Sixty-four "glossary items," which are approximately 200 words in length, have brief explanations, and cite two bibliographic references, are provided. Finally, 90 glossary items, with 50-word definitions are included. Many entries include *see also* references to terms defined elsewhere in the encyclopedia. Within entries, words defined elsewhere are in capital letters. A detailed subject index with extensive subheadings is included, providing specific additional access to the entries. Throughout, the writing is clear and relatively jargon-free, whenever possible.

489. Turner, Jeffrey S. **Encyclopedia of Relationships Across the Lifespan.** Westport, Conn.: Greenwood, 1996. 495p. index. $99.50. LC 95-573. ISBN 0-313-29576-X.

Social relationships occur across the lifespan in a wide variety of social institutions, such as the family, work, school, peer groups, the community, health care institutions, and more. This encyclopedia provides descriptions of hundreds of key concepts, themes, theories, or policies on the developmental aspects of these relationships. Topics of both historical and contemporary interest are included, as are those focusing on international or multicultural themes or comparisons. Sociologists studying marriage and the family, social psychology, and gerontology will find important concepts and processes addressed here. Terms are arranged alphabetically, and their descriptions range in length from one to two pages. Terms are also accompanied by references for further reading. Cross-references direct the user from unused to preferred terms. Overall, the entries are multidisciplinary, reflecting the insights of sociology, history, anthropology, demography, and many of their specializations. A selective bibliography of 220 recent references is appended, as are directories of relevant journals and organizations. A thorough subject index is also available.

World Wide Web/Internet Sites

490. **Social Psychology Network.**
Available: http://www-osf.wesleyan.edu/psyc/psyc260/
(Accessed: December 31, 1996).

Information on social psychology, psychology, and Wesleyan University is provided on this homepage. The social psychology information includes links to relevant Web sites; guides to social psychology Ph.D. programs, research groups, and journals; links to the homepages of social psychologists; and lists of textbooks and courses in social psychology.

SOCIOLOGY OF EDUCATION

Indexes, Abstracts, and Databases

491. **Sociology of Education Abstracts.** Vol. 1- , No. 1- . Abingdon, Oxfordshire, United Kingdom: Carfax Publishing Company, 1965- . quarterly. $464.00/yr. ISSN 0038-0415.

This is probably the major resource, along with the *ERIC* database, for identifying book and journal literature in the sociology of education. It has two main strengths. First, it covers relevant literature published worldwide. Second, many of the 150- to 200-word abstracts are written by educational sociologists, including members of the editorial board. Works from a variety of theoretical perspectives in the sociology of education are represented, with particularly good coverage of British, Australian, and American scholarship. While the abstracts are not evaluative, they are well written and particularly descriptive. Other abstracts are either full or, in some cases, abbreviated versions of the author's abstract. Approximately 600 items each year are abstracted. Each issue includes both author and subject indexes, with cumulative indexes in the last issue of each volume.

Handbooks and Yearbooks

492. Richardson, John G., ed. **Handbook of Theory and Research for the Sociology of Education.** New York: Greenwood, 1986. 377p. index. $79.50. LC 85-931. ISBN 0-313-23529-5.

Though 10 years old, this handbook provides a useful review of key research and theoretical developments in the sociology of education. It has a number of interesting features. First, it draws on British, French, and American sociologists, many of whom are quite well known in the sociology of education (e.g., Basil Bernstein, Pierre Bourdieu). Second, it addresses important topics in the field, which are reflected in the book's four major parts: history and social origins of education; socialization processes and educational outcomes; educational transmission and reproduction; and methodological and theoretical issues in the sociology of education. Each of these parts has from two to four articles on more specific topics. Most importantly, the articles span the various theoretical perspectives in the field, including the "new" sociology of education and its related conflict theories. These articles are fairly sophisticated, so the handbook is most appropriate for upper-level undergraduate and graduate students in the sociology of education. A more readable overview of the field can be found in a good sociology of education text, such as Christopher Hurn's *The Limits and Possibilities of Schooling* (3d ed., 1993).

World Wide Web/Internet Sites

493. **Education Policy Analysis Archives.**
Available: http://olam.ed.asu.edu/epaa/
(Accessed: February 3, 1997).

This is the Web site for a peer-reviewed scholarly journal that focuses on a broad range of policy issues of sociological interest (e.g., educational reform and educational inequality). The site tells one how to subscribe and submit articles to the journal. A related e-mail discussion list or listserv (*EDPOLYAN*) that includes ongoing discussion of compelling policy and sociological topics is provided. This list is available at listserv@asu.edu and can be joined by sending the message SUB EDPOLYAN YOUR NAME.

494. **SOCED** (Sociology of Education).
Available: MAJORDOMO@LISTS.STANFORD.EDU
(Accessed: December 31, 1996).

SOCED is a mailing list in the sociology of education. Occasional job listings are provided, though the traffic on the list has been very modest. To subscribe at the above address, send the message *subscribe soced firstname lastname*.

SOCIOLOGY OF ORGANIZATIONS AND GROUPS

Bibliographies

495. Peters, Jacob, and Doreen L. Smith. **Organizational and Interorganizational Dynamics: An Annotated Bibliography.** New York: Garland, 1992. 270p. index. (Garland Library of Sociology, Vol. 25; Garland Reference Library of Social Science, Vol. 641). $48.00. LC 92-10773. ISBN 0-8240-5304-4.

The primary focus here is on identifying sociological and related research "in the areas of organizational transformation, interorganizational relations, and organizational effectiveness" (p. xi). Included are references to 555 books, edited collections, and journal articles, with most items having been published between 1975 and 1990. All items are in English and most have been published in North America. Chapter one provides an overview of the issues and strategies involved in organizing and compiling the bibliography. The entries are arranged alphabetically by author within the remaining three chapters. Chapter two is on organizational transformation and has subsections on organizational change, organizational culture, and organizational power. Chapter three addresses interorganizational relations, with subsections on interorganizational analysis, interlocking directorates, and joint ventures. Chapter four has entries on organizational effectiveness. Substantial, descriptive abstracts are provided for all entries. Author, journal, and subject indexes are also included.

Handbooks and Yearbooks

496. **Research in the Sociology of Organizations.** Vol. 1- . Greenwich, Conn.: JAI Press, 1982- . annual. $73.25. ISSN 0733-558X.

This annual presents state-of-the-art articles in organizational sociology. The (average) eight or so articles per issue focus on such topics as networks, bureaucracy, power, and other methodological and theoretical issues. Contributors are drawn from the fields of sociology, psychology, business, administration, organizational behavior, and related fields. Some volumes do have special themes (e.g., social psychological processes in organizations; labor relations and unions).

World Wide Web/Internet Sites

497. **Center for the Study of Group Processes.**
Available: http://www.uiowa.edu/~grpproc/
(Accessed: February 3, 1997).

Developed by the Sociology Department at the University of Iowa, this site has information about the Center, group processes research, and local (Iowa) and national news and announcements. It also includes the peer-reviewed electronic journal, *Current Research in Social Psychology* (entry #155).

SOCIOLOGY OF RELIGION

Bibliographies

498. Blasi, Anthony J., and Michael W. Cuneo. **Issues in the Sociology of Religion: A Bibliography.** New York: Garland, 1986. 400p. index. (Garland Reference Bibliographies in Sociology, Vol. 8; Garland Reference Library of Social Science, Vol. 340). LC 86-1292. ISBN 0-8240-8585-X.

Almost 3,600 books, articles, book chapters, dissertations, and theses are included in this bibliography. While the focus is decidedly sociological, some references from the anthropological and political science literature are included if their methods and focus are sociological. The entries are arranged under an extensive subject classification structure of chapters, sections, and subtopics. Chapter one, on structures, includes sections on social psychology and attitudes, roles, organization, politics and religion, and stratification. Chapter two addresses processes and contains sections on conversion, role entry and exit, deviance and legitimization, organizational change, social movements, secularization, the Protestant ethic, and societal evolution. Chapter three focuses on disciplinary conceptualizations and includes sections for the definition of religion, religiosity, practices and ritual, typology, and theories and problematics. Within all chapters and sections, numerous subtopics for the further classification of entries are available, which are then arranged by author. Brief overviews precede all chapters and sections, as well as some subtopics. Some references in the bibliography are briefly cited under more than one subtopic, with a cross-reference to the entry number for the full citation. An author index is also provided, as is a rather brief subject index.

499. Blasi, Anthony J., and Michael W. Cuneo. **The Sociology of Religion: An Organizational Bibliography.** New York: Garland. 1990. 459p. index. (Garland Library of Sociology, Vol. 18; Garland Reference Library of Social Science, Vol. 612). $76.00. LC 90-40684. ISBN 0-8240-2584-9.

Unlike the authors' other bibliography (see entry #498), which was organized around themes in the sociology of religion, this bibliography is organized around "specific religious organizations and traditions" (p. xix). Over 3,200 references to books, articles, chapters, theses, and dissertations are included, with the most recent references dating from 1988/89 and the older references extending back decades. The bibliography is organized into five parts. "The first part consists of three chapters that list studies of the great Asian traditions, including the classical Hindu and Buddhist faiths and their variegated descendants. The three chapters of the second part feature sociological accounts of various aspects of the Hebrew, Jewish, and Islamic traditions. The third part, the volume's most extensive, contains six chapters, one dedicated to studies of early Christianity, three to those of Roman Catholicism, and one each to studies of Anglican and Byzantine Christianity respectively. Part IV includes nine chapters, each differently focuses on denominations and movements which belong . . . to the Reformation family of Christian traditions. The final and residual part is composed of . . . the so-called new religions, and other religions not quite so new, such as the Mormon and Baha'i" (p. xix). Some of the references are briefly annotated; others are cited in more than one section. Author and subject indexes are also provided.

500. Choquette, Diane, comp. **New Religious Movements in the United States and Canada: A Critical Assessment and Annotated Bibliography.** Westport, Conn.: Greenwood, 1985. 235p. index. (Bibliographies and Indexes in Religious Studies, No. 5). $65.00. LC 85-9964. ISBN 0-313-23772-7.

The focus here is not only on the growth and influence of various new religious movements, religious cults, and sects (e.g., the Unification Church, Hare Krishna, UFO groups, est, and the Church of Scientology), but also on the renewed interest among North Americans in some Eastern religions (e.g., Hinduism and Buddhism). Included are references to 738 books, journal articles, dissertations, conference papers, and unpublished reports from the 1960s through 1983. A variety of disciplinary perspectives are represented here, including history, psychology, sociology, theology, and anthropology. References are listed by author under 12 subject headings covering not only the above disciplines, but also reference works, the cultural background of new religious movements, legal studies, personal accounts, and the spiritualization of knowledge. The sociology/ anthropology chapter has subsections focusing on cult and sect theories; conversion, brainwashing, and deprogramming; and individual groups and movements. Paragraph-long, descriptive annotations accompany all references. An appendix selectively lists publishers of new religious movements books. Author/title and subject indexes are also available. The introduction provides a discussion and classification of various types of new religious movements.

501. Homan, Roger, comp. **The Sociology of Religion: A Bibliographical Survey.** New York: Greenwood, 1986. 309p. index. (Bibliographies and Indexes in Religious Studies, No. 9). $75.00. LC 86-18471. ISBN 0-313-24710-2.

Homan has included over 1,000 references to books and articles on a wide variety of topics in the sociology of religion. Entries are arranged alphabetically by author under 24 major subject headings. Included among these headings are religion and social class, religion and the state, typologies of religious organization, sects and cults, secularization, religiosity and religious behavior/attitudes, Marxist critique, recruitment and socialization, and religion in particular geographic regions. English language and non-English language sources are included and all entries receive paragraph-long, evaluative annotations in English. Author, title, and subject indexes are also included. An interesting and lengthy introductory overview of the field is also provided. Though a bit dated, this is a useful retrospective bibliography to the late 1950s.

502. Saliba, John A. **Social Science and the Cults: An Annotated Bibliography.** New York: Garland, 1990. 694p. index. (Sects and Cults in America: Bibliographical Guides, Vol. 17; Garland Reference Library of Social Science, Vol. 564). LC 90-32106. ISBN 0-8240-3719-7.

Substantial social science and sociological literature relating to the study of cults, sects, and new religious movements is available. This bibliography cites 2,219 references to books, book chapters, and journal articles published from the 1930s to 1988. Excluded are works from the psychological, legal, and popular literature, as well as works on religious movements in Africa, Asia, and the Third World. The bibliography is comprised of four main chapters. Chapter one cites bibliographic sources (books, articles, bibliographies, encyclopedias, manuals, and periodicals) that were used to compile the references cited here; all but the periodical titles are annotated. Chapter two includes references to the historical literature on religious movements, covering the period from the 1930s through the 1960s. This literature predates the recent interest in cults and establishes some of the theoretical perspectives and classic studies used in evaluating current movements. Chapter three covers general background literature on social movements, communal groups, etc., as well as works on the theory and methodology of studying cults, sects, and new religious movements. Chapter four includes references to studies on specific cults, sects, and movements. All entries are descriptively annotated. Both author and subject indexes are included. Book-length bibliographies on specific cults, sects, or movements (e.g., Scientology, Unification Church, Baha'i, and Jehovah's Witnesses) can be found in this Garland bibliography series.

503. Wolcott, Roger T., and Dorita F. Bolger, comps. **Church and Social Action: A Critical Assessment and Bibliographical Survey.** New York: Greenwood, 1990. 256p. index. (Bibliographies and Indexes in Religious Studies, No. 15). $49.95. LC 89-28565. ISBN 0-313-25086-3.

Sociologists of religion and social movements should be interested in this bibliography's focus, which is on organized religion's active role in promoting social change. References addressing the church's humanitarian and social work activities, or its defense of vested interests, are excluded. In all, 748 references to books, book chapters, monographs, and journal articles are included; all receive paragraph-long descriptive annotations. Citations are organized alphabetically by author within five subject chapters: religion in modern society; survey research and organizational studies; religious social movements - United States; comparative studies; and historical studies. The chapter on comparative studies has subsections for general and theoretical works, South East Asia, Central and South America, Muslim countries, Europe, and other areas. The historical chapter includes subsections on not only general and theoretical works, but also peasant tribal revolts, reform and independence movements, the formation of modern societies, and confronting social problems. A lengthy introductory survey discussing all of these subject categories is provided. Author, subject, and title indexes are included.

Handbooks and Yearbooks

504. Utter, Glenn H., and John W. Storey. **The Religious Right: A Reference Handbook.** Santa Barbara, Calif.: ABC-CLIO, 1995. 298p. index (Contemporary World Issues). $39.50. LC 95-44344. ISBN 0-87436-778-6.

Sociologists of religion, political sociologists, and sociologists of social movements may all find material of interest in this handbook. It provides a variety of textual, directory, and bibliographic information that should be particularly useful to students. The information is organized into seven chapters: introduction, chronology, biographical sketches, survey data and quotations, directory of organizations, selected print resources, and nonprint resources. The chronology of key events is historical to the early nineteenth century, while the biographies include both historical and currently living individuals of note. Both the attitudes of and quotations from conservative Christians are broken down by key topics, such as abortion, anticommunism, capitalism, education, and politics, among others. The organization directories include both conservative Christian organizations, and their critics, in two separate lists. The chapter of print resources is an annotated bibliography of books either by or about the religious right. These are arranged by author under a few broad subject categories, including a category for biographies. An annotated list of relevant periodicals is also included. The nonprint resources chapter is also annotated and separately lists resources that are for or against the religious right. It also lists and annotates radio and television programs, CD-ROMs, diskettes, databases, and some e-mail discussion lists. A glossary is provided, as is a detailed index to names, subjects, and titles.

World Wide Web/Internet Sites

505. **Weberian Sociology of Religion.**
Available: http://acs4.bu.edu:8001/~moriyuki/
(Accessed: February 3, 1997).

Included here is information on Max Weber and his work on the sociology of religion, annotations of his major works, some of his relevant writings, and other information on Christianity and Japanese religions.

SOCIOLOGY OF SPORT AND LEISURE

Guides

506. Shoebridge, Michele, ed. **Information Sources in Sport and Leisure.** London: Bowker-Saur, 1992. 345p. index. (Guides to Information Sources). LC 91-21637. ISBN 0-86291-901-0.

Arranged into a collection of bibliographic essays, this covers a wide variety of bibliographic sources, organizations, and background information on major topics in sport and leisure. The 16 chapters are each written by an expert in the field and provide not only an overview of the topic, but also brief references to key books, journals, and other information sources. Many of the chapters touch on subjects that have sociological relevance, such as government and sport, history of sport, sociology of sport, and leisure. Chapters on statistical sources and North American information sources are also included. The guide's value is increased by its inclusion of European and Australian sources. A list of international organizations is appended, as is a name/title/subject index.

Bibliographies

507. Wise, Suzanne. **Social Issues in Contemporary Sport: A Resource Guide.** New York: Garland, 1994. 789p. index. (Garland Reference Library of Social Science; Vol. 595). $130.00. LC 93-29608. ISBN 0-8240-6046-6.

Intended primarily for undergraduates, graduate students, and researchers new to the field, this annotated bibliography cites over 2,400 books, articles, government documents, conference papers, and other materials on social issues in sports. Coverage is from World War II to the present, though most of the references were published since 1970. Research and popular writing from all of the social sciences is included. The references, which are descriptively annotated, are listed by author within 15 subject chapters: general sources, representative biography, drugs, economics of sport, sport and education, fans, gambling, labor relations, sports law, mass media, sport and politics, race relations, violence, women, and youth. An additional chapter ("addenda") of other references is included, as well as lists of selected organizations/research centers and selected journals. Major sport sociology journals, such as *Arena Review*, *Journal of Sport and Social Issues*, and *Sport Sociology Journal* were systematically combed for articles. Much to interest sociologists is included, particularly such subjects as fan violence/hooliganism, racism/race relations, socialization, and gender roles. A subject index is included, though some headings (e.g., "football") would benefit by subheadings.

Indexes, Abstracts and Databases

508. **Physical Education Index.** Vol. 1- , No. 1- . Cape Girardeau, Mo.: BenOak, 1978- . quarterly, with annual cumulations. $195.00/yr. ISSN 0191-9202.

Though indexing articles primarily in the areas of sports, fitness, exercise physiology, sports medicine, coaching, and related areas, this index also identifies sources relating to sport sociology and sport psychology. Up to 200 journals are scanned for references, which are arranged in the index by title under an extensive list of subject headings. Beyond headings for sports psychology and sports sociology, one can also look under more specific topics (e.g., lifestyle, leisure, demographics, eating disorders, and attitudes). Citations include the author, article title, abbreviated journal title, volume, date, and pages. A preliminary section translates journal abbreviations into complete titles.

509. **SPORT.** Ottawa, Ontario, Canada: Sport Information Resource Center, 1949- . monthly updates. DIALOG file #48.

Arguably, this is one of the best indexes, abstracts, or databases for the study of sport. While much of the information covered here is on sports, physical fitness, sports medicine, and exercise physiology, information on psychology, leisure, and related sociological topics is also available. More than 1,000 sport periodicals, from a number of countries and in many languages, are indexed. Theses and monographs are included and are covered back to 1949, while journal citations are included from 1975 to the present.

510. **SPORT Discus.** [CD-ROM]. Norwood, Mass.: SilverPlatter Information Inc., 1975- . quarterly updates.

Begun in 1994, this CD-ROM is the equivalent of the *SPORT* database (see entry #509) provided through the DIALOG database service. It indexes articles in approximately 1,200 sports journals, covering such topics as fitness, coaching, exercise physiology, biomechanics, and more. Also covered are topics related to sport psychology, sport sociology, leisure, and attitudes and behaviors relating to sport.

STRATIFICATION AND INEQUALITY

Bibliographies

511. Chalfant, H. Paul, comp. **Sociology of Poverty in the United States: An Annotated Bibliography.** Westport, Conn.: Greenwood, 1985. 187p. index. (Bibliographies and Indexes in Sociology, No. 3). $59.95. LC 84-25191. ISBN 0-313-23929-0.

This is an important, albeit selective, bibliography on poverty, covering works published since the early 1970s. Sociology is construed broadly to include economics, social work, and social psychology. A total of 621 books and articles are arranged into seven major chapters on stratification, ideology, and poverty; measurement of poverty; economics of poverty; status, power, and poverty; poverty among racial and ethnic minorities (arranged by group); correlates of poverty; and alleviation of poverty. Correlates covered are education, health, mental health, crime, law, family, and housing. All entries are descriptively annotated.

512. Feinberg, Renee, and Kathleen E. Knox. **The Feminization of Poverty in the United States: A Selected, Annotated Bibliography of the Issues, 1978-1989.** New York: Garland, 1990. 317p. index. (Garland Reference Library of Social Science; Vol. 530). LC 90-2869. ISBN 0-8240-1213-5.

Over 500 books, book chapters, articles, ERIC documents, reports, and government documents are cited in this bibliographic guide to the feminization of poverty. Major print indexes and electronic databases (e.g., *Sociological Abstracts*, *PAIS*, and *Ageline*) were searched for relevant sources, as were some alternative sources (e.g., *The Left Index*, and *Alternative Press Index*). Both scholarly and some popular magazine articles are cited. Newspaper articles and dissertations are excluded.

The references are arranged under 18 subject chapters: poverty in America; feminization of poverty; families headed by women; children of poverty; child support; child care; women's employment; comparable worth/pay equity; Reaganomics; women of color; older women; social security, pensions, and retirement; teenage mothers; health, nutrition, and hunger; housing and homelessness; welfare; welfare reform and workfare; and family policy. Each chapter is preceded by a one- or two-page subject overview. References are accompanied by paragraph-long descriptive abstracts. Additional access to the entries is provided by an author index and an arbitrary subject index. Important authors and a variety of sources are cited, making this a valuable guide to a timely social policy issue.

513. Kinloch, Graham C. **Social Stratification: An Annotated Bibliography.** New York: Garland, 1987. 357p. index. (Garland Library of Sociology, Vol. 11; Garland Reference Library of Social Science, Vol. 393). LC 86-32024. ISBN 0-8240-9805-6.

Kinloch has cited and briefly annotated 1,744 sources dealing with virtually all aspects of social stratification. The entries, mostly journal citations, are drawn from "the major social science literature and published primarily between the 1960s and 1980s" (p.

xv). They are arranged under a detailed list of major chapter headings and subtopics, with the six major chapters covering general bibliographies and research trends, theoretical and conceptual issues, methodological issues, historical studies of stratification, stratification in the United States (the largest chapter), and stratification in other societies. The extensive list of subtopics covers every aspect of stratification research. The chapter on stratification in the United States has approximately 60 subtopics covering minorities, elites, attitudes, the family, education, religion, deviance, medicine, and more. The chapter on other countries has subtopics for specific countries, as well as for country comparisons. Within these subtopics, sources are listed alphabetically by author. A final chapter lists relevant publications and addresses. Author and subject indexes are included, though the latter is somewhat unnecessary given the book's extensive topical arrangement. Overall, this is an excellent source for the time period covered.

514. Nordquist, Joan, comp. **The Feminization of Poverty.** Santa Cruz, Calif.: Reference and Research Services, 1987. 64p. (Contemporary Social Issues: A Bibliographic Series, No. 6). $15.00. ISBN 0-937855-11-1.

Gender is a significant factor in the incidence of poverty. In 1988, 57.1 percent of those in poverty were female, and 38.2 percent of White and 56.3 percent of African American female-headed households were in poverty (*Encyclopedia of Sociology*, Vol. 3, pp. 1529-30). The effect of gender is compounded by such factors as age, race, marital status, class, and ethnicity. This bibliography selectively cites the literature on this important topic from approximately 1977–1987. References are listed alphabetically by author in three sections. Section one cites background books on such topics as "women in the labor force, comparable worth, discrimination in employment, poverty in America, and the contemporary family" (p. 6). Section two focuses specifically on the feminization of poverty, with subsections on general treatments, minority women, older women, divorced women, and statistics sources. Monographs and articles/book chapters are listed separately. Section three lists related bibliographies and a directory of activist organizations. The sources cited here are excellent and only modestly dated. The guide to relevant government statistics sources, such as *Current Population Reports*, is also valuable.

515. **Poverty in Developing Countries: A Bibliography of Publications by the ILO's World Employment Programme, 1975-91.** Washington, D.C.: International Labor Office, 1992. 152p. index. (International Labour Bibliography, No. 12). $16.00. ISBN 92-2-108248-2.

The amount of poverty in developing countries is staggering, with anywhere from 50 to 70 percent of rural populations in Asia, Africa, and Latin America being poor. Over the years, the World Employment Programme of the International Labor Office (ILO) has sponsored research on the extent of and trends in poverty in developing countries, as well as on policies for its reduction. This annotated bibliography is a guide to 350 of those research reports published between 1975 and 1991.

The bibliography is divided into four sections. Section one is the collection of bibliographical references and abstracts arranged alphabetically by author or corporate author. Sections two through four are the author, corporate author, and subject/geographical indexes. Under each index heading, not only relevant entry numbers are included, but also the first line of each work's title. While the bibliography is easy to use, it does have a few small problems. First, some abstracts are useful descriptive paragraphs, while others are simply lists of keywords. Second, the readability of both types of abstracts is compromised by the use of slash marks around keywords. Overall, this bibliography should be appropriate for those studying poverty or economic development in developing countries.

World Wide Web/Internet Sites

516. **Social Inequality and Class, Stratification and Poverty.** Available: http://www.pscw.uva.nl/sociosite/TOPICS/Inequality.html#CLASS (Accessed: February 3, 1997).

All four of the above topics are covered in this subsection of the *SocioSite* Web site, which is out of the University of Amsterdam. Information on these areas includes lists, book summaries, book excerpts, bibliographies, position papers, links to other Web sites, and more.

THEORY

Bibliographies

517. Clark, Michael. **Michel Foucault, An Annotated Bibliography: Tool Kit for a New Age.** New York: Garland, 1983. 608p. index. (Garland Bibliographies of Modern Critics and Critical Schools, Vol. 4; Garland Reference Library of the Humanities, Vol. 350). LC 82-48274. ISBN 0-8240-9253-8.

Though not current, this bibliography is comprehensive through the early 1980s and, consequently, is a major resource for scholars of Foucault and poststructuralism. It includes over 2,500 published items through 1981, with additional major items for 1982 and 1983. Also included are sources found in the national bibliographies of France, Germany, the United States, and Great Britain. References span the social sciences and humanities and may be in any of seven languages. The descriptive annotations, however, are all in English. Three major parts comprise the bibliography: primary works, secondary works, and background works. "Primary works" is arranged chronologically and is comprised of five subchapters: books and collections of essays; prefaces, translations, and books edited; essays and review articles; reviews; and interviews, miscellaneous. "Secondary works" is arranged alphabetically by author and also has five subchapters: books and collections of essays, special journal issues; essays and review articles; reviews; dissertations; and miscellaneous. Finally, the "Background Works" chapter includes sections for books and essays in which Foucault is discussed, though Foucault may not be a major focus of the item. The book provides a brief biography of Foucault, as well as a lengthy introduction. Five indexes covering authors, book titles, article titles, journals, and topics are also included.

518. Deegan, Mary Jo, ed. **Women in Sociology: A Bio-Bibliographical Sourcebook.** New York: Greenwood, 1991. 468p. index. $79.50. LC 90-43376. ISBN 0-313-26085.

Deegan's work documents "the lives and work of founding women in sociology" (p. 6), covering the 150 years from 1840 through 1990. It includes discussion about both their lives and their "social thought." A total of 51 women are covered, including such notable names as Hannah Arendt, Jane Addams, Charlotte Perkins Gilman, Helena Lopata, Alva Myrdal, Alice Rossi, and Helen Lynd. The women sociologists ultimately included in this work were identified through either the recommendations of other sociologists or extensive research; all met at least one of five criteria to be considered a sociologist. The introduction discusses these criteria, as well as the these women's place in the historical development of sociology. The essays themselves range from five to ten pages, with an additional few pages of references. All of the essays include sections for a biography, major themes in that sociologist's work, and critiques. Accompanying bibliographies of works by and about the individual and her work are also included. Name and subject indexes are appended.

519. Egan, David R., and Melinda A. Egan. **V. I. Lenin: An Annotated Bibliography of English-Language Sources to 1980.** Metuchen, N.J.: Scarecrow, 1982. 482p. LC 82-659. ISBN 0-8108-1526-5.

Almost 3,000 English-language sources about V. I. Lenin are included in this bibliography. Covering a wide range of political perspectives, they are drawn from "books, essays, chapters from general studies, periodical articles, reminiscences, interviews, addresses, doctoral dissertations, reviews of major Lenin studies, and introductions to Lenin's works" (p. vii). Lenin's writing is excluded, but little else is. This bibliography is international in scope, including many Soviet-era interpretations of Lenin's work.

The entries are arranged alphabetically by author under an extensive number of chapters and subtopics. Books and essays have Library of Congress call numbers, and the contents of anthologies are listed. The annotations are descriptive, and author and subject indexes are included. This is an excellent source for those interested in both Leninist theory and practice and revolutionary social change.

520. Eubanks, Cecil L. **Karl Marx and Frederich Engels: An Analytical Bibliography.** 2d ed, New York: Garland, 1984. 299p. index. (Garland Reference Library of Social Science, Vol. 100). LC 81-43337. ISBN 0-8240-9293-7.

This second edition adds 1,000 new entries to the first edition (1977). Its purposes remain the same: to be a comprehensive listing of various editions and translations of the writings of Marx and Engels; and to provide a comprehensive listing of works dealing with or elaborating upon their writings. Books, articles, monographs, book chapters, and dissertations are included. Marxist-Leninist literature is considered too derivative and is, therefore, excluded. The entries are arranged into four sections: the works of Marx and Engels (with separate listings for each author's individual and collected works, as well as their joint works); books on Marx and Engels; articles on Marx and Engels; and dissertations on Marx and Engels. Within each section, entries are arranged alphabetically by author. There are two introductory bibliographic essays (from both editions) that are quite useful, as well as newly added subject indexes to books, articles, and dissertations. Because it is now a bit dated, this is no longer a comprehensive bibliography of secondary works on Marx and Engels. However, it remains an important guide to many classic analyses of their work. Furthermore, the comprehensive listing of primary works by Marx and Engels is as valuable as ever. Graduate students and faculty will find this most useful.

521. Kivisto, Peter, and William H. Swatos, Jr. **Max Weber: A Bio-Bibliography.** New York: Greenwood, 1988. 267p. index. (Bio-Bibliographies in Sociology, No. 2). $59.95. LC 88-24656. ISBN 0-313-25794-9.

Both English translations of Weber's work and a "comprehensive, annotated bibliography of secondary literature" (p. 8) are included in this bibliography. Textbooks and book reviews (of primary and secondary works) are excluded, while dissertations and theses are included selectively. Overall, the book has two parts. Part one includes a biographical essay, an essay on Weber's reception in Anglo-American sociology, and a discussion of various Weber archives. Part two, the largest, includes seven chapters. The first of these lists Weber's works in English translation, along with notes describing additional features of the edition or translation. The next chapter lists collections "on and out of Weber's work" (p.58). The 764 books, chapters, and articles cited in the last five chapters focus on different subjects concerning Weber and his work: biography and intellectual history; methodology; religion; politics and social classes; and modernity, rationalization, and bureaucracy. All entries in these chapters receive brief, descriptive annotations. An author index is provided, including editors and individuals mentioned in abstracts, and a name/subject index. This is an essential research tool for advanced students and faculty researching Weber.

522. Kurtz, Lester R. **Evaluating Chicago Sociology: A Guide to the Literature, with an Annotated Bibliography.** Chicago: University of Chicago Press, 1984. 303p. index. (The Heritage of Sociology). LC-84-53. ISBN 0-226-46476-8.

This is an analysis of and guide to further research on the Chicago school and its place in U.S. sociology. The first part of the book is an overview of the Chicago school's development, key individuals, philosophical foundations, theoretical perspectives, areas of research, and approaches to social change and collective behavior. The second half of the book is a bibliography on the Chicago school, its members and their works. Over 1,000 books, articles, dissertations, etc., are arranged alphabetically by author. Most entries are annotated and all were published before 1983. A name/subject index is included.

523. LaPointe, Francois H. **Georg Lukacs and His Critics: An International Bibliography with Annotations (1910-1982).** Westport, Conn.: Greenwood, 1983. 403p. index. LC 83-5613. ISBN 0-313-23891-X.

Lukacs, a Hungarian social theorist, is considered an important figure in the development of Marxist theory. Not surprisingly, his work has generated considerable secondary literature. Though somewhat dated, this partially annotated bibliography is a comprehensive guide to that literature for items published through the end of 1982. References in many languages are included, adding to the bibliography's value. Approximately 2,000 entries arranged into four parts are included. Part one includes references to books and reviews, with subdivisions for books in English, German, French, Italian, Spanish, and other languages. If the books were reviewed, references to the reviews are included. Some books are extensively abstracted and may even include a list of chapters. An additional section lists special issues of journals devoted to Lukacs; the constituent articles are listed. Part two covers worldwide dissertations and theses on Lukacs; abstracts from *Dissertation Abstracts International* are included for some of these. Part three lists essays and articles on Lukacs, with a further breakdown by language (English, German, French, Italian, Spanish, and other). Part four lists items in which Lukacs is compared to other theorists. This section is arranged alphabetically by the names of the other theorists, with references listed under those names. An index for authors and editors is included, though unfortunately no subject index is available.

524. Nordquist, Joan, comp. **Antonio Gramsci.** Santa Cruz, Calif.: Reference and Research Services, 1987. 60p. index. (Social Theory: A Bibliographic Series, No. 7). $15.00. ISBN 0-937855-12-X.

525. Nordquist, Joan, comp. **Georg Lukacs.** Santa Cruz, Calif.: Reference and Research Services, 1988. 64p. index. (Social Theory: A Bibliographic Series, No. 11). $15.00. ISBN 0-937855-20-0.

526. Nordquist, Joan, comp. **Hannah Arendt.** Santa Cruz, Calif: Reference and Research Services, 1989. 64p. index. (Social Theory: A Bibliographic Series, No. 14). $15.00. ISBN 0-9378455-26-X.

527. Nordquist, Joan, comp. **Herbert Marcuse.** Santa Cruz, Calif.: Reference and Research Services, 1988. 60p. index. (Social Theory: A Bibliographic Series, No. 9). $15.00. ISBN 0-937855-16-2.

528. Nordquist, Joan, comp. **Jacques Derrida: A Bibliography.** Santa Cruz, Calif.: Reference and Research Services, 1986. 57p. (Social Theory: A Bibliographic Series, No. 2). $15.00. ISBN 0-937855-02-2.

529. Nordquist, Joan. comp. **Jean Baudrillard: A Bibliography.** Santa Cruz, Calif.: Reference and Research Services, 1991. 55p. index. (Social Theory: A Bibliographic Series, No. 24). $15.00. ISBN 0-937855-47-2.

530. Nordquist, Joan, comp. **Jean-Francois Lyotard: A Bibliography.** Santa Cruz, Calif.: Reference and Research Services, 1991. 60p. index. (Social Theory: A Bibliographic Series, No. 21). $15.00. ISBN 0-937855-41-3.

531. Nordquist, Joan, comp. **Jürgen Habermas: A Bibliography.** Santa Cruz, Calif.: Reference and Research Services, 1986. 60p. (Social Theory: A Bibliographic Series, No. 1). $15.00. ISBN 0-937855-00-6.

532. Nordquist, Joan, comp. **Jürgen Habermas (II): A Bibliography.** Santa Cruz, Calif.: Reference and Research Services, 1991. 68p. index. (Social Theory: A Bibliographic Series, No. 22). $15.00. ISBN 0-937855-43-X.

533. Nordquist, Joan, comp. **Max Horkheimer.** Santa Cruz, Calif.: Reference and Research Services, 1990. 63p. index. (Social Theory: A Bibliographic Series, No. 18). $15.00. ISBN 0-937855-35-9.

534. Nordquist, Joan, comp. **Max Weber.** Santa Cruz, Calif.: Reference and Research Services, 1989. 80p. index. (Social Theory: A Bibliographic Series, No. 13). $15.00. ISBN 0-937855-24-3.

535. Nordquist, Joan, comp. **Michel Foucault: A Bibliography.** Santa Cruz, Calif.: Reference and Research Services, 1986. 59p. (Social Theory: A Bibliographic Series, No. 4). $15.00. ISBN 0-937855-06-5.

536. Nordquist, Joan, comp. **Michel Foucault (II): A Bibliography.** Santa Cruz, Calif.: Reference and Research Services, 1992. 76p. (Social Theory: A Bibliographic Series, No. 27). $15.00. ISBN 0-937855-53-7.

537. Nordquist, Joan, comp. **Talcott Parsons.** Santa Cruz, Calif.: Reference and Research Services, 1987. 60p. index. (Social Theory: A Bibliographic Series, No. 8). $15.00. ISBN 0-937855-14-6.

538. Nordquist, Joan, comp. **Theodor Adorno.** Santa Cruz, Calif.: Reference and Research Services, 1988. 52p. index. (Social Theory: A Bibliographic Series, No. 10). $15.00. ISBN 0-937855-18-9.

539. Nordquist, Joan, comp. **Theodor Adorno (II): A Bibliography.** Santa Cruz, Calif.: Reference and Research Services, 1994. 72p. index. (Social Theory: A Bibliographic Series, No. 35). $15.00. ISBN 0-937855-69-3.

All of these bibliographies in Nordquist's *Social Theory* series are arranged similarly. They typically are 70 pages long and include approximately 500 unannotated references to books, articles, reviews, and other sources by and about the theorist. In some cases, works in languages other than English are also cited. The bibliographies are organized into four sections. Section one usually cites books written by the theorist, while section two lists the theorist's articles or essays. Sections three and four cite books and articles about the theorist, respectively. In some of the bibliographies, the different sections are accompanied by their own keyword indexes. These are important bibliographies not only because they provide access to the literature by and about traditional and contemporary theorists, but also because they span a wide range of theoretical and ideological positions.

540. Perrin, Robert G. **Herbert Spencer: A Primary and Secondary Bibliography.** New York: Garland, 1993. 1,005p. index. (Garland Reference Library of the Humanities, Vol. 1061). $150.00. LC 93-12108. ISBN 0-8240-4597-1.

Spencer is one of the important nineteenth century early sociologists, best known for incorporating Darwinism and natural selection into his views on societal evolution. This bibliography is an extensive guide to works both by and about Spencer. It is organized into two major sections. Section one lists works by Spencer and includes correspondence, manuscripts, books, pamphlets, articles, and letters. The second section cites books, articles, reviews, and dissertations about Spencer. These are organized into chapters by subject, including categories for biographical and general studies, philosophy–religion, philosophy–ethics, biology, psychology, economics, politics and political science, sociology and social thought, education, art/literature/style, music, and miscellaneous. Virtually all entries, except dissertations, receive brief, descriptive annotations. In all, over 2,000 primary and secondary sources are cited. A lengthy introductory chapter provides an overview of Spencer's life and work. Supplementary material includes a chronology of Spencer's life, a list of periodicals cited, and a name index.

541. Schultz, William R., and Lewis L. B. Fried. **Jacques Derrida: An Annotated Primary and Secondary Bibliography.** New York: Garland, 1992. 882p. index. (Garland Bibliographies of Modern Critics and Critical Schools, Vol. 18; Garland Reference Library of the Humanities, Vol. 1319). $150.00. LC 92-12592. ISBN 0-8240-4872-5.

Though most influential in the area of literary criticism, deconstructionism has also had an impact in the social sciences, as seen in some of the work of sociologist Anthony Giddens, among others. This is a comprehensive guide to over 4,000 works by and about deconstructionism's principal exponent, French philosopher Jacques Derrida. The guide is divided into major sections for primary and secondary sources. Primary sources are further subdivided into books and chapters, articles, interviews, and reviews and translations by Derrida. Both the book and article sections include subsections for works in different languages (i.e., English, French, German, Italian, or Japanese). Many, though not all, of these primary sources are briefly annotated. The secondary sources are subdivided into sections for books, chapters, articles, dissertations, reviews, and background articles and reviews. As with the primary sources, the books, chapters, and articles are further subdivided by language. Most of these sources are annotated. The introduction includes a useful overview of the controversial nature of Derrida's work, as well as a categorization and discussion of many issues addressed in the secondary literature. Author and name indexes are provided.

542. Simich, Jerry L., and Rick Tilman. **Thorstein Veblen: A Reference Guide.** Boston: G. K. Hall, 1985. 240p. index. LC 84-25177. ISBN 0-8161-8358-9.

This is a comprehensive annotated bibliography of books, portions or chapters of books, articles, reviews, dissertations, and other sources on Veblen written between 1891 and 1982. Both English-language and some foreign-language sources are included. The entries are arranged first chronologically, then alphabetically by author. Within each year, the entries are numbered; the combination year/entry number is used in the index. The descriptive annotations are generally a paragraph long and well written. The editors also provide a selective list of major writings by Veblen; they do not explain why more of Veblen's work is not cited. A thorough author/title index that also includes personal names as subjects and a selective number of other subject headings is also included.

543. Steinhauer, Kurt, comp. **Hegel: Bibliography.** New York: Bowker, 1981. 896p. index. $129.50. LC 81-194446. ISBN 3-598-03184-X.

Admittedly, this bibliography on Hegel and the philosophy of German idealism is not for everyone. But for those interested, for example, in fully understanding the roots of Marxist theory, this could be valuable. Over 12,000 entries, representing a variety of countries and languages, are included. Citations are, for the most part, in the language of origin. The main body of the bibliography has two sections: works by Hegel and secondary sources on his work. The primary sources are arranged by complete works, selected works, single editions, and correspondence. Secondary sources are arranged chronologically from 1802 through 1975. An author/editor/translator index, a keyword index, and a list of periodicals and series are included. Effective use of this bibliography would require a knowledge of German. A follow-up volume by Steinhauer, *Hegel Bibliography, Pt. 2: Background Material on the International Reception of Hegel Within the Context of the History of Philosophy*, is forthcoming from K. G. Saur in 1997 (ISBN 3-598-10787-0).

Handbooks and Yearbooks

544. Rasmussen, David M., ed. **Handbook of Critical Theory.** Oxford: Blackwell, 1996. 426p. index. $74.95. LC 95-49861. ISBN 0-631-18379-5.

Included here are 16 essays providing critical analyses and overviews of the various theories and theorists that comprise the history and current state of critical theory. Among the theorists and schools covered are the Institute of Social Research and the Frankfurt School, Jürgen Habermas, Theodor Adorno, Max Horkheimer, Michel Foucault, Karl-Otto Apel, poststructuralism, and postmodernism, among others. The chapters fall under sections for philosophy and history; social science, discourse ethics, and justice; law and democracy; civil society and autonomy; pragmatics, psychoanalysis, and aesthetics; and postmodernism, critique, and the pathology of the social. A final chapter provides a bibliography of the primary writings of the Institute of Social Research and important critical theorists, as well as secondary writings on aspects of critical theory. A thorough subject index is provided. This is a sophisticated treatment of critical theory and is suitable for specialized graduate students, researchers, and faculty.

Dictionaries and Encyclopedias

545. Bottomore, Tom, ed. **A Dictionary of Marxist Thought.** 2d ed. Oxford: Blackwell, 1991. 647p. index. LC 91-17658. ISBN 0-631-16481-2.

This second edition expands upon the first (1983) by adding almost 50 new entries and expanding or revising numerous others. The entries are written by a stellar group of contributors, including Bottomore, David McLellan, Ralph Milliband, Ernest Mandel, Paul Sweezy, John Rex, David Harvey, Istvan Meszaros, Russell Jacoby, and Immanual Wallerstein, among others. Some of the new entries address Marxism in various countries or regions, analytical Marxism, liberation theology, market socialism, dependency theory, modernism and postmodernism, and even particular works (e.g., Antonio Gramsci's *Prison Notebooks*). The lengthy, signed definitions are accompanied by brief bibliographies of suggested readings. The dictionary also includes biographies of well-known contributors to Marxist thought; newly added biographies treat Jürgen Habermas, Raymond Williams, Nicos Poulantzas, and Joan Robinson, to name a few. The definitions are mostly self-explanatory, though they do include cross-references to terms defined elsewhere. While clearly written, the essays vary in difficulty, with entries in economics and philosophy often presuming some background knowledge. Appended bibliographies of the cited works of Marx, Engels, and others are provided. A thorough name/subject index is included.

546. Carver, Terrell. **A Marx Dictionary.** Totowa, N.J.: Barnes and Noble, 1987. 164p. index. LC 86-22172. ISBN 0-389-20684-9.

Karl Marx is one of the major, founding theorists of sociology. However, it is not an easy matter for sociology students to become conversant with his ideas, which are often quite complex. This dictionary is intended to render Marx more understandable to undergraduate students by straightforwardly discussing 16 central concepts in his work. Those concepts are: alienation, base and superstructure, capitalism, class, communism, dialectic, exploitation, fetishism of commodities, ideology, labor, materialism, mode of production, revolution, science, state, and value. For each concept, a three to ten page essay discussing its origin and meaning in Marx's work is included. The essays also cite key works in which Marx developed the concept and they highlight in boldface terms those that are treated elsewhere in the dictionary. Suggestions for further reading that include both works by Marx, with relevant page references, and secondary sources about that particular concept are also included. Carver also provides an introductory historical overview of Marx's life and works. Supplements include a bibliographical essay of works by and about Marx, a bibliography of Marx's writings, and a subject index.

The importance of these 16 concepts in Marx's work cannot be disputed. While the essays are very well written, they are probably best suited not for introductory course "beginners," but for upper-level undergraduates in sociological theory, social change, or social stratification.

547. Payne, Michael, ed. **A Dictionary of Cultural and Critical Theory.** Oxford: Blackwell, 1996. 644p. $74.95. LC 95-8003. ISBN 0-631-17197-5.

This is an excellent guide to the concepts, theories and theorists within cultural and critical theory. Sociologists may be particularly interested in the essays on such topics as modernity, structuralism, postmodernism, phenomenology, poststructuralism, race-class-gender analysis, alienation, deconstruction, base and superstructure, Marxism and Marxist criticism, social formation, subcultures, and other concepts. In addition, biographical essays on important theorists are included, such as Marx, Derrida, Habermas, Lyotard, Lukacs, Arendt, Baudrillard, De Beauvior, Gramsci, and more. All essays are signed and range in length from a few paragraphs to seven multicolumn pages. Within essays, concepts and individuals defined elsewhere in the dictionary are capitalized. Each essay is accompanied by a brief author/title list of suggested readings; a complete bibliography is found in the back of the volume. An introductory essay provides a broad overview and categorization of theorists and theories. A subject index for additional access to the entries is also included. The concepts treated here are not for beginners, but for more advanced students of cultural and critical theory.

548. Turner, Bryan S., ed. **The Blackwell Companion to Social Theory.** Oxford: Blackwell, 1996. 484p. index. $24.95. LC 95-9586. ISBN 0-631-18401-5.

Focusing on recent developments in social theory, this volume is a collection of introductory essays providing overviews of a variety of contemporary theories. The 15 signed essays fall under five categories: foundations; actions, actors, systems; the micro-macro problem; historical and comparative sociology; and the nature of the social. Within these categories are essays on such topics as classical social theory, critical theory, systems theory, structuralism, rational choice theory, theories of action and praxis, historical sociology, feminist social theory, cultural sociology, psychoanalysis and social theory, postmodern theory, sociology of time and space, and social theory and the public sphere. While the focus is contemporary theory, some effort to connect these theories to their classical sociological roots (where appropriate) is made. These essays are thought provoking and well written. However, they presume a level of knowledge appropriate for advanced students and faculty. A subject index helps in tracking down particular concepts and theorists mentioned throughout the volume.

World Wide Web/Internet Sites

549. **Dead Sociologists Index.**
Available: http://diogenes.baylor.edu/WWWproviders/Larry_Ridener/DSS/INDEX.HTML
(Accessed: December 31, 1996)

Information about and writings by 12 of the major sociologists in the history of the field are covered in this Web site. Those sociologists are Comte, Durkheim, Marx, Spencer, Simmel, Weber, Veblen, Cooley, Mead, Park, Pareto, and Sorokin. For each sociologist, information about the person, a summary of some of their major insights and ideas, and some original works are included. Much of this information is drawn from Lewis Coser's *Masters of Sociological Thought* (2d ed., 1977).

550. **The Durkheim Pages.**
Available: http://www.lang.uiuc.edu/RelSt/Durkheim/DurkheimHome.html
(Accessed: February 3, 1997).

This Web site includes a biography of Durkheim, a time line of important events for Durkheim and the Third French Republic, a biographical dictionary of his antecedents and contemporaries, a glossary of important terms, bibliographies of primary and secondary works, a list of lectures Durkheim gave at Bordeaux and Paris, a list of Durkheim scholars, directions on how to subscribe to the discussion list, *Durkheim* (Available: MAJORDOMO@LISTSERV.CSO.UIUC.EDU), and information on how to subscribe to the print annual, *Durkheim Studies*.

551. **Literature and Process Sociology.**
Available: http://www.arts.ubc.ca/german/lps/elias.html
(Accessed: February 3, 1997).

Included at this site are guides to literature in the field, as well as detailed information about Norbert Elias. Categories for news and events, principal figures in the subject area, course descriptions, and guides to related Web sites are also provided.

552. **Marx and Engels' Writings.**
Available: http://english-www.hss.cmu.edu/marx/
(Accessed: February 3, 1997).

This Web site includes: full text of 40 works by Marx and/or Engels; a full-text biographical archive of shorter and book-length biographies; a photo gallery of Marx, Engels, Marx's family members, and Marx's antecedents, contemporaries, and notable intellectual descendants. Keyword searching of the texts is also available.

553. **The Marx/Engels Archive.**
Available: http://csf.Colorado.EDU/psn/marx/
(Accessed: February 3, 1997).

Included in this Web site are the full text of 62 works, interviews, and essays by Marx, Engels, or Jenny Marx; biographical material and photos of, as well as texts by, related writers (e.g., Trotsky, Lenin, and Luxemburg). Keyword searching of texts is available.

554. **Norbert Elias and Process Sociology.**
Available: http://www.usyd.edu.su.au/su/social/elias/elias.html
(Accessed: February 3, 1997).

Elias is known not only for his work in process sociology, but also in historical sociology and sociological theory. This site has information on the Elias-I listserv, as well as guides to Elias archives. Lists for upcoming conferences and calls for papers, descriptions of research in progress, and bibliographies are also included.

555. **Society for the Study of Symbolic Interactionism.**
Available: http://sun.soci.niu.edu/~sssi
(Accessed: February 3, 1997).

A variety of information here is related to symbolic interactionism and, more generally, qualitative research. The site describes how to access the SSSITALK discussion list and provides an archive of recent traffic. Information on conferences, papers, and debates in the field and on the teaching of symbolic interactionism is included. Links are provided to the SSSI Gopher site, as well as to other relevant resources, such as the Participatory Action Research Network and *Qualitative Report*, an electronic journal of qualitative research.

556. **Sociological Theories.**
Available: http://www.pscw.uva.nl/sociosite/TOPICS/Theory.
html#KNOWLEDGE
(Accessed: December 31, 1996)

This guides the visitor to other Web sites that are categorized under six subjects: General, Knowledge, Time, Ethnomethodology, Marxism, and Sociologists. For each, anywhere from one to ten Web sites are identified; these, in turn, can lead to many more related sites. The "Knowledge" category identifies sites relating to the sociology of knowledge. Across all sites, a variety of types of information is identified, including theses, book chapters, bibliographies, newsletters, organization Web sites, interviews, and more.

557. **Sociologists: Dead and Very Much Alive.**
Available: http://www.pcsw.uva.nl/sociosite/TOPICS/Sociologists.html
(Accessed: February 3, 1997).

This is a subsection of a Dutch sociology Web site, *SocioSite*, that includes texts, information, and discussion by and about 38 well-known living and dead sociologists. Along with Weber, Marx, and Durkheim, one also finds information about Bourdieu, Giddens, Wallerstein, and Paul Willis, among others. For each theorist one may find excerpts from texts and guides to related Web sites.

URBAN SOCIOLOGY AND COMMUNITY STUDIES

Bibliographies

558. Husted, Deborah. **Women and Urban America: A Selected and Multidisciplinary Bibliography of Materials Published Since 1960.** Monticello, Ill.: Vance Bibliographies, 1988. 157p. (Public Administration Series: Bibliography, #P2440). ISBN 1-55590-840-3.

Included here are research-oriented books, articles, and chapters that explicitly or implicitly examine the role of women in urban environments, as well as the effect of such environments on women. Popular works, newspaper articles, and government documents are excluded. Most cited works were published in the 25 years prior to the bibliography's publication date. The citations themselves are arranged by author under approximately 20 subject headings. These include such topics as aging and widowhood, demography and fertility, criminal and social problems, economic conditions, environments, ethnicity/race relations, family, health, immigration, marriage and divorce, and social structure/mobility/networks, among others. Occasional chapters include subtopics.

559. Momeni, Jamshid A. **Housing and Racial/Ethnic Minority Status in the United States: An Annotated Bibliography with a Review Essay.** New York: Greenwood, 1987. 310p. index. (Bibliographies and Indexes in Sociology, No. 8). $65.00. LC 86-27089. ISBN 0-313-24820-6.

Researchers and policy makers specializing in urban sociology, race and ethnic relations, or population and demography may find this bibliography useful. Its purpose "is to facilitate and stimulate fresh research on minority housing and its socioeconomic, legal, humanitarian, and political consequences in the society" (p. xix). It includes 1,007 annotated references to books, articles, and reports. References are arranged by author within 12 subject chapters, including discrimination, segregation, redlining, rental housing, public housing, elderly housing, and homelessness, among others. The paragraph-long abstracts were either written by the compiler or taken from the original source; in some cases, longer source abstracts were condensed. Author and subject indexes are included, as well as a lead essay that discusses minority housing characteristics as indicated by the 1980 Census.

560. Sala, Christine M. **Edge Cities.** Knoxville, Tenn.: Council of Planning Librarians, 1995. 32p. index. (CPL Bibliography, No. 317). ISBN 0-86602-317-8.

Reflecting the increasing suburbanization of the United States, this bibliography focuses on what have been referred to elsewhere as "edge cities." While coverage is interdisciplinary (e.g., architecture, urban planning, and urban sociology), items are treated that should interest and be appropriate for sociology students. Included are references and abstracts of 130 books, journal articles, and newspaper articles. Forty of the references were published prior to 1991, though mostly in the late 1980s, with the rest published after that date. References are arranged by author within chapters for the year of publication. Some citations also include an indication of the NEXIS or DataTimes database file one could use to obtain the full-text of the document. Additional chapters are available for 1) reviews of Joel Garreau's *Edge Cities: Life on the New Frontier*; 2) databases; and 3) newsletters. Place name and author indexes are also provided.

561. Tambo, David C., Dwight W. Hoover, and John D. Hewitt. **Middletown: An Annotated Bibliography.** New York: Garland, 1988. 180p. index. (Garland Reference Library of Social Science, Vol. 446). LC 87-34582. ISBN 0-8240-5839-9.

Robert and Helen Lynd's Middletown books are classics of sociology and community studies. They have spawned popular and scholarly reaction for over 60 years, including follow-up research on Middletown during the 1980s. This bibliography provides brief annotations for 799 popular and scholarly works discussing the Middletown research and its successors. Books, reviews, journal articles, magazine articles, newspaper articles, and dissertations are included. Arrangement of the entries is chronological from 1924 through 1987. Excluded are references in which Middletown is only tangentially treated. A subject index is included. The Center for Middletown Studies, which was established in the 1980s, sponsored this book.

Indexes, Abstracts, and Databases

562. **Index to Current Urban Documents.** Vol. 1- , No. 1- . Westport, Conn.: Greenwood, 1972- . quarterly, with annual cumulations. $425.00/yr. ISSN 0046-8908.

This indexes seemingly obscure publications from local governments on a variety of topics relating to urban life, services, and management. Some county, state, and other government-related publications are also included. The citations can be found through either the geographic index or the subject index. The former is arranged alphabetically by city (U.S. and Canadian), then by author (usually an agency); the latter is arranged by city within each subject heading. Most entries are held in the Urban Documents Microfiche Collection, the holdings for which are contributed by dozens of libraries and agencies. The order number for the document, and the number of fiche it occupies, are included with the citations.

563. **Sage Urban Studies Abstracts.** Vol. 1- , No. 1- . Thousand Oaks, Calif.: Sage, 1973- . quarterly. $345.00/yr. ISSN 0090-5747.

Approximately 250 books, book chapters, journal articles, government publications, and other items are abstracted in each issue. Entries are arranged alphabetically by author under 15 chapter headings, which include such topics as trends in urbanization, urban development, crime, social services, social issues, theory and research, and more. Besides a paragraph-long abstract, each citation also includes approximately five subject headings that are used in the subject index. This index provides significant coverage of numerous sociological concepts, including race, ethnicity, gender, socioeconomic status, social mobility, and social networks. Besides the subject index, an author index is also provided, and both are cumulated in the last issue of each volume. A source list cites all of the journals from which citations were drawn.

564. **Urban Affairs Abstracts.** Washington, D.C.: National League of Cities; Louisville, Ky.: Center for Urban and Economic Research, University of Louisville, 1971- . monthly, with annual cumulation. $300.00/yr. ISSN 0300-6859.

An interdisciplinary guide to literature on urban affairs, this index includes references and abstracts from journals of sociology, business, education, economics, law, criminal justice, political science, public administration, and social policy. The citations and descriptive abstracts are arranged alphabetically by title under an extensive list of subject headings and subheadings. Of particular interest to sociologists should be headings for aging, demography, crime, community development, health, sociology, minorities, public policy, and women, to name a few. The sociology heading includes such subtopics as caregiving, families, homelessness, poverty, and quality of life. Supplementary indexes for authors, geographic regions, and subject descriptors are included. A "Periodical Guide" listing the journals indexed is also appended.

WOMEN'S STUDIES

Bibliographies

565. Gabaccia, Donna, comp. **Immigrant Women in the United States: A Selectively Annotated Interdisciplinary Bibliography.** New York: Greenwood, 1989. 325p. index. (Bibliographies and Indexes in Women's Studies, No. 9). $79.50. LC 89-17191. ISBN 0-313-26452-X.

Sociology has had a long-standing presence in the scholarly writing on immigrant women. However, this bibliography reflects a growing diversity of the literature, incorporating references from sociology, social work, psychology, history, and literature, among others. It includes references to over 2,000 scholarly books, articles, and dissertations arranged by author under 12 chapters. These chapters are: bibliography, general works, migration, family, work, working together, body, mind, cultural change, biography, autobiography, and fiction. The diversity of perspectives reflected here may help present a broader picture of the experiences of immigrant women. The inclusion of biographies and autobiographies helps to illuminate "female subjectivity, experience, and voice" (p. x). Similarly, the citing of literary works may provide additional insight that may not be gained by other kinds of scholarship. Most references are annotated, though these are usually no more than a sentence or two in length. Author, person, group, and subject indexes are available.

566. Huls, Mary Ellen. **United States Government Documents on Women, 1800-1990: A Comprehensive Bibliography.** Westport, Conn.: Greenwood, 1993. 2v. index. (Bibliographies and Indexes in Women's Studies, No. 17 and 18). $159.00. LC 92-38990. ISBN 0-313-29016-4(set).

Covering almost 200 years and 7,000 documents, these two volumes are an excellent guide to government publications dealing with women. Volume one addresses social issues and is arranged into 21 subject chapters, most of which are of sociological interest. These chapter topics include discrimination and women's rights, educational equity, health, fertility and maternity, divorce and child support, public assistance and poverty, violence against women, female offenders, and more. Volume two deals with labor and includes chapters on women in the labor force, employment discrimination, pay equity, industrial health and safety, household employment, and child care and eldercare, among others. Within all chapters, references are arranged chronologically, then alphabetically by the governmental body that represents the corporate author. Many of the citations are annotated, and virtually all include a SuDoc (Superintendent of Documents) number to aid locating the item in library collections. Supplementary personal author and subject indexes are included.

567. Watson, G. Lleywellyn. **Feminism and Women's Issues: An Annotated Bibliography and Research Guide.** New York: Garland, 1990. 2v. index. (Garland Reference Library of Social Science, Vol. 599). LC 89-23327. ISBN 0-8240-5543-8.

Many areas of sociological interest are addressed in this massive, retrospective bibliography, with sources dating back to the 1960s and 1970s. The 7,364 references to books, book chapters, and journal articles are arranged by author within 15 subject chapters: historical/psychological perspectives; critique of patriarchy; capitalism; work; family crises; education; sexism; sex-role socialization; sexuality; health; religion; politics; the legal system; sports; and women cross-culturally and minority women. Each of these chapters, in turn, has numerous subtopics. Many entries are briefly annotated. Entries may also include cross-references to other chapters and subtopics to which they relate. The subject classification scheme is sufficiently detailed to allow for focused subject searching. Unfortunately, no author index is available. A partial list of relevant periodicals is appended.

Indexes, Abstracts, and Databases

568. **Women Studies Abstracts.** Vol. 1- , No. 1- . Rush, N.Y.: Rush Publishing Co., 1972- . quarterly, with annual cumulations. $148.00/yr.(institutions). ISSN 0049-7835.

Approximately 400 or more books and articles are cited and selectively annotated in each issue. References are listed alphabetically by author under about 30 subject categories, including such sociological areas as education and socialization, sex roles, family, violence against women, prejudice and sex discrimination, employment, sexuality, society, interpersonal relations, and more. Most abstracts come from either the source journal or from an abstractor. For other references, a brief, descriptive phrase or sentence accompanies the citation. A separate section lists book reviews, which are not abstracted. Each issue of the index lists the specific journals and issues that were scanned for references. Author and subject indexes, which are cumulated in the last issue of each volume, are also included.

569. **Women's Studies Index.** Vol. 1- . New York: G. K. Hall, 1989- . annual. $175.00/yr. ISSN 1058-8369.

Over 80 popular and scholarly journals, mostly American, are scanned each year for the articles cited here. The references themselves are arranged by title under an extensive alphabetical list of subjects and authors. Library of Congress subject headings are used, with "see" and "see also" references to other terms. Specific subject headings for book, film, music, play, and video reviews are also included. Among the sociological headings are such terms as class differences, divorce, family structure, family roles, aging, sexuality, gender differences, race relations, postmodernism, and poverty. In fact, most sociological specialities are reflected in the many and varied subject headings. The journals indexed, as well as their specific volumes and issues, are noted in a "List of Periodicals Indexed." A list of subscription addresses for these journals is also available.

Handbooks and Yearbooks

570. Schmittroth, Linda, comp. and ed. **Statistical Record of Women Worldwide.** Detroit: Gale, 1991. 763p. index. $89.50. LC 91-4175. ISBN 0-8103-8349-7.

This includes 814 tables of social and economic data profiling women around the world. Approximately half of the tables cover the United States, with some breakdowns by city and state; the other half cover international populations, primarily by country or region. Both government and nongovernment sources are consulted; this is not a "repackaging" of Census data, according to the editor. U.S. statistical tables are historical (to 1970) in some cases; international data are not. Furthermore, some tables include comparative (i.e., by gender, race, or ethnicity), or forecast data.

The tables are grouped by subtopic under 14 major categories: attitudes and opinions; business and economics; crime, law enforcement, and legal justice; domestic life; education; health and medical care; income, spending, and wealth; labor, employment, and occupations; the military; population and vital statistics; public life; sexuality; and sports and recreation. Numerous subtopics are included under each category, with multiple tables of data on each subtopic. The data source for each table is noted with the table and in a supplementary "List of Sources Consulted." A subject/geographic index is available. The majority of tables are directly relevant to various sociological subtopics. Beyond the data included here, one might benefit by identifying important source documents.

571. Taeuber, Cynthia M., comp. and ed. **Statistical Handbook on Women in America.** 2d ed. Phoenix, Ariz.: Oryx Press, 1996. 354p. index. $54.50. LC 96-1521. ISBN 1-57356-005-7.

Approximately 350 tables and charts in this handbook are organized into four chapters profiling the demographic, employment/economic, health, and social characteristics of women. Most of the data are drawn from government sources, including the Census, the Current Population Reports series, the Survey of Income and Program Participation, the 1990 Census, and the National Center for Health Statistics, among others. Within the four chapters, tables are further arranged by subtopics, many of which are of sociological interest. "Social Characteristics" includes data on marriage and divorce, living arrangements, educational attainment, crime, and more. "Employment and Economic Status" covers earnings, unemployment, poverty rates, labor force projections, and working mothers, among others. A few tables contain data for 1994, though in most cases, 1993 data are the most current. Also, historical data are included in many of the tables. The data sources are fully cited with each table or chart. Furthermore, every chapter is introduced by a summary of its various subsections. A glossary of terms and a detailed subject index are provided.

572. **The World's Women 1970-1990: Trends and Statistics.** New York: United Nations, 1991. 120p. $19.95. ISBN 92-1-161313-2.

573. **The World's Women 1995: Trends and Statistics.** New York: United Nations, 1995. 188p. $15.95. ISBN 92-1-161372-8.

These two statistical handbooks are international in scope, of sociological interest and, in the case of the 1970–1990 volume, somewhat historical in focus. They include comparative data and analysis on a range of topics dealing with the lives of women in political, economic, and social settings. The volume for 1995 includes six topical chapters that are very similar to those in the 1970–1990 volume: population, households and families; population growth, distribution and environment; health; education and training; work; power and influence. Within chapters, very readable prose is interspersed with tables and charts to give succinct overviews of the topic. Chapters do include subsections to help focus the analysis. For example, the chapter on health has sections on life expectancy, the health of boys and girls, health risks and causes of death, reproductive health, and disability. Appended to each chapter are bibliographic notes and tables of data. Also included for each volume is a list of the statistical sources consulted. A more detailed and extensive version of these data are available on a United Nations CD-ROM source, *Women's Indicators and Statistics Database (Wistat).*

Dictionaries and Encyclopedias

574. Humm, Maggie. **The Dictionary of Feminist Theory.** Columbus, Oh.: Ohio State University Press, 1990. 278p. LC 89-16237. ISBN 0-8142-0506-2.

Key concepts, theories, and individuals in feminist theory are covered here, with definitions ranging from a paragraph to more than a page. Of special interest to sociologists are the definitions of "conventional" sociological terms, such as class, alienation, knowledge, religion, or racism. These definitions focus on feminist interpretations and uses of the concepts, often contrasting these uses with their more traditional definitions. This is consistent with the book's goal of showing "how feminist theory both challenges, and is shaped by, the academy and society" (p. ix). Even concepts rooted in more radical social theories do not necessarily do justice to feminist analyses of these subjects. The definitions include references to key works, which are fully cited in the bibliography at the end of the volume. While the preface and rationale for the dictionary at times seem intended for a more sophisticated reader, the definitions themselves are consistently clear, well written, and understandable for undergraduates, graduate students, and general readers.

575. Tierney, Helen, ed. **Women's Studies Encyclopedia.** New York: Greenwood, 1989. 3v. index. $59.95(vol. 1); $59.95(vol. 2); $65.00(vol. 3). LC 88-32806. ISBN 0-313-26725-1(vol. 1); 0-313-27357-X(vol. 2); 0-313-27358-8(vol. 3); 0-313-24646-7(set).

These three volumes focus on recent feminist research dealing with a broad range of topics and from diverse disciplinary perspectives. Because of this breadth of coverage, each volume is devoted to a subset of disciplines. Volume one covers the sciences; volume two is devoted to history, philosophy, and religion; and volume three covers literature, the arts, and learning. Though the entries are fairly substantial, ranging from 750 to 1,500 words, their intended audience is educated nonexperts, not researchers. This explains the paucity of further references listed at the end of many of the articles. For undergraduate sociology students, very readable introductions to any number of interesting subjects are included. For example, volume one includes entries on sex-role socialization, the sexual division of labor, sociobiology, gender roles and stereotypes, poverty, and feminist theory, among others. Volume two primarily includes essays on various religions, countries, cultural practices, and women's movements in different countries; many of these entries are historical. Each volume includes a selected bibliography and a combined name/title/subject index.

World Wide Web/Internet Sites

576. **Women Issues - Feminism.**
Available: http://www.pcsw.uva.nl/sociosite/TOPICS/GenderWomen.html#WOMEN
(Accessed: February 11, 1997).

A subsection of the *SocioSite* Web site, this provides links to a variety of other Web sites on women's studies, feminism, work and labor, health, and more. A guide to listservs or discussion lists is provided, as well as links to other major directories on women's studies and feminism, such as that found on Yahoo. This site is international in scope. It is part of a larger section, titled *Sex-Gender, Queer, Feminism and Woman Issues*, that has links on gender and homosexuality.

AUTHOR/TITLE INDEX

Numbers refer to entry numbers. Those with an *(n)* refer to annotations.

SUBJECT INDEX

Numbers refer to entry numbers. Those with an *(n)* refer to annotations.